Dave 'Harry' Bassett was manager of Wimbledon FC from 1981 to 1987, overseeing their rise from the Fourth Division to the top of the First Division in just five seasons. Formerly a player at Wimbledon, then assistant manager at the club, he was an integral part of the team when they were elected to the Football League under Allen Batsford in 1977, and took over as manager from Dario Gradi in January 1981. He went on to manage more than 1,000 games for Wimbledon, Watford, Sheffield United, Crystal Palace, Nottingham Forest, Barnsley, Leicester City and Southampton, with a record seven automatic promotions, including back-to-back promotions twice, also never done before.

Wally Downes was the first Wimbledon apprentice to make it into the first team following their election to the Football League in 1977. He made his debut on 11 May 1979, scoring his first goal just three days later, and went on to make over two hundred appearances for the Dons in an injury-blighted career, captaining the club, before joining his mentor Dave Bassett in the dugout. He has since managed Brentford and been on the coaching staff of Crystal Palace, Reading, Southampton, West Ham United and QPR, helping them win promotion to the Premier League.

The Crazy Gang

The True Inside Story of Football's Greatest Miracle

Dave Bassett and Wally Downes

BANTAM BOOKS

LONDON • TORONTO • SYDNEY • AUCKLAND • JOHANNESBURG

TRANSWORLD PUBLISHERS
61–63 Uxbridge Road, London W5 5SA
www.penguin.co.uk

Transworld is part of the Penguin Random House group of companies
whose addresses can be found at global.penguinrandomhouse.com

First published in Great Britain in 2015 by Bantam Press
an imprint of Transworld Publishers
Bantam edition published 2016

A CIP catalogue record for this book
is available from the British Library.

ISBN
9780857503251

Typeset in 12/15pt Bembo by Falcon Oast Graphic Art Ltd.
Printed and bound by Clays Ltd, Bungay, Suffolk.

1 3 5 7 9 10 8 6 4 2

Contents

Acknowledgements

This book would not have been possible without everyone associated with Wimbledon Football Club down the years – the players, the staff, the fans. Thank you to everyone who has supported the Dons in whatever way they have done. Thanks too to everyone at AFC Wimbledon, particularly Ivor Heller, and to Tony Stenson, Mick Pugh, Steve Elson and Giles Elliott for helping to put the book together.

The Crazy Gang story would simply not exist without all those ex-players and staff who gave their time to contribute to the book. It's been a pleasure to meet up again with so many of you. So here's a special thank-you to, in the order that their reminiscences appear in this book: John Leslie, Steve Ketteridge, Steve Galliers, Dave Beasant, Glyn Hodges, Francis Joseph, Geoff Taylor, Gary Peters, Steve Hatter, Nigel Winterburn, Mark Morris, Mick Smith, Paul Fishenden, Alan Gillett, John Fashanu, John Gannon, Kevin Gage, Andy Sayer, Derek French, Vinnie Jones, Andy Thorn, Andy Clement, Vaughan Ryan and Lawrie Sanchez.

Dave Bassett and Wally Downes,
London, September 2015

Foreword
Shcrazies

Steven Howard, chief sportswriter of the Sun

WE WERE IN a bar in Spain a week before Wimbledon played Spurs in the FA Cup quarter-final at Plough Lane. It was March 1986 and it didn't seem life could get much better for a club that had fought its way through the footballing jungle from Fourth Division to First in just four seasons. Not surprisingly, the boys were in a playful mood. On one side of the bar were Tony Stenson and myself, the two tabloid journalists who probably knew Wimbledon best. On the other, the squad and manager Harry Bassett. It couldn't have been much after seven in the evening, but they already had a glint in the eye.

Harry let out a shout of, 'Right, let's have a bundle,' – or some other such key phrase – and the entire squad took part in the sort of loose maul normally associated with heavy men on a rugby field. Everybody and everything went flying. Elbows were in ears, someone's finger was in someone's nose. The noise was stupendous. I think they called it 'bonding'.

We ordered another San Miguel and left them to it.

Later, on the way back to the hotel we were sharing with the team, I said, 'I wonder what they've done to my room?'

It didn't take long to find out. As the lift arrived on the ground floor and the doors opened, there it was. My room. Well, quite a bit of it. All my clothes, shoes, the entire contents of the bathroom, a couple of chairs, a light-stand and, yes, even the bed. Sort that out.

Yes, the Crazy Gang were in town.

I would later discover that the perpetrator was a certain Nigel Winterburn.

Ah, young Winterburn. I once interviewed Dave Beasant towards the end of the remarkable rise from the foothills of the Football League, and we were discussing players' nicknames. Beasant was famously 'Lurch', and Mark Morris 'Wear 'Em Out Wilf' because he never stopped running in training. Then we came to Winterburn. 'What's he called?' I ventured.

Beasant smiled and said, 'With a name like Nigel, he doesn't need a nickname.'

On another occasion, I was with Beasant, Wally Downes and Stewart Evans in a pub opposite the training ground at the start of the A3 at Robin Hood Gate. Here were two of the founding members of the Crazy Gang, two men who, with Harry, Mick Smith, Steve Galliers and Alan Cork, had done so much to make the club what it was – and what it was still to become.

No one was spared as we ran through the team. Least

of all themselves. How Beasant had stopped coming into training on his moped because the players kept filling his crash helmet with talcum powder . . . how, when Glyn Hodges won his first cap for Wales, the FAW had to sew two together as one wouldn't fit. How John Fashanu turned up in such a flash motor on his first day, Wally stole the keys. How Wally himself was far past his best and just hanging around for Harry to move on so he could take over as manager. They said he had started just eight games that season and the Dons had lost the lot.

At the end, Downes would put his finger on the secret of their success when he said, 'We have no respect for anyone. If we were stupid enough to respect the opposition, they would murder us.'

Except, of course, they did respect each other. In fact, they would trust each other with their lives.

Not long after that chat, Wimbledon would go on to win promotion to the old First Division with a side that included former youth players Hodges, Kevin Gage, Andy Thorn, Mark Morris, Brian Gayle and Paul Fishenden. Cork and Winterburn had come on free transfers; Beasant for £1,000 from Edgware and Steve Galliers for £1,500 from Chorley. Only Lawrie Sanchez and Fash had cost real money. And that for me makes the journey from the Southern League to FA Cup winners inside a decade the most spectacular story in the history of English football. At the centre of it all were the Crazy Gang.

Of course, they polarized opinion like no other team

except, perhaps, Don Revie's Leeds or George Graham's Arsenal. The red tops, generally, loved them. They were manna from heaven – the street urchins who blew a raspberry at all and sundry, especially those they felt were a little above themselves. The broadsheets and the more conservative tabloids were torn. They looked down their nose at the route-one football Wimbledon tended to play in the First Division, having had quite enough of it with Watford. Yet those in the broadsheets who had been paying any attention were right behind them on the romantic roller-coaster ride up from the Fourth to First.

Once the Dons were there, though, many papers professed alarm at the table manners of these young upstarts when they finally took their place in the grand banqueting hall alongside the Liverpools, Manchester Uniteds and Arsenals. 'Don't they know how to behave themselves?' Probably, but they didn't want to.

At the same time, they were not exactly helped by journalists whose behaviour alternated between what might be termed enterprising and, er, a little unscrupulous.

I once met a young Vinnie Jones at the Watford Hilton and emerged with a story published under Vinnie's byline and the headline: I TOLD DALGLISH I'D RIP OFF HIS EAR AND SPIT IN THE HOLE. That earned Vinnie the first of many fines and, looking back, I rather led him down the path.

But Vinnie was very forgiving, and he was still

providing me with exclusives in the week of the FA Cup final against Liverpool, the never-to-be-forgotten afternoon of 14 May 1988.

I still remember the intro: 'While John Barnes and Liverpool were in a studio putting the finishing touches to "The Anfield Rap", Vinnie Jones was making a recording of his own entitled "You'll Never Walk Again".' It was intended as a joke. Then Vinnie tackled Steve McMahon.

While others prevaricated over the Crazy Gang, their strengths and weaknesses, some saying there was little moral justification for either the way they played or the strokes they pulled, I was a pushover. Brought up on Wimbledon Common, there had been enough left in the estate of my actor grandfather, Leslie Howard – his films included *Gone With the Wind*, *The First of the Few* and *Pimpernel Smith* – for my father to buy a large house next door to Cannizaro Park. What was then an old people's home would eventually be turned into the Cannizaro House Hotel, from where Bobby Gould would send his players out for a couple of beers round the corner at the Dog and Fox the night before he unleashed them on four-times European champions Liverpool.

But it was an earlier Wimbledon appearance at Wembley that first brought the club national recognition. That was the day in 1963 when Eddie Reynolds became the only player to score four goals with his head as the Dons beat Sutton United 4–2 in the Amateur Cup final.

Roy Law, who sadly left us in 2014, skippered the club that season and performed outstandingly in a career of some 644 games between 1955–72. These days he would be on £100,000 a week.

In the early Seventies, I would join the *Wimbledon Borough News* just in time to hitch a ride on the Allen Batsford juggernaut that would win three successive Southern League titles before finally breaking into the Football League in 1977.

At the heart of that team was Bassett, who had arrived with Batsford in 1974 from Amateur Cup winners Walton & Hersham, along with defenders Dave Donaldson and Billy Edwards. Strikers Keiron Somers and Roger Connell, who had decamped from Walton to Hendon for a season, would also rejoin their old boss. These players were in a distinctly superior category to anything Wimbledon had seen before. Harry was a fine player, though never blessed with the greatest pace. As one opposition player after another ended up in the Wandle behind the goal at the Speedway end of Plough Lane, Harry would turn to the match official and say, 'Not my fault, ref. Just couldn't quite get there in time.'

Harry's midfield partner was Selwyn Rice, a farmer's boy from Devon. Here were two players for whom the expression 'they never took prisoners' was coined. Even if those prisoners happened to be Billy Bremner and Johnny Giles: it was during this period Wimbledon had the most famous result of their non-league history – a goalless draw with champions Leeds at Elland Road. I was there with Wimbledon estate agent Bob Holmes and vividly recall the endless conga round the Dragonara Hotel eight hours or so after Dickie Guy had saved Peter Lorimer's penalty to earn a remarkable goalless draw. On the train back to King's Cross, Rice put his right peg on the table, pulled up his trouser leg, pointed at various battle wounds and said, 'That was Bremner, that was Hunter, that was Giles . . .'

If the Crazy Gang started anywhere, it was here with Rice and Bassett. Well, certainly its spirit. This was exactly the same iconoclasm with which the Wimbledon team of the next decade would approach the huge challenges they faced then overcame. The main common denominators were a sense of fun and a total lack of fear.

Though even I was surprised by the events of one game that old Batsford team played the following season.

It was at Plough Lane, against Wealdstone, and was supposed to celebrate the Dons just retaining the Southern League title. They won 4–1 but somehow managed to get involved in a game where *six* players were sent off – three from each side. Maybe only the Crazy Gang would understand that.

Years later, I asked Harry how he had escaped being red-carded. 'I was suspended, wasn't I, son,' he said.

And so into the league they went, though Batsford would resign after just six months, with Dario Gradi taking over with Harry as his number two. The following season, Cork would celebrate his second season at the club with 25 goals, Galliers would be player of the year and a 17-year-old Downes would score his first for the club in a 1–1 draw with Barnsley that ensured promotion to the Third Division. It was all starting to take shape. Now we were starting to see the first fully paid-up members of the Crazy Gang. For me, the team that epitomized it was the side of the early to mid-eighties.

Yes, Fash and Vinnie would be allowed to hijack the 2014 BT documentary that annoyed so many people connected with the club.

But significant as their contributions were – and Vinnie, of course, did return to the club subsequently in his career, while Fash played 276 games – they were late additions to the story.

For me, and so many Wimbledon fans, it was Beasant, Cork, Downes, Hodges, Evans, Morris, Mick Smith, Gary Peters, Steve Galliers, Steve Ketteridge, John Leslie, Kevin Gage and even Winterburn who were the real heroes of this particular tale.

First, there was the great day in May of that 1983–84 season – perhaps one of the most auspicious in the whole history of the club. It's also one that has slipped under the radar in terms of what it actually meant. Even younger AFC Wimbledon fans might have heard of the famous Sanchez winner at Huddersfield in the pouring rain in 1986 that saw the Dons finally ascend to the First Division. But even some of their elder brethren might have forgotten the 2–1 win at Sheffield United that clinched promotion to the Second Division two seasons before. Certainly, no one outside the club would recall it. But in many ways it was as important to Wimbledon as that Mark Robins winner in the FA Cup at Nottingham Forest had been to Alex Ferguson and Manchester United in 1990. Or the Clive Walker goal at Bolton in 1982–83 that prevented Chelsea tumbling into the old Third Division and towards financial meltdown. Even the late Paul Dickov equalizer for Manchester City against Gillingham in the Second Division play-off final in 1999 that continued a run that would end with City being showered with Sheikh Mansour's billions and turned into a global giant.

To a lesser extent but just as important to Wimbledon's little band of brothers, that 2–1 win in front of 22,850 at Bramall Lane was key in maintaining a momentum that would see them reach the First Division within two seasons. Cork would score the second, one of 33 for the season in a career that would see him emerge as Wimbledon's top scorer in professional football.

The success story, of course, could never last. While a club like Sheffield United could attract 22,850 to a Third Division promotion battle, the Dons would struggle along on 8,500 in the First.

They were also massively betrayed by Sam Hammam. Here was a man who, in my opinion, took all and gave nothing. And sold the club down the river. Sure, he will say he was the face of the club, 'the head of the family', protecting it against all the sharks in the football fish tank. But, for me, it was all for his own benefit. He gloried in the big time, the Crazy Gang headlines and his own role at the centre of it. But when the going got tough, off he went, destroying the club in the process. He moved Wimbledon to Selhurst Park before later selling Plough Lane to Safeway for £8.5 million.

He would then make the best part of £30 million flogging Wimbledon to some naïve Norwegians. So he got the glory days and the best part of £40 million. Almost all of it profit, seeing as Ron Noades once told me he had sold the club to Hammam for just five figures.

I once turned up at Hammam's house and was served a cup of tea in finest porcelain by his butler as I waited for the fella. Yes, a bloody butler! Everything the Crazy Gang fought against.

But Hammam wasn't the only person to use Wimbledon for his own ends, though no one quite cashed in like him. I will never forget Fashanu's first game for the club after signing for a club record £125,000 from Millwall in March 1986, a purchase that helped get Wimbledon over the line and into the First Division. It was a 1–1 draw at Fratton Park, with Fash coming on in the second half, elbowing Porstmouth's Kevin Dillon in the face and turning a competitive game into a free-for-all that ended in a 22-man brawl in the tunnel. Welcome aboard, Fash.

Afterwards, we all presumed he would be keeping a low profile. Little did we know.

The Portsmouth press area in a labyrinthine main stand was one of the more difficult to get to, but Fash found it. As we went off to track him down, he came walking towards us, bold as brass. 'Hello, chaps,' he said. 'I think you might want to speak to me.'

From that moment, Fash took over. Yes, he always seemed to be part of the Crazy Gang – and used it to his own advantage – but he wasn't, really. He was his own person and thought himself a little above it all. In the end, Fash got out of Wimbledon exactly what he needed to further his career both on and off the pitch.

My own favourite memory of him will not be one he would personally care to remember. It was the sight of Fash, a man who loved no one more than himself, going arse-over-tit back over the wall he was sitting on at the old A3 training ground while conducting a live TV interview. It was a priceless moment of hubris.

As I draw to a conclusion, I have to end with Bassett, the man who created the Crazy Gang, added to it and sustained its irreverential spirit. His 13 years at the club as skipper, assistant manager and manager was an astonishing period. Though his players and the old fans know exactly what he did for the club, he never received the credit he deserved from the outside world. In Wimbledon's first season among the elite, they finished 6th, performed doubles over Manchester United and Chelsea, won at Liverpool, West Ham and Spurs and reached the quarter-final of the FA Cup for the first time in their history. Yet the manager of the year was

Howard Kendall, as Everton won the title for the second time in three seasons. An outstanding feat, but was it better than Harry's?

Perhaps Harry was with the wrong club. Or in the wrong era.

In more enlightened times, George Burley would win the award for finishing 5th with Ipswich (who were relegated the next season). Alan Pardew would win it when he also finished 5th, with Newcastle in 2011–12, while Tony Pulis would be manager of the year for saving Crystal Palace from relegation as they ended 11th in 2013–14.

Harry would have to make do with a special award as *Sun* manager of the year in 1986 – and a peck on the cheek from a Page Three girl.

And then he left for Watford and missed out on the glory of Wembley the following season.

It was a difficult choice for a man with Wimbledon in his DNA – and vice versa – but, finally, he was getting a salary more commensurate with his ability.

His relationship with Hammam, I believe, had also become stretched, with the owner – like so many other owners – wanting more of the credit for Wimbledon's success to be apportioned to him rather than the manager. In his place came Bobby Gould, whose main qualification for the job appeared to be the fact he was loopier – and I say that in a nice way – than anyone already at the club.

Gould did, though, have a forensic knowledge of

players in the lower leagues, and immediately brought in John Scales and Terry Phelan. He was also wise enough to appoint Don Howe as his number two. I also liked the fact he displayed the Gobbledygook Award he won for his programme notes with some pride on his desk.

But as he led the Crazy Gang out at Wembley, I spared a thought for Harry up in the TV gantry.

Down below were his boys and his team. Two of the latest additions – Jones and Wise – would have a profound influence on Wimbledon returning to Plough Lane with the trophy. At the end, Beasant would go up to receive the Cup from Diana, Princess of Wales.

It really was a fairytale. Amazingly, the frog had turned into a prince.

In closing, I am sure that older Dons fans (like me) would want to pay tribute to some of the earlier heroes who made the club what it was and what it is. The likes of Ian Cooke, the striker who took time off from a life in banking to score 297 goals in 615 appearances that straddled amateur and semi-pro football and whose grandson has played for the youth side. And cricket-loving Bernie Coleman, an astute, influential member of the old TCCB and Surrey but, more importantly, a wise, sympathetic(!) host at the Dog and Fox, who bailed the club out in the seventies. Then there was Ron Noades, who did so much to get the club in the league, and Eric Willcocks, 'Mr Wimbledon', who served the club so selflessly over a remarkable 60 years. And, finally, Dickie Guy. I was there at Elland Road when he saved that

Peter Lorimer penalty – conceded, I believe, by a certain H. Bassett – in a game that made him the star he always deserved to be.

More importantly, I was also there a few seasons ago when Dickie, now club president, saw the Dons beat Luton Town to regain membership of the Football League. It was a crucial game after their miraculous, Phoenix-like rise from what even the most optimistic thought was oblivion. At the end, Dickie, who has struggled manfully with cruel ill health over the last few years, was in tears, overcome by the emotion of it all. At his side, in his embrace, was his wife Josie, who had given him – and continues to do so – the love and warmth of all those at Wimbledon, who owe this most unassuming of men the support he deserves.

This, of course, is a book about the Crazy Gang and its founder members – like Harry, Wally and Corky, and the others who bought into the whole experience and made teammates and fans alike believe that, yes, we can do it.

But let's not forget the others.

Prologue

Dave Bassett

> *I am not surprised by these achievements. After all, if we can sell Newcastle Brown to Japan, Bob Geldof can have us running around Hyde Park, and if Wimbledon can make it to the First Division, there is surely no achievement beyond our reach.*
>
> Text of a speech given by the Prime Minister, the Rt Hon Margaret Thatcher, FRS, MP, at a dinner hosted by the CBI on Thursday, 22 May 1986.

THAT'S WHAT SHE said. I puffed my shoulders. It made me realize we were recognized as a success. Wimbledon are truly a remarkable story, perhaps one of the greatest success stories in the history of the game. It's a story that will certainly never be repeated: a homespun, cash-strapped, often down-at-heel club rising from the Southern League to the old Division One in nine years and staying for more on low crowds, even lower wages, and then winning the FA Cup.

We got criticized by the media and weak-minded opposition, hounded and accused of betraying football. What total rubbish. We fought, we planned, we analyzed, and yet were still branded a long-ball side. That was not an issue or a problem. It worked. Today, if a player hits a glorious 50-yard pass, it's considered skill. We had an academy before they became fashionable, producing footballers who went on to become internationals.

We were different, I accept that. A lot of us were in the last chance saloon, but we also believed. We believed, given another chance by people who believed in us, that we could make a new life for ourselves. It was a magic, intoxicating formula that changed the face of football. We didn't hide behind the media hymn sheet. I managed and played to a style that suited us and within our own financial compass. We were fighting against the odds on average earnings of £100 a week.

Yes, we took rules to the nth degree; yes, we stole traffic cones for training because Wimbledon didn't supply them. We competed on the training ground. I encouraged it. During the time Dario Gradi was manager, I often took the training and we'd have a free-for-all rugby scrum. Dario wondered how we finished so dirty, so covered with cuts and bruises. It was a hangover from my days as a Wimbledon player, under Allen Batsford as manager. He was a lovely, quiet man but also had a ring of steel about him. I was his direct opposite – always noisy, causing mayhem. But he turned his back on our antics because he believed it was forging something special.

One of my first targets was keeper Dickie Guy. He was always dressed like he'd just stepped out of a tailor's shop window. I soon put a stop to that by cutting his ties, suits and ruffling his well-coiffured hair. I conned him the day we played Leeds in the FA Cup by getting a friend to say he was from the BBC and asking him for an interview in the hotel lobby – '... and, by the way, could you please put on a suit and tie?' So down he pranced, looking pleased with himself at the thought of being a star. He waited ... and waited ... until we all arrived, asking how it went. It finally dawned on him that he had been duped. Eventually he got the right hump with me and offered to fight me, putting up his hands like an old-fashioned prize fighter. I couldn't stop laughing. In the end Dickie joined in the antics and once nailed my best shoes to the dressing-room wall.

The strongest survive. We loved it. We all had stories to tell. Mine began forty years ago, when I had a dream. It started in the wake of non-league Wimbledon beating Burnley to take on Leeds in the FA Cup – games that live on in the memory to this day because TV continues to show Dickie Guy making his penalty save. Those games were eye-openers for me. We played hard and almost achieved the impossible because at that point Leeds were *the* club, one bristling with international stars. We knew we couldn't beat them for skill, but decided to match them in everything else.

Allen Batsford, a true legend in the making of Wimbledon, gave us a plan and we stuck at it. After the match I went home and analyzed the game and decided that if and when I became a manager I would follow the Leeds ethos. I liked the way they played, I liked the way they supported each other. If one player was in trouble, another would soon arrive to help out. They had bundles of skill, but they also never forgot what a team is all about. Leeds were going to be my blueprint.

Eventually, my chance arrived and the work started. It was no fluke we achieved so much in such a short time. Our plan was to produce a group of young, mostly home-grown players who bought into my ideas. I am proud to say that when I left Wimbledon they were 6th in the table, had reached the quarter-finals of the FA Cup, and in the side were 13 of the 21 players who began the journey with me. Brian Gayle, Kevin Gage, Andy Thorn, Mark Morris, Wally Downes, Glyn Hodges, Paul Fishenden, Vaughan Ryan, Simon Tracey, John Gannon, Andy Sayer, Andy Clement and Dennis Wise – all take a bow.

There were others along the way, like Gary Peters, Steve Ketteridge, Stewart Evans, Steve Hatter and Mick Smith, who must also not be forgotten. The likes of Dave Beasant, Alan Cork, Nigel Winterburn, Stevie Galliers, Lawrie Sanchez, Carlton Fairweather, John Fashanu and Vinnie Jones were to follow. We could also boast nine players who played in all four divisions for the club

– Beasant, Smith, Downes, Cork, Hodges, Galliers, Gage, Morris and Fishenden.

When the side eventually broke up and players were sold, the club banked £7.2 million from transfers. Not a bad return. What's more, the well was also being replenished with quality replacements, the likes of Dean Blackwell, Chris Perry, Neil Sullivan and Neal Ardley.

We had fun, but there was a lot of hard work and planning that went into those years. We were a good, well-run club living within our means. We defied critics who said that we couldn't play in the Fourth Division by getting to the Third. We defied them again when they said we weren't good enough for the Third by getting to the Second. And then Division One.

There certainly weren't the devious plots that have been depicted elsewhere. I would never have tolerated those ideas. I read that we'd flood the opposition dressing room, rip out toilet seats, and block drains to make the place stink. Total and utter rubbish. Lies. Can you imagine the likes of Alex Ferguson and Brian Clough arriving at our old Plough Lane ground and putting up with that? They would have verbally bashed us and reported it to the league. And rightly so.

If things happened after me then I can't answer for that, although I'd certainly struggle to see the likes of Bobby Gould and Don Howe tolerating those kind of antics. But not in my time. Never. We had laughs and japes, but we were never a dressing room full of bullies. I did push some barriers to create a band of brothers, but it was only within our own confines, not at the expense of others. We did it to build up the hype, to let other people think we weren't prepared. But we were organized, believe me.

Can you imagine that lot putting up with the kind of things John Fashanu said on TV during that BT Sport documentary called *The Crazy Gang*? As far as I'm concerned Fash did a good job for me, but we weren't thugs and he wasn't the Crazy Gang leader. He wasn't around when it started, and it was winding down when I left. Fash made it plain to me when he joined the club that he wasn't buying into the Crazy Gang ways and wanted no part of it. The same with Lawrie Sanchez. I had no problem with that.

I had some wonderful staff in the likes of Alan Gillett, a good coach and voice of reason when I might have lost it on occasions. There was also the physio, Derek French, a larger than life character who had the ability to make even the injured players leave his treatment room smiling. Geoff 'Ballbag' Taylor was our master of spotting talent and developing the youth players, whose part in Wimbledon's rise to glory should never be underestimated. There's also no forgetting Sid Neale, our kit man, a wonderful character who lived with us throughout those years without getting a penny in wages, as did Joe Dillon and Geoff 'the Adder' Priest, coming in every day to do things for us, for nothing.

My game plan was built on the words I once heard from country singer Dolly Parton, when she appeared in a film with the likes of Jane Fonda. Dolly admitted to being star-struck by those around her and said the only way she could truly compete was to learn the lines of everyone around her, knowing she could fill in at any time. That struck a chord with me. It was one of the reasons we spent pre-season training at various army camps around both England and Europe. They were tough 'beasting' days but I wanted to build characters. I also wanted bonding. I wanted mates who would rush to the rescue of mates if they ever felt they were in trouble. It was Leeds thinking again. Like the SAS, we would never leave a mate behind.

Some players saw our army-training trips as hell on earth. Steve Ketteridge hated heights but by the end he was abseiling down mountains like a veteran; Andy Sayer hated tunnels, but he finished up being called 'an underground sewer rat'. Then we sat down afterwards with army specialists – in particular a guy called Dick Parker, who was so enthusiastic and became so immersed in our spirit that thereafter he arranged all our trips. We analyzed the players, making sure they were not square pegs in round holes. We wanted them to feel comfortable in uncomfortable positions, so they could take this on to the field and be happy wherever and whenever they played.

We also had fun – and some scary moments. I remember one occasion Corky, Frenchie, Wally and myself being dropped off by the army in a remote part of the Mendip Hills with just a map and a compass to get home. We soon got lost and decided to cut across a field. We were halfway there when a farmer raced out, shouting, waving his shotgun and telling us to get off his land. We ignored him, and told him to fuck off, only to get pellets fired over our heads. We ran for our lives. Now that was real character building!

I like to think we were ahead of our time. I had every player going to Lilleshall to gain their FA preliminary coaching badge to get a wider picture of the game. We made video clips and analysis of ourselves and opponents before almost anyone else was doing this. We were never given any credit for it. It didn't matter – I was of the opinion that this was the way forward to be successful. But critics accused us sometimes of being tough, although they forgot teams like Spurs had Graham Roberts and Paul 'Maxy' Miller in their side – ditto Steve McMahon and Jimmy Case at Liverpool. You had to stand up for yourselves, as all the top teams had players who could look after themselves: Derek Mountfield, Pat Van Den Hauwe and Peter Reid at Everton; Norman Whiteside, Remi Moses and Bryan Robson at Manchester United.

We achieved something unique in football. Many said it wasn't easy on the eye, but we were successful. We were hated. But we will never be forgotten, even though we were never given due credit.

I was quite surprised when I heard that *The Crazy Gang* documentary had won an award at the Sports Journalists' Association dinner. As far as I was concerned, they made out that we were a team of thugs who would do anything to win a football match, but that just wasn't the case. I felt extremely disappointed by it and betrayed by the programme makers who, it seemed to me, had not done their homework on the years before the 1988 Cup Final.

They had, in my opinion, an agenda whereby they wanted to sensationalize some of the stories that Vinnie and Fash had, and made them the centre of attention when the film was released. Good men and good players such as Glyn Hodges, Steve Galliers, Kevin Gage, Mark Morris and Brian Gayle were all ignored because the programme makers wanted a dramatic film.

It frustrated me because there was no mention of the stats man Neil Lanham, sitting in the stands each week to record free-kicks, corners and throw-ins. There is no mention, either, of the money we invested on video equipment for our analyst Vince Craven, which was twenty years before ProZone was developed. I read Wisey's transcript of his interview for the documentary and it irritates me that his anecdotes, for example, about Don Howe showing tapes of Arrigo Sacchi's Milan team, with Franco Baresi, Alessandro Costacurta, Ruud Gullit and Marco van Basten in their pomp, were left on the cutting-room floor.

I watched the film with Neil Ashton, a football journalist with the *Daily Mail*, who went on to write a piece about it. I felt let down. The Crazy Gang tag suited Sam Hammam and the legend lived on long after I left the club. Fash embellished stories and attempted to glamourize something that was a very special part of our lives. When Fash joined Wimbledon, he told the dressing room: 'I am not in the Crazy Gang, do not cut up my clothes and I won't cut up yours'. Then to claim in the documentary that he was the leader is wrong because in my time this wasn't correct.

In my opinion Fash embarrassed himself during the interview about the Cup Final, claiming he told John Barnes in the tunnel that he said things to the Liverpool winger that 'only a black man could say to another black man'. They then showed a picture of the two teams in the tunnel and Fashanu doesn't say a word to Barnes. It's all in his head. Barnes later confirms in his own interview that Fash didn't say anything to him while they were waiting for referee Brian Hill to lead the teams out.

My phone was lighting up with text messages during the programme, with former players telling me how disappointed they were with the tone. So in the aftermath of *The Crazy Gang* documentary, Wally Downes and I sat down and decided that we wanted to set the record straight on our time at Wimbledon. And the more that we remembered those times – from 1977 when the club was elected to the Football League, to ten years later when I left and Wally's injury-blighted playing career was coming to a close – the more we realized what an incredible story it was.

That was how this book came about. But we also realized that we couldn't write the story without the testimony of the players themselves. Many of those players had got in touch to say, 'Hold on, that wasn't what happened,' or ask why they hadn't been featured in the show too. So over the course of a few months, we got together, had some laughs, more than a few drinks, and shared our Crazy Gang memories. These are all in this book, along with chapters by Wally and me. And, by the way, it's the question I'm always asked, but no, I can't remember when people started calling me Harry – I got the nickname passed down from my dad, Harry.

We hope you enjoy the book. It's the real Crazy Gang story.

1
A Dirty Bastard

Harry

I WAS FIRST OFFERED the job of Wimbledon manager by chairman Ron Noades, following on from Allen Batsford, the man who took the club into the Football League. Allen had taken me – a wild man, an in-your-face, Nobby Stiles type of player (without the same skills) – and turned me into a leader. He made me his captain at both Walton & Hersham and Wimbledon. I gave out a lot of verbals, and not just to the opposition. He turned a blind eye to my wild behaviour because he knew I cared for our cause. We both wanted to be winners. We reaped rewards together. I went on to win ten England amateur international caps and lifted the FA Amateur Trophy under his command. There were 42,000 at Wembley the day Walton beat Slough Town in 1973.

Wimbledon were in the Southern League when we both got there, and local rag and bone men had more money to spend than we did. Allen turned us into a formidable force, and when he left I was really disappointed. He was treated shabbily. Even a promise of a testimonial to the man who took us into the Football League was denied him. His funeral, on a snowy day, was one of the low points of my life.

You could hardly say I was destined for the top of the football world, but you don't spend years in the Athenian League battling away for the likes of Walton without learning a few things. It was as a midfielder that I got my reputation for being an enforcer: hard, tough, or as I once described myself, '. . . enthusiastic without much talent . . . a bit of a dirty bastard'. This always stood me in good stead – still does – but I actually started out playing up front for Roxeth Manor school in south Harrow, then for Harrow schoolboys. It was in my early non-league days at Hayes, Wycombe Wanderers and Hendon where I learned my more knucklesome trade. That was after I'd failed to make the grade at Chelsea, who were the top youth team in those days.

At Walton, people could well forget, we got some great results too. The season after we won the Amateur Cup, we pulled off one of the most famous FA Cup shocks, holding Brighton to a 0–0 draw then thrashing them 4–0 in the replay at the Goldstone Ground in front of a crowd of 10,000. The match had to kick off at 1.45 on a Wednesday afternoon due to one of those 1970s power crises, but even the Brighton management team of Brian Clough and Peter Taylor couldn't use that as an excuse.

The match report in the Brighton *Argus* makes for some interesting reading in terms of my future management career: 'In midfield, they were outsmarted. Only in terms of fitness were Albion superior, and they relied too much on running Walton off their feet. Walton absorbed the pressure like a sponge, had men of heart and character, and not a few players who showed a greater desire for the ball when it was obvious someone was going to get hurt . . .'

'A bunch of bloody amateurs, and they beat us 4–0,' Cloughie later wrote in his autobiography. 'I've had some bad days in football but that must have been one of the worst.' He was clearly forgetting some of the batterings my Wimbledon later gave Forest . . .

So it was no surprise when, in the summer of 1974, the now Wimbledon manager Allen Batsford signed five of us from Walton – me, Dave Donaldson, Billy Edwards, Roger Connell and Keiron Somers. I think I was on £45 a week as a part-time player. But that was where it all started for Wimbledon, the winning habit which we would take all the way up the divisions. We were champions of the Southern League in 1975, then again in 1976, with the Southern League Cup as icing on the cake, then again in 1977, with a record 63 points. We were unstoppable.

It was only towards the end of the third of those league titles that we began to think that we had a chance of being elected into the Football League – there was no promotion and relegation like now; you had to be voted in, and someone else voted out. But this time the establishment could no longer ignore Wimbledon. At the annual meeting of the Football League on 17 June 1977, at the Café Royal in London, it was announced that we had taken the place of Workington in the Fourth Division, getting 27 votes compared to their 21. The dream had finally come true.

Ron Noades, as Wimbledon chairman, was obviously instrumental in our election to the Football League, mounting a huge publicity campaign on our behalf, and he was going to get his way come what may, by fair means or foul. One way of doing that was to produce a brochure with a picture of Plough Lane at night 'showing the quality of our floodlights'. That was just a little bit of a porky pie. They were crap!

Non-league football may have been part-time, but it wasn't a joke. It laid the foundations of what was to come. The game was never just a hobby to me. We were all part-timers at Wimbledon but we were dedicated and fit, and the reason we were able to beat teams like Burnley – the first time a First Division club had been beaten by a non-league team on their own ground in 55 years – and draw with Leeds United was that we fancied our chances against professional opposition. You've just got to take the opportunity when the situation arises.

There was also an incredible amount of football to fit in, even though we were only part-time players. In fact, during that 1974–75 season when we came to national attention, in addition to winning the league and the 42 games that involved, we had a total of 19 Cup ties, reaching the Fourth Round of the FA Cup (having started in the preliminary round), the quarter-finals of the FA Trophy, the semi-finals of the Southern League Cup, and winning the London Senior Cup. And players nowadays complain of being tired and overworked!

As I later said, 'I like to think I've always had a professional attitude towards football, and so have the players I've been associated with.' And that attitude was about to be tested in the Football League for the first time, along with John Leslie, another of the players making the transition upwards. He certainly saw some ups and downs in his eight years at the club. Here's the first of those Crazy Gang players' memories.

John Leslie

They were great days, great fun. I left Wimbledon with a heavy heart, leaving only because I needed more money to pay my mortgage and support two growing kids.

I joined Wimbledon in the Southern League, signed by Allen Batsford. I joined from amateurs Dulwich Hamlet where I got fed up waiting for my £15-a-week wages. I would have to go to manager Jimmy Rose and ask to be paid and he, often reluctantly, would pull out a wad of notes and roll them off. So when Wimbledon came in for me it was a chance to earn more, not much more, but be paid regularly. I lived at the time in

Plumstead in south-east London and getting to their Richardson Evans training ground wasn't easy, although I could do it then in an hour and half. I wouldn't dream what time it would take now.

Our tactics were simple. Boot it up to the attackers. I would draw my defender then turn and run behind him as the ball was hoofed over his head. Even then it was fun days. I remember our keeper Dickie Guy walking past me with a bucket of water and wondering why. He had seen Dave Bassett going into the toilet, one of those old-fashioned ones with no top. Guy waited until Dave was sitting down, stood on the seat of the other cubicle and chucked the water over him. Dave said a few choice words and then came storming out of the cubicle, trousers down by his ankles, waving toilet paper with something nasty on it, trying to stick it on Dickie's head!

There were some tough games in the Southern League. I remember the boys telling me before I arrived that Harry once laid out Wealdstone player John Watson and was sent off. On another occasion, I watched him leave a pass alone, waiting for his opponent to run by him, and as he did so Dave ran straight into him, knocking him flat out. He immediately started walking to the dressing room, not waiting for the red card. He said afterwards there had been previous.

I also recall playing against Wealdstone during the 1975–76 season when six players were sent off, three from each side (a league record), including me. Danny

Light spat in my face and I retaliated. Before the match Wimbledon had been presented with the league trophy and Wealdstone needed points to avoid relegation. We beat them 4–1.

We finally reached the Football League and were still part-timers. I worked for a heating company. Still do today. But after a few months chairman Ron Noades decided we would go full-time because the teams we played against were fitter and better. I reckon few teams trained harder than us. We needed to be fit to compete. We also needed to be fit because of the way we played. Allen was still ordering us to whack the ball forward.

Money was tight in those days. I remember trying to board a coach to an away game when the coach driver, one who took us to all the matches, said we couldn't get on. I asked why not and he said, 'Because you haven't paid us for previous trips.' Ron was called and had to write out a cheque there and then so we could board. It was like that at hotels too. We rarely stayed in the same hotel more than once, and the ones we did were mainly out of town because we hadn't paid up. I remember going to one hotel, booking in and then slipping downstairs for a chat. When I returned I couldn't find my room. The number on it didn't match that on my key. The lads had stolen my key and swapped my door for another one. I never left my key around again.

When Dario Gradi took over, he used similar tactics but had more ambition. Allen was happy to remain where we were. Dario wanted to push on, and our training changed slightly. Then came Harry. He was a joy. He was still a player at heart and wanted us to have fun. His training was just as fierce and passionate but there was always a smile about the place. Despite my long journey every day, I always wanted to get to training and never missed a day. Same as the others. Every day was different and we didn't want to miss it. I had played my first game with Harry against Chelmsford. He had told me before the game he was fast. I never saw it!

Harry has been an important part of my life. He owned an insurance brokerage and he sold a policy to me after I bought my house. I also spent the night after my wedding with Harry in a Huddersfield hotel getting ready for a game. Ron Noades had driven me and him to Yorkshire in his Rolls Royce.

I once asked Harry for more money at a time when Brentford wanted to sign me. My contract was up and they offered me a rise and a three-year deal. I accepted. Then when that ended I asked for a rise and Harry said he couldn't do it because I was already the highest earner and money was tight, but he did say he would pay me extra out of his own money to stay. But he also told me Gillingham were interested, and did I fancy going to a trial? I played one game and they signed me for £15,000.

I got my rise, but at what cost? I was leaving a club who supplied me with the best footballing days of my life. Days of fun and thunder, but never any evil. I left as the last remaining member of the team which joined the Football League in 1977.

2

The Mischief Begins

Harry

'DISGRACEFUL' WAS ALLEN Batsford's choice of word when asked to describe Wimbledon's first ever league match, against Halifax at Plough Lane on 20 August 1977. It was a bit harsh – even if we did concede a late goal for a 3–3 draw having just taken the lead with a spectacular Roger Connell strike – as I'm sure the crowd of 4,616 enjoyed the momentous occasion, and a six-goal thriller. The goals we conceded were shit though.

The size of that attendance at Plough Lane, of hardened Dons fans 'mingled with a section of "curiosity" spectators', as Steve King, the editor of *Dons Outlook* ('still only 20p'), wrote in the September issue of the monthly magazine produced by the supporters' club, which I have kept to this day, showed that 'Wimbledon Football Club's future looks extremely prosperous, and barring any major catastrophe, the way is clear ahead for future soundness financially and on the field.' If only we all knew what a journey it would be . . .

The team against Halifax, for the record, was Dickie Guy, Jeff Bryant, Dave Galvin, Dave Donaldson (at 35, the oldest player to make his debut in the Fourth Division), Glenn Aitken, Geoff Davies, Steve Galliers, Willie Smith, Roger Connell, Billy Holmes and John Leslie. Galliers had been signed from non-league Chorley for the princely sum of £1,500, and was one of three new signings, along with Galvin and Smith, to make their league bows. From this point onwards Steve Galliers will be referred to by his official nickname of 'Midget'. And little could Midget have known that just nine years later he'd be playing First Division football under a Wimbledon manager called Harry Bassett.

But where was I, the Dons' skipper, on that historic occasion against Halifax? Yes, nigh on fourteen years at Wimbledon as player, captain and (later) manager, and I only go and miss that part of the club's history – suspended. As I have said, I was a bit of a dirty sod, and usually missed the beginning of the season due to a suspension hanging over from the last campaign, as was the case on this occasion. It was a bit gutting – and still rankles, in fact – but sometimes that's the way the cookie crumbles, as they say.

Instead, after coming back from my ban, I was turning out for the reserves three days later along with Billy Edwards, our player of the season from the previous campaign, in a 2–1 win against Northampton. Jeff Bryant, a former Fulham player, got the honour of becoming the Dons' first ever goalscorer in league football, despite having broken a couple of teeth in a pre-season friendly. It was a bit of a scrambled effort, but they all count.

I had actually scored – not that many of the players would believe me now – four days earlier in the second leg of a League Cup match against Third Division Gillingham, which we won 4–2 on aggregate to get the season off to a cracking start. My goal at Plough Lane came against the run of play, but once Roger Connell had put us ahead with what Allen Batsford described as 'a goal in a million', there was no looking back.

Billy Holmes had scored Wimbledon's first ever goal as a league club, in the first leg, for his place in the record books, converting a Willie Smith free-kick. We missed Billy when he moved on to Hereford halfway through that season, and he's no longer with us, sadly, but he was a real character with great skill who loved football and swore like a trooper. Mind you, he didn't like getting his knees dirty, so we'd throw him in a pond at training.

Our reward for the win over Gillingham was a plum tie at White Hart Lane in the second round of the League Cup, and a chance to match up against a young Glenn Hoddle and Steve Perryman. Dickie Guy, ever-present for seven seasons and in his testimonial year to boot, had lost his place by then after Allen held him responsible for a 4–1 thumping in the league at Brentford in front of more than 11,000. He had not missed a league game since 1968 before then! Richard Teale was between the sticks, but anyone could have been in goal to be fair, as they wouldn't have stopped Spurs and John Duncan's hat-trick of headers. Still, if nothing else, a mini League Cup run meant Wimbledon were on the map as a league club.

Wimbledon had always had a reputation as a good team for a Cup shock, particularly after our run in the 1974–75 season. There was the famous win over Burnley, of course, called at the time 'the most sensational result in post-war FA Cup history', with Micky Mahon getting the only goal of the game at Turf Moor, and, of course, Dickie's performances against Leeds were probably when most of the country first heard of our exploits. I'll skip over my role in those two games, shall I? At Elland Road I brought down Eddie Gray for the penalty which Dickie famously saved from Peter Lorimer, then in the replay at Plough Lane Johnny Giles' shot deflected in off me. Still, those games must have earned the club something in the region of £10,000 at a time when the club's budget ran to about £450 a week!

Then even the season we were elected into the Football League we ran a Middlesbrough team featuring Graeme Souness in midfield close in a Third Round replay at Ayresome Park. That came after a disciplined defensive performance gave us a goalless draw at Plough Lane, where I was described in the programme notes as 'a student of the game and a great character'. It was a dreadful decision that gave Boro the penalty in that replay too – man falls over on snow-covered pitch – but it showed the famous fighting Wimbledon spirit was alive and well. I don't know how Roger Connell stayed on the pitch, in fact.

But if it was no great surprise to see us get beat 4–0 at Tottenham in the League Cup, losing 3–0 at Enfield in the First Round of the FA Cup was a fucking embarrassment. It probably summed up that first league season – we'd made the step up, but fell far short of what was expected of us. We failed to win any of our first seven league games before finally beating Northampton. We failed to win many friends too; after a draw against Darlington, their manager Peter Madden described us as 'the worst side I have ever seen for conning the ref'. What a load of crap.

Of course, being part-time players effectively made us one of the underdogs in the division – we had been the first part-time club ever to be admitted into the Football League. I had my own insurance business, which kept me busy throughout my career in tandem with football; Wally had his family fruit and veg stall; and Dave Donaldson supplemented his wages as a footballer by working for British Airways. How he managed to arrange his flight schedule to get to games, I'll never know.

We often lost players because they couldn't commit to the rigours of league football. Wimbledon stalwart Ian Cooke, for instance, had left the club in the summer of 1977 to go to Slough Town in the Isthmian League, as he couldn't get sufficient time off from the bank where he worked to take part in the additional afternoon training sessions that we had to implement to try to catch up with better-funded rivals and to improve our fitness, which simply wasn't up to scratch for this level. We were so hard up that the club even organized pitch-side donations of pennies from fans to bolster the budget.

Watford, under Graham Taylor, ran away with the division and we finished in mid-table in our first tilt at this level, but there were a couple of noteworthy debuts that are part of the history of the Crazy Gang. In October, a schoolboy by the name of Lawrie Sanchez made his debut for Reading against us on a wet and windy Saturday at Elm Park. I decided to give him a few welcoming digs and kicks and he took it well and just got on with the game. Years later, Vince Craven, who lived near Reading, was to recommend him to me again. Reading wanted £32,000 but we offered £29,000 cash and they accepted straight away. Lawrie was to go on and establish himself. He wasn't a hardcore Crazy Gang member, more on the fringes of things – although he did once take down a Christmas tree in a hotel foyer.

Then, in February 1978, 18-year-old Alan Cork made his Wimbledon bow in a 0–0 draw with Scunthorpe. Corky had impressed Dario Gradi when the two of them were at Derby, and was brought in to replace the misfiring Phil Summerill, a fans' favourite but not a prolific finisher, who had not scored for 12 games. The Dons' fans were not enthused by Corky initially – he hadn't done anything at Derby – but how wrong they were. He went his first five Wimbledon matches without scoring but bagged a goal at the sixth attempt, in a 3–1 win against Bournemouth. The rest is history.

By now, Dario was the Wimbledon manager. He had come in as Allen Batsford's assistant in October, but took over when Allen resigned in the new year. The final straw for Allen was when we had a 'mare at Swansea, me personally, and Dickie too, and it wouldn't be long before that goalkeeping legend played his last game for the club, Ray Goddard arriving from Millwall to take his place. In fact, I seem to remember Dickie being dropped for the final time after turning up late to a game. To be fair to Dickie, though, he didn't enjoy that season much; the part-time game was more his thing. The day job may have been working as an export booking clerk with the Port of London Authority, but his save from Lorimer – and the rest – assures his place in history.

We were truly crap against Swansea, losing 3–0 with our confidence in tatters, but the real reason for Allen's departure was a series of rows with the chairman, Ron Noades, mostly about finances. It had all come to a head when we played at Rochdale on Boxing Day, losing 3–0 in front of three men and a dog to a team that were bottom of the league. As Allen later recalled, 'We had terrific spirit but no money. Because a team bus cost too much, Ron ordered the players to drive to Rochdale, just like a pub side.' Mind you, even when we did have a bus, like on that trip to Swansea, it could be a shambles

– we left Dave Galvin behind at a service station and he missed the match!

We drank like a pub team too. Roger Connell, top scorer as usual that season (but for the last time) with 15 goals, summed it up when the 1977–78 squad had a get-together twenty years later: 'Gazza couldn't survive our lifestyle. Girls and drinking were the main subjects for us.' For Roger, that would lead to several run-ins with Allen Batsford, and he was transfer-listed before Dario restored him to the number nine shirt alongside Corky.

But that was our culture, and a lot of that came from the Walton boys – me, Roger, Dave Donaldson and Billy Edwards. Billy – who was a policeman, on the beat at Plough Lane after he retired from playing – drew a comparison with the later generation of the Crazy Gang when we all met up in 1997. 'They are a better team now but not as hard,' he told the *Mail on Sunday*. 'Vinnie Jones is a pussycat compared with us. I had such a short fuse I once butted my teammate John Leslie in training. I've done some terrible things, over-the-top tackles and calling referees names that would have earned me red cards today. If anyone got physical with us, we'd gang up on them and they'd live to regret it. The tackling was much harder.' And that from a player who used to play for cultured old Tottenham in the Second Division before heading to Walton . . .

For the likes of Corky, and others who would arrive in the coming years, joining the club was a culture shock. 'One minute I'm knocking about with Roy McFarland,

Colin Todd and Kevin Hector, the next I'm plunged into the hard-drinking, hard-living lifestyle at Plough Lane,' Corky said. 'I was paid so badly in that first season of league football that the club fixed me up to work on a building site to supplement my earnings.' Corky did later admit, however, that 'the odd £50 note would fall into my possession from Sam Hammam. He used to walk about with £5,000 in notes sticking out of his pockets!'

Corky – he was a bloke who could only see dark clouds on a summer's day.

The other major change at Wimbledon in 1978 was that I had now embarked upon my managerial career, as Dario's assistant, a role I took up in February, while still playing. Allen had been a great mentor in setting me out on this road. While he witnessed me pulling back the windscreen wipers on the cars of teammates, blocking in someone who I knew wanted to get away early, and generally messing around, I also understood that you didn't mess with him, and he taught me good things. I would often, even as a player, go to midweek matches and watch the opposition, to check out their tactics as well as the man who I was expected to mark the following Saturday.

Ron Noades had actually offered me the manager's job before Dario, but I had turned it down, thinking the time wasn't right. And I think that was definitely the correct decision. There were other factors too. Dario had been appointed as Allen Batsford's assistant, but on a higher wage. Allen had steered the club into the league but I thought his authority was undermined by Ron – even after we got into the Football League he had to wait for a full-time contract. It was, in my opinion, a kick in the teeth to a decent man, and it was no wonder it took us eight games to record our first win. I felt a sense of loyalty to Allen, of course – to a man who had influenced my career so much.

Looking back on it now, though, I suppose it was the perfect storm for what Wimbledon would become. Dario used me much as I would later employ Wally, as his eyes and ears on the pitch. I was 33, so knew my way around the game, even if I had little practical coaching experience. But by April my playing career was being wound down. I was aware my legs were going, and Dario concurred: after a 5–0 thumping of Southport and a home win over Stockport, in which Les Briley scored his first goal for the Dons, that was my lot as a first-team player.

I left first-team action to turn out for – and run – the reserves, and I was content doing that. I could sense raw talent, smell the hunger of youngsters who wanted to succeed because they believed there was nothing else. And, of course, I could have a lot of fun doing it, with all the opportunities for pranks it presented – although that was nothing compared to what a young apprentice at the club, by the name of Wally Downes, was about to instigate.

While I would go on to manage Wimbledon, Wally

would manage the dressing room. He was the club's pumping heart, my go-to guy and perfect disciple. He was a bright boy who played the role of mischief-maker and was my aide-de-camp throughout the club's rise, fall and rise. He was madcap, a crazy horse, and if something happened then you could bet his thumbprints were not far away.

He is one of eight in his extended family named Wally, and most of them were market traders from Shepherd's Bush. He was signed by Wimbledon as a 16-year-old after impressing Ron Noades and scout Alan Smith while playing for West London Boys against Merton at Craven Cottage. Wally was the club's first professional, joining us when we had just been elected into the Football League in 1977. He had seen all his mates gobbled up by other clubs and thought his chance had gone, until Ron came to his rescue. Eventually. He was approached with an offer . . . and that was that. Wally waited. Nothing. Accepting his moment had passed, he took a job in a record company and was ready to join Alan Smith, who by then had taken over at Dulwich Hamlet, until Ron arrived at his door. Wally was turfed out of the living room as his dad and Noades opened talks. Wally was eventually offered £5 a week and an apprenticeship. His dad later walked around in an expensive suit, shoes and overcoat. Wally never looked back, and the rest is the history you are about to read.

Wally's antics are legendary – from tying up a player on a roof rack and driving him down the busy A3, to once causing the whole team to be thrown off the team coach. In the latter case we were driving back from a reserve-team game and we stopped off for fish and chips. We got them in a big square box, and when he finished his Wally put the box over the driver's bald head – I think his name was Brian – but because there were still odd chips and bits of batter in the box, his head started to burn, and even though we were hurtling down the motorway he was forced to make an emergency stop. The driver then ordered everyone out, leaving us stranded on the hard shoulder. Not surprisingly the driver quit soon after.

But Wally is the nearest thing to me in football. Competitive, ambitious and loyal; niggling, often in your face and, if I'm honest, a pain in the arse at times. But while I was a very competitive player, a dirty bastard, Wally had better ability, and used it to create mayhem and then leave the stage. Like me, though, Wally also wanted to learn, to be a winner and to plough his own furrow in life and football.

I turned a blind eye to some of Wally's antics because I liked mavericks. Allen Batsford allowed me rope because he knew I cared for the team. He'd come down hard on anything that he believed stretched decency, but overall he secretly enjoyed the playground foolishness. I believed that if you created a bond in the dressing room, you take it on to the pitch. So I allowed Wally and others certain licence to play silly buggers, but they all knew when to stop.

Wally was a grammar school boy, although I am not

sure how many days a week he attended. I think he discovered the 'one term a year' routine. But he was bright, sharp as a tack, and ready to go. His first love is QPR, but Ron and Wimbledon gave him his chance, and for that, I know, he is eternally grateful. He'd work on the fruit and veg stall – so he said, I never saw proof of it – before catching the bus to our training ground just off the A3, by the Robin Hood roundabout. I always thought that was an apt place for us because we were always robbing the rich!

I knew we had signed Wally but I wasn't particularly aware of him at the time. Back then I didn't just run the reserve team and my insurance brokerage, I also kept an eye on Nelson's, the nightclub on the bottom floor of our wobbly stand at Plough Lane, where players and fans would mix, and the Sportsman pub, also attached to the ground. It was where the players would rush to after a game, mingling with punters and enjoying a laugh. Imagine that today. Coincidentally, board meetings would start at 2 p.m. and usually finish around 11 p.m.

But, as I said, I really didn't take much notice of Wally until Dickie Guy came to me and said, 'That new apprentice is not shy. Christ, where did we get this kid from? Does he ever stop talking?' So I took notice. I liked the guy. He would arrive every day with a smile, albeit a mischievous one, and learn. Reputations meant nothing to him. He got stuck in from the moment he arrived – after eating a full English breakfast, mind you. There was a café at the training ground, where the players paid for their own meals. And they weren't pasta and chicken.

I noticed in Wally a kind of confidence and a sharp tongue. He liked a laugh but also knew when it was time to get serious. In fact, he was better than me because not only could he play, he was also more streetwise. No one got the better of young Wally Downes. He listened, learned but also had the mental strength to say what he thought. Most of the team at that time were in their thirties, and often put Wally in his place, but at the same time he never stopped picking their brains.

From an early age Wally continually suffered with a knee injury and that, I believe, stopped him from really going on to become a very, very good player. I always had Wally in my side when he was fit, though, so much so that I even changed tactics to suit him, moving him to sweeper around 1982. It wasn't something I was truly happy about, though, and eventually I went to the side and said it's not working and we're switching to 4–4–2. Wally basically disliked that. I could see the look on his face and to my mind he was thinking, 'Well, that's me finished. Non-league here I come.' But he bought into my idea, backed me 100 per cent even.

Wimbledon was the ideal place for a lad like Wally to grow up and learn. Wally accepted my change of tactics and changed his game to suit, and it's fair to say he never once let the club down. In fact, he lifted it with his banter and skill. We became close and I often heard players ask him 'Where's your dad today?' He took it well, but then would get his revenge with a bit of mischief. You often wondered how so many shoes were filled with a brown, sticky substance.

Wally was the Crazy Gang.

Later on, he quickly became firm friends with Vinnie Jones, and the pair ran riot. They would strip rooms, hang hotel beds out of windows and go around wearing balaclavas and throwing buckets of water over people they didn't like, particularly news reporters who turned up at the training ground. The laces of newcomers were constantly cut to pieces. I recall Vinnie telling me how he and Wally once set alight a plastic bag owned by Eric Young. When Young signed he used to have one of those bags that kids carry with the name of your favourite club on the side. His was Brighton, and despite repeated warnings of what would happen to the bag he continually arrived with it. That was enough for Wally and Jonah. They both stood up in the changing room, doused the bag with lighter fuel and put a match to it. It filled the entire room and the café next door with so much billowing, black smoke that the whole place had to be evacuated.

Derek French, the physio, constantly used to tell me he was working with hooligans and reeled off names like Downes, Morris, Smith, Peters and Cork, but he added, 'If I ever go to war I want them by my side.' Nice to see Wally maintained my traditions and carried on the legacy.

When I became manager of Sheffield United one of

the first things I did was to take Wally with me, signing him on a free transfer. Although he was approaching the end of his playing life, I knew he still had much to offer – both on and off the field. He was a dressing-room character but, just as important, someone who I could trust. And that's still the case today. At Sheffield United, Wally was sent off twice in a short time, against Leeds and Bradford, and claimed afterwards that it was a West Yorkshire conspiracy. But Wally achieved far more off the pitch, until he broke his ankle in a pre-season friendly against our neighbours Sheffield Wednesday. He never played for me again and left at the end of that season to coach at Crystal Palace. Wally later became manager of Brentford and was a coach under Steve Coppell at Crystal Palace and Reading. He was also a coach under Alan Pardew at Southampton and has had spells at West Ham and QPR. You don't get those types of jobs, and respect, by just being a joker. He has great knowledge of the game and we are still close to this day.

So close, that I even allow him to beat me at golf sometimes.

3

The Sorcerer's Apprentice

Wally Downes

I BEGAN LIFE AT Wimbledon on £5 a week and left, a decade later, earning £300 a week. In between I broke both my ankles twice, and often thought I was going to be kicked out. There was also the small matter of playing with a split knee-cap – that needed an op and made me look slightly wonky throughout my career.

I wouldn't have changed it for the world. Wimbledon was my life, my saviour, and I like to think I repaid them with honours and laughter. I was proud to be their captain. I arrived at the club in the dying days of them being in the Southern League, training on Tuesdays and Thursdays, playing mostly in the Suburban League. It was a joy.

One of my mum's sisters had two fruit and veg stalls, one in Shepherd's Bush market and a massively busy one in Kilburn. I'd get up before school and go to pull the barrow out in the Bush, put all the 'flash' up – that's the array of fruit and veg – then shoot off to school before coming back later to help put it away. I loved the job, interacting with the public, being part of a vibrant market, always busy and taking money. I even continued while I was playing for Wimbledon, in the same manner: open up, go to work, come back, collect the take, order for the morning, pack it away and go home and rest. Quite a heavy workload for an aspiring footballer, but I wouldn't have swapped it for the world; it's part of who I am and who the family are – and the wages weren't exactly great at Wimbledon!

When I was 14, I had been invited to train with QPR. I was obviously absolutely ecstatic to play for the club I supported, but unfortunately it didn't work out. All of my teammates for first Hammersmith and then west London schools – and I mean ALL of my teammates – had been taken on on schoolboy forms. I knew I was one of the best behind Mark Lovell, who had been made the Fulham youth-team captain, so just had to sit and suffer while they all had the kudos of being at a football club. I didn't know what I had done to deserve this snub, but I had clearly done something, or had upset someone, and to this day don't know what. Although, looking back, I suppose I was far too opinionated and mouthy for my age for the clubs that were looking. So when Wimbledon came in, I was obviously pleased as punch.

West London Schools were playing our last two representative games, in 'the Tommy Trinder Cup'. For any youngsters who don't remember him, Tom was an old comedian. He was also chairman of Fulham, and every year Merton Borough would play West London in a two-legged affair – the first at Plough Lane in the borough of Merton and the second at Craven Cottage in west London. It was always the last game of the season and had always been a nice way to thank the players from each team for representing them for the previous five years. I can't remember the score at Plough Lane but it must have been close as we went into the return at Craven Cottage very determined. Most of our side were on Fulham's books at the time – Mark Lovell, Robbie Wilson, Nicky Martin, Peter Johnson – and Merton had the likes of Micky Fillery, who was at Chelsea, and Chris Dibble, who was at Millwall but later had a year with us at the Dons.

It was to be my last game for the group and I had no idea who or where I was gonna play next, as I was still surplus to any football club's requirements. Anyway, I had a good game, we won and, luckily, Ron Noades and Alan Smith, who was managing the reserves, were at the game, on the lookout for a couple of youngsters to take on. They said I had 'bossed it', which I took as a massive compliment considering the opposition. I was invited to evening training a couple of days later, and was surprised to be thrown in with the first-team squad. And so it was by the skin of my teeth I'd made it on to someone's books!

Ron Noades was to play a big part in my life, later signing me as a coach at Crystal Palace under Steve

Coppell, who'd seen me play loads of times. Steve hated defensive coaching and I was put in charge of that area. It worked well and we continued together in the same vein at Reading, where we won promotion to the Premier League. Ron also made me his manager at Brentford after he took over there.

I played regularly for the youth team at Wimbledon, but after one game Allen Batsford said to me, 'We need to get your knee done.' I didn't realize until then I had a problem. I was sent to Great Ormond Street Hospital and they discovered I had a broken knee cap and that it had happened several years before, when I was 13 or 14. I had an operation to take half of the knee away. I hobbled around all summer and spent most of my time at Headley Court, the famous RAF rehabilitation centre in Surrey, where servicemen and women were also sent to recover from hideous injuries. Most had lost limbs, and seeing their spirit and admiring their courage made me realize how lucky I was. I had started working on the fruit and veg stall at the age of 11, and this gave me the confidence to talk to people – it cemented the outgoing personality that clearly hindered my schoolboy career but helped me enormously later on. Going to Headley Court showed me another side of life.

I had a job at CBS Records, not in the recording department, I might add (this was pre-boy band), and continued my rehab at the club. When I was fit enough I would work Saturday mornings and come in to be the 13th man if required. This proved quite lucrative, as I could sell any records that the players had ordered. When I wasn't needed for the game, I went and played for my mate's pub team.

I didn't really know Dave Bassett at that stage but as time went on we seemed to click. I think he saw me the same way as Allen Batsford saw him. During one of my many comebacks, when we were in the Second Division, he came to me and told me that Joe Kinnear, who was then manager at Doncaster, would like to take me on loan. I spoke to Joe and his first words were, 'Sorry, but I can only offer you £600 a week.'

Six hundred pounds a week! More than I ever earned at Wimbledon, in fact, it was twice what I was on and they were two divisions below! Sadly, the move never took place.

I had played around 250 games by the time I turned 23, but only about 15 in the five years that followed. My career at Wimbledon was defined on 7 April 1984 when I broke my ankle playing at home against Hull. This is my only regret of my life at Plough Lane. It was to happen three more times. Although I was to return, I wasn't the same player, yet Harry continued to believe in me. We had a great relationship. He was one of the boys, but we all knew he was also the manager.

Dave made a fun speech at my testimonial dinner, a boxing night at the Hilton Hotel, but he also got into trouble for dropping his trousers. It was his party piece. That night I was given £3,000 to hold (a decent sum in

1987), the result of an auction. Instead of handing it over the next day to my committee, I headed to the upstairs bar with pals . . . and you can guess the rest. I'm sure it's still the only testimonial to end up in the red.

Asking Harry for a rise was like squeezing blood from a stone. He invented the flick-a-coin technique, saying if he won 'you get nothing'. We swore he had a double-headed coin because he rarely lost. I went to him one day and asked for a few bob extra in wages and he said no. In the end, we settled for me always having Monday off so I could work on the family stall to make up my wages. Can you imagine Wayne Rooney negotiating a similar deal with Manchester United? Yet we didn't mind. We loved the place and him. It was hard work too because we were certainly made aware results mattered most.

Harry always made sure we had fun, creating mayhem before gently disappearing. He loved throwing pebbles in the pond and watching the ripples. His days as reserve-team coach under Dario Gradi were a hoot. He made the mistake one day of turning up in a yellow top. It didn't stay that colour for long. As soon as we were out of sight of the dressing room, he was jumped on and rolled into a muddy pool of water.

He didn't really change when he became manager. Except this time I was THE NEW HIM. He encouraged me to rib players, particularly newcomers. When Dave Beasant arrived, Harry approved of me winding Beasant up. In training I would turn to Harry and look at Dave and say, 'Where did you get him from?' or 'Send him back to non-league!' I nicknamed him 'Lurch' after the butler from the TV show *The Addams Family*, and it stuck.

Lurch rarely carried any money with him, except the correct amount when he needed a drink and a snack after training. If you ever asked him for money, he'd reply he couldn't because he never carried more than a pound in his pocket. He made the mistake of telling me that his mum left a pound behind the clock on the mantelpiece for his daily spending money. From then on, fans would shout at him, 'Got your quid from behind the clock!'

One day I caused Lurch to boil over. Harry ordered a one-to-one session against him and ordered us to try to take the ball round him. That was the plan. When my turn came I would get within 20 yards of him and either chip the ball over him, or curl it into goal – basically do anything but follow orders. I could see steam coming from Lurch's ears. Harry was loving every minute. By the fifth or sixth time I had scored, Lurch raced from goal to try to get the ball, but I whacked it straight in his stomach. He accused me of not having the bottle to take him on. Next time, I did, but Lurch came out with a two-footed tackle and caught me on my damaged knee. A few inches lower and it could have ended my career there and then. But did it stop me? Never.

Pranks were part and parcel of our daily lives, from spreading Deep Heat on underpants – we got Harry with that once, and he was literally hopping mad on the touchline – to knotting trousers and cutting clothes to shreds. I never, ever, burnt clothes. Honest.

Alan Cork was also not slow in coming forward, but another great prankster was Steve Parsons, a long-time friend from Shepherd's Bush. We went to Dave Beasant's 21st in a hall, and he spent the night hitting his head with pints of beer. No one was safe. Mouthy apprentices were pelted with rotten eggs and flour and then ordered to clear the mess up.

Talking of 21st birthdays, Wisey's was a hoot! We had it in a hall in Notting Hill after an away game – it was a great bash, with lots of Den's mates who he'd grown up with, as well as all his football mates. Typically these halls had a time for throwing out, and I think Dennis had secured an extra half hour with the caretaker. When this time came around, the do was still in full swing and nobody looked like leaving. The caretaker came in and demanded the music be switched off, but we weren't too keen and, after a short discussion, it was decided we could have a last half hour. Lovely . . .

That half hour whizzed past and the party had escalated superbly. We wanted another hour. The caretaker was adamant this would not happen, so the attitude adjuster (in the form of 50 quid) was brought into play and we got the extra hour . . . marvellous!

The party was now heaving, just getting to full tilt, when he was over again, dead on the hour! He wanted the music off again; we've been nice and got half an hour, then negotiated the £50 – no mean sum for a caretaker for an hour's work in those days – and here he was, back again, wanting to sling us out! This time he was very adamant – but so were we – and he started to get a little bit vocal now and was causing a bit of a scene. So to avoid any animosity, we went back into the store room so we could hear what he had to say without the thumping disco beat. He was still proving slightly intransigent, so we sat him down, tried to get him to relax . . . My exact memory of the next few minutes is a bit fuzzy, but somebody spotted some gaffer tape on the shelf, and the next thing you knew the caretaker was wrapped up on the chair, and we had the extra couple of hours that were required. Luckily the music kept his protests from us! A wonderful time was had by all, and he got another hundred quid for the inconvenience, and was highly delighted. I've always thought he'd have been better to just join the party!

After me, Glyn Hodges was the first kid to get a break in the first team. The senior squad were very protective of him, as he was so young and so gifted. That wasn't the case with his peers, who used to slaughter him. He was known as 'Dario's pet'. They hammered him. He once had a very severe haircut that made his head look a bit too big. Guppy (Mark Morris), Fish and the rest were merciless about this, and one way or another it got round to the first team, whereupon it was decided to measure Hodges' head, and, sure enough, he had the biggest bonce at the club. Hodges held the title for years, despite administering what became known as 'the bootlace test' to measure every new signing's head. When Sanch turned up he finally lost the title.

Playing Bristol City away one season we were warming up (i.e., smashing balls at Lurch) when the opposition ran out to do the same at the other end. We did a double-take. Being the young piss-takers that we were, we zoned in on their keeper, John Shaw – he was completely bald! It wasn't that cool to have the shaven head in those days – you didn't see many, the comb-over was still pretty fashionable! Frenchie was in his first season with us and had bought all of his high-tech, top-of-the-range physio equipment from Barnet FC – essentially, a bag with an old ball bladder filled with water and a sponge. In the middle of winter that sponge of freezing water would get most players up a bit lively. Anyhow, one thing led to another and it was decided that we should try to put Baldy off, get at him, generally fuck with him about his wiggy slap head. So, just while Hodge was preparing to take a corner early in the second half, I pulled Frenchie's ball bladder from out of my slip and stuck it on my head. I went and stood right by Shaw. He dissolved in laughter, the ref got the hump and made me remove it, but we scored from the corner. That said, John had the last laugh: we got done 4–1, but still shared a beer after the game.

The early years were great, but as time went on Wimbledon knew they had to sign decent players to move on, and the likes of Tommy Cunningham, Tony Tagg, Chris Dibble, Les Briley and Paul Denny arrived.

It simply meant us youth team players – Andy Thorn, Hodges, Paul Fishenden, John Gannon, Mark Morris, Kevin Gage, Steve Ketteridge, Andy Sayer and myself had to raise our game or move out. And we soon realized we weren't that bad and could easily hold our own with the more experienced arrivals. From a youth team squad of 13 put together by Harry, Gage, Morris, Fishenden, Hodges and myself played for Wimbledon in all four divisions. Alan Cork and Dave Beasant, although not home-grown players, were also around in those early days and also played for the club from top to bottom. Not many clubs then and now could boast that.

Long journeys home on the train from places like Rochdale and Halifax could get riotous. There was no exclusivity, no players' carriage back then – we were all in with the fans. Only a couple of hundred went to the games, but about 50 of those would be on the train. We would inevitably end up draining the buffet car dry and have a right old sing-song with them, win, lose or draw. On a good night this would continue on the coach from the train station back to the Sportsman pub or the dance floor at Nelson's. In a sense we were actively encouraged to be binge drinkers in those days, but boy would we have to sweat it out on Mondays. It was a different time, and attitudes to refreshment weren't as enlightened, but most teams did the same, so I suppose you could call it a level playing field!

Siege mentality has become a fashion item at clubs these days. Sir Alex Ferguson used it during his days at

Manchester United. We had that mentality from day one in the league. We had the lowest gates, the smallest ground and lowest wages. Friendship, spirit and 'us against them' were the things that bound us together. What Wimbledon achieved is something remarkable, and will never be repeated again.

Anyway, back to where it all started. So after rejecting the record company for an uncertain life in football, I carried on working on the family stall, getting up at 3 a.m., going to the market to buy the fruit and veg, return, lay it out and then jump on a 72 bus from the Bush to Wimbledon's training ground on the edge of Wimbledon Common. Richardson Evans was owned by the council and used by local teams over the weekends. The 'dining room' was a roadside café, which we shared mostly with lorry drivers. It didn't feel strange to us, sharing cuppas with truckers, because we didn't know any different. As noted, most of us were in the last chance saloon anyway, so this was the Ritz as far as we were concerned. Work, if you can call it that, was a fun place to be. I went every day with a smile on my face. I have been at a lot of clubs since and witnessed moaners, groaners and lots of unhappy people. I never witnessed that at Wimbledon. It was Butlin's without the sea, but we also took playing, training and learning seriously. When we finished, well, that was different.

At training one evening, I knew I was joining a club that was some distance off the wall. Harry knew that when we were done I usually caught the bus home, but on this occasion he asked Roger Connell to take me home. Roger was a Spice Boy before they invented Old Spice. He had the mullet, the short shorts and fancy sports car. The lot. He was the business. He would often go out down the West End on a Thursday night and turn up to be the star player on the Saturday. When Harry asked him to give me a lift home, I could see the despair in his face. 'Me? Super Rog? Giving a 16-year-old, scruffy, £5-a-week apprentice a lift home? Whatever next? Oh, I suppose so.' So we climbed into his car. We had little to talk about because I was the rookie, the boot cleaner, general dogsbody. He was a first-team player. Eventually he broke the ice by asking what I had in my bag. Now my bag was full of the previous day's takings on the stall and I hadn't had time to bank it. So I had taken it to work on the bus. I mentioned this to Roger. Five hours later I'm a 16-year-old drinking champagne in Ronnie Scott's, getting chatted up by a 30-year-old Essex girl. I thought, 'This is the life for me.' I couldn't wait for training to come around again next Tuesday evening.

Wimbledon here I come. The ground rules had been laid.

As Harry mentioned at the start of the book, we've been gathering all the ex-players to tell their part in the Crazy Gang story. So now it's time to hand over to another of my fellow players. Here's Ketts with his memories.

Steve Ketteridge

Me and Corky came down from Derby. Corky stayed but Tommy Docherty called me back – I think he just wanted to confirm how shit I was before he properly bombed me. I remember four months later I came back down, probably aged 17 or 18, and went straight in the reserves with Harry, which was an experience in itself. It was a massive culture shock because we had come from the youth team at Derby. I remember playing my first game with Harry and he used to wear this massive sovereign ring. As a midfielder you used to look up to see the ball coming down from a goalkick and suddenly I heard CRACK! And there is a bloke bleeding out of his mouth . . .

Harry and Dario were chalk and cheese. They were both so professional but so different. Dario was a great coach in how he developed players, and Harry was a winner and a man's man. Harry knew what the old Liverpool team with Jimmy Case and Souness was about, but Dario wouldn't have that – that was the difference. They took different paths but were both very successful.

Dario used to quite like me as a player, but I was still a kid – I was 17 and looked 14, but I had Wally and there were always stories from the minibuses. Harry used to get us nicking cones for training off the roadworks on the A3 because we couldn't afford to buy them. They were formative trips in the reserves. Harry came from non-league and I had been at Derby with players like

Charlie George, Colin Todd and all them superstars. I arrived at Wimbledon and there was Roger Connell and Dickie Guy, and I don't mean it disrespectfully, because they were good footballers, but they all had other jobs. Dave Donaldson was a fucking pilot!

Wally, even at 17, was a strong character, and he made you grow up. If you couldn't survive the chat and piss-taking you were pushed out – and that was just in the reserves. As we rose through the ranks, people got bigger and stronger, and if you were a weak person you stood no chance – no matter how good you were. I don't think we ever lost any really good players because of that – mainly because we never paid enough money to have any really good players in the first place!

The senior players were non-league players, and we were arriving from bigger clubs. With Dario in charge the transition to professionalism was happening. By the time me and Wally got in the team there were more professionals.

When I joined Palace later on there were a lot of senior pros who had played at a higher level and were out for themselves, but at Wimbledon we were all together. At other clubs it was a case of 'you're on your own' – you were judged on what you did as individuals. At Wimbledon, if you were having a nightmare you would certainly be told about it, but at the same time the team would pull together even tighter to get us through. There was a team ethic and we used to get through it, somehow. I don't know how.

Harry was always so organized. He was doing things that were so far ahead of their time. People were called clever when they started doing things ten years after Wimbledon did them. We were watching videos of ourselves and our opposition when they were still in black and white. We had a fat goalkeeper – the Flying Pig – in the reserves and his dad was a sergeant at Wimbledon police station, so we used to use his CCTV cameras to film matches and training!

I remember either the first or second time we got relegated and me and Harry went for a run. And toward the end of the season I had done my ankle ligaments and I thought I was going to get released. I remember going on the run and praying – because I had two young kids – I would not be given the elbow. But Harry said, 'You've grown up and there's more to come from you,' and he gave me a new one-year contract – but there was no rise, of course!

4
The First of Many

Harry

Les Briley took over from me as Wimbledon captain for the start of the 1978–79 season. He had been our record signing, at no less than £16,000, when he had signed from Hereford the previous season – they were a Second Division team at the time, so he was quality. Les would go on to form a dynamic partnership with Midget (aka Steve Galliers) in midfield. They were chalk and cheese, though. Les was a great provider, and an all-action player too, whereas Midget buzzed constantly around the field with non-stop aggression: 'a tigerish midfield player who loves to get into the thick of the action', as that September 1977 issue of *Dons Outlook* called him under the headline THIS BOY'S DYNAMITE. 'Although he hasn't scored yet, he is playing with tremendous enthusiasm and should be a vital member of the squad.'

We had first come across Midget playing for Chorley in the FA Trophy, and a right little menacing fucker he was. He's such a major player in the Crazy Gang story we'll let him take over from here.

Steve Galliers

I was at Chorley and we drew Wimbledon in the FA Trophy. Our manager then went to watch them play and said they had the dirtiest midfield player he had ever seen – Harry Bassett. When the game came, I thought to myself, 'If I don't give this bloke some I'm going to get slaughtered.' But as it happened Harry was playing on the other side of midfield and I was up against Glenn Aitken instead, and I kicked shit out of him, thinking it was Bassett, but Glenn was never that sort of player.

We ended up playing them three times. It was 2–2 at Wimbledon, then we got them back to Chorley where the average gate was 600, but they had 6,500 who saw another 2–2 draw, and then we had a replay at Walsall and Chorley took 19 coaches of fans down, which wasn't bad for a village team from the Cheshire League.

At the end of that season Wimbledon got in the league and they signed me for £1,500 and I was given a £35-a-week contract. I drove down in my Mark One Cortina but didn't have a map so I ended up lost in Tottenham. The first person I met was Ron Noades and he drove me to Richardson Evans in his Range Rover. I stayed with Allen Batsford for two weeks and then I moved in with the programme editor Eric Wilcox – it was supposed to be for two weeks and it ended up being for five years. They couldn't get rid of me!

Allen saw something in me that he thought he could work with but then it didn't work out for him and I felt sorry for him when he left because he had worked hard to get us into Division Four, yet halfway through the season he was gone. If we had been full-time from the start it might have been better for him, and he could have been more fairly judged. We got in the league and thought, 'Oh shit, we need to get a team together.' We were part-time so we very rarely trained together, and then we got hammered away at Enfield in the FA Cup, when they were a good side.

We went full-time then even though some of the boys like Dave Donaldson and Jeff Bryant stayed part-time. Really, it was from then that we became more organized and had a good run at the end of the year. But I hardly played during that period because Dario didn't like me, he didn't rate me at all. Dario was going to sell me at the end of that season to Wycombe for £500, but Harry said, 'He has a year left, you might as well see how he develops.' Or at least that's the story I was told.

Dario was a good coach and there wasn't a great change in personnel – all we needed was a bit of direction and thought in what we were trying to achieve. The following season we were more organized and we got some new players in, people like Steve Perkins, Paul Haverson and Tommy Cunningham.

I knew Ron Noades and Harry had a good relationship, they seemed to get on well. Ron was a qualified coach as well, and he rated Harry because he had not only been a good player but was a student of the game – he was interested in learning football. We would finish training and Harry would go and do extra coaching with the young lads.

If you look at the people there, there was a cross section. Wimbledon at that time did not have quite enough players coming through from the youth team, but Peter Prentice and John Sparks were very good at getting young kids in from around the borough, and kids that Chelsea and QPR had let go. I say there was a collective of different types, but they almost all had a point to prove. All they needed was direction, and that is what they got.

Dario only liked nice footballers and nice boys, whereas Harry could see beyond that. But they were a good combination because of that, not in spite of it. Harry treated you like a man and expected you to behave like a man, but he was a bit of a big kid himself. Often he would start the antics that went on and then stand back and let it kick off. There was always something happening on the away trips. There would always be somebody stripped naked in a lay-by, or on top of the minibus. It was never major stuff. It was young lads letting off steam. Unruly teenagers, basically.

I went on my first trip abroad with Wimbledon, and after about ten minutes sitting in the sun I thought, 'This is boring.' So I said to Roger Connell, 'What do you normally do when you go away?' and he turned to me and handed me a Cuba Libre and said, 'You drink one of these.' That was about one o'clock in the afternoon and by seven that night I had fallen off the barstool and was carried up to bed just as Dario was coming down to dinner. So you can probably see why he wanted to sell me.

I went on eight Magaluf trips with Wimbledon and they were just mental, young lads having a good time. I didn't think it was ever evil. Just like any jokes or pranks, there is a line that when crossed makes things not funny any more, but it was never the case during my time – which ended in '88–'89 – that we overstepped the mark.

I socialized with Harry and Roger and Dave Donaldson, but when I came down to London I was young and naïve. I was from 'up north' and hadn't long left my little village, and they looked after me – not in a parental way, but they just included me. Harry talks a lot but he isn't one to put an arm round you and coddle you.

Harry is a very intelligent bloke and, psychologically, he always knew what buttons to push. In all my years there I cannot remember a time when he ever said, 'Well done.' But you knew yourself, and if you weren't doing well then you were out of the team. He was a student of the game and could talk about it for hours, but I never really listened because I was never that interested in it, to be honest. I enjoyed playing, but I was never interested in putting cones out for other people or anything else like that.

Corky was a really nice bloke. He was another who thought a lot about the game and was an intelligent footballer who liked a drink as well. Corky never changed. He was never up in the air or down in the dumps, he was 'steady Eddie', and one of the best finishers I've ever seen. They went in off his toe and head and shin but he also scored some great goals; he was just a natural goalscorer. It was his movement and the way Harry worked it. We always had two good people out wide who could cross it. People would say we just lumped it, but there was thought behind what we did and we knew what we had to do in certain areas of the pitch.

Corky had a nice Austin Allegro car one year, brown I think. But he wanted a new car because it kept breaking down, so they drove it over to Edgware and they tried to set it on fire but they couldn't get it to light on the first go. So they went back, and as they got near the car it exploded.

I struggled in my first season. I had been playing in Blackburn reserves since I was 15 against the likes of Liverpool and Manchester United. I didn't understand the training ethos and the eating right; watching the others helped but it took me a year to buy into it. I used to get kicked to shit all the time. My first game for Blackburn reserves was against Macclesfield in pre-season, and I had my nose broken after 15 minutes. I wasn't one who went looking for confrontation but

I soon learned to look after myself because in that era you had to.

After games it wasn't an uncommon sight to see people having stitches put in their eye, and cuts . . . things like that. Harry would plant a seed in your mind when we were travelling up north to games. He would say, 'Be careful today because these lot are expecting a load of southern softies.' That's all he said, but that made us refuse to be intimidated by the northern teams, which had happened to us in the past.

It was a different game then. I don't even watch football now because it's such a different sport – there is no tackling. I prefer rugby, where you get physicality and honesty. I used to get into trouble for back-chat – my quickest booking was 15 seconds at Huddersfield for giving the ref a mouthful. We used to get fines for dissent, and that was one of the times I fell out with Harry – his rule was you would never get fined for a tackle, only back-chat. When we were in the Second Division, once we were playing up at Middlesbrough. We were 2–1 down and a bloke was fannying around with the ball so I went through him near the touchline and I got booked and fined 50 quid. Because Harry went back on his word we fell out.

We knew when we were travelling up north who the hard players were up there. When Billy Whitehurst was at Hull he was an animal, a man-mountain, but Harry would say, 'Don't wind him up, just say, "Hello, Bill".' If we didn't cross him he was good as gold, but if you got into him he was like a man possessed.

Reaching the top division was joyous, but it had been something we had worked for – that success didn't come without any thought and planning. Over the years, after Harry took over, we had almost constant success; before that we did have to cope and deal with some failure.

When it finally came to me leaving Wimbledon for good I had played 16 games before I injured my knee, and Vinnie came into the team. Harry had Vinnie on a tight rein at the start, and Vinnie was always all right, but he had a wicked temper – I saw him do things that I am sure he wasn't proud of, but he had a good heart and was a nice lad.

We used to get one-year contracts, so when we were in the Fourth Division our main focus was just getting another contract. We weren't thinking about promotion or the First Division. And then when we were getting promoted we knew we were getting a tenner rise at the end of the season and that was the big deal. I don't think we were ambitious. I think we believed we were better than other people thought and said we were.

I remember watching Wally play Southern Counties and he looked like a Beckenbauer for his age group. Glyn Hodges was talented, as were Winterburn and Gage and Cork – we had good young players who were ambitious. Hodge wasn't lazy, he was big; he had an amazing left foot and he never missed those cross-field passes or shots that either went in or Corky got on the end of. Francis Joseph was not the toughest bloke in the dressing room – he made out he was tough, and a bit of a gangster, but really he was a wimp! He was such a genuinely nice guy and I had many a good night out with him. He would get all soppy when he had a drink.

Fash had an aura about him, and even after all he had achieved in football his opinion of himself was probably higher than it should have been. But, to his credit, even though he didn't drink he would come with us on a night out, and I found him all right. I don't know what happened later on but I think once they were labelled 'the Crazy Gang' they had to play up to it.

There were a lot of good people; we were not stupid. Sanch was a well-educated man and he wouldn't stand for it. He wouldn't try to stop people doing things, but he just wouldn't get involved in it. That was your choice: you got carried along with it or you didn't. The way I look back on it is, we were good mates. You could take anyone out of the 20 of us and room with anyone and get on fine, go for a pint; there weren't any cliques, we all got on really well.

The Crazy Gang label made people do stupid things. I am sure if we tried to do the things we did then now, we would get in a lot more trouble than we did – everything getting reported on social media.

Bassett never pulled any punches and his volleys could be brutal and me and him would fall out a lot. Sometimes, if we got beat, he would tell us we weren't fit enough or didn't care enough, and that simply was not true. He didn't do it all the time, but you knew if we'd had a bollocking it was likely he would still have the hump on Monday morning. Harry would drop me quite regularly if I didn't play well, but generally I played. It was good that nobody felt immune to being dropped. Harry would always give someone else a chance – if you didn't do it you were out.

I knew every Wimbledon fan by name at the start, that was one of the best things about it. We would go up on the train with the fans and have a drink with them on the way back. At the start of the first season in the league things weren't going very well, and they seemed to single Harry out for a lot of stick. I remember once at Plough Lane he went in the crowd to talk to a few of them. It wasn't aggressive, but he just spoke to them. People either loved or hated Harry, but I think they all liked him in the end, and quite rightly so.

I left in a dark time, because Corky had suffered a really bad break and Dave Clement had died; that was such a shame because he was such a nice man, and when you see his boy now he is the spitting image of him. No one saw it coming.

When we got in the First Division people thought we would go straight back down, but after about ten games we were doing OK. The results meant the media couldn't stick it to us much, but with every bad result it seemed to be, 'Right, let's hammer them.' I am sure the other boys have said they never found the same camaraderie or will-to-win at any other club they went to. I think people underestimated us: we had talented players, we always scored goals, we never went to draw 0–0 or keep it tight. That was the result of our years working together, and it gives me a tremendous amount of pride that no one can ever take away from us. We had good and bad times, but we laughed through it all.

When we were shit, Harry used to give it to us something rotten in the dressing room. There was one game at Oxford when we lost by three or four goals, but at half-time I thought I had done all right. But he slaughtered us and sent us straight back out on the pitch to stand around, embarrassed, in front of our own fans.

We didn't help ourselves at times, of course. I used to room with Wally, which meant that sometimes in evening matches we weren't in the best of shape, as we spent all day wrestling. He always wanted to wrestle between 12 and 3 p.m. – we were supposed to be sleeping but he just got in one of those moods so I had to take him down. Professional footballers, eh?

Harry

I should add that Midget could surprise us – and the fans – too. As Charlie Addiman once wrote in the *Dons Outlook*, 'It's so often that one hears of footballers caught boozing it up in various spots that I can tell a tale with a slight difference. One night in a bierkeller in Richmond, vast amounts of overpriced lager were being quaffed at an alarming rate, and in the middle of this drunken orgy was our own Steve Galliers . . . sipping orange juice.'

Dario had us fired up on more than just Quosh, though, when the 1978–79 season kicked off, and a draw at Aldershot was an encouraging start to the campaign. What followed was even better – four wins on the spin and an unbeaten run of 13 league games to set us right on course for promotion to the Third Division. And that was despite getting absolutely mauled by Everton at Goodison Park in the League Cup, 8–0, with England striker Bob Latchford scoring five times, after Dario had expressly told everyone in the dressing room before the game 'at all costs avoid an early goal'. It wasn't Dave Donaldson's finest hour and a half.

Corky was banging in the goals left, right and centre – OK, mostly with his head. He got a hat-trick against Northampton, and after we bounced back from the Everton debacle by winning 1–0 at Stockport, there was talk that scouts were on his trail from higher division clubs. How different would the Wimbledon story have been if any of that reported interest had materialized into something concrete?

We went top of the table after that match, in which Ray Knowles made his debut. He was a hard bastard who had come in from Southall, having spent the majority of his career in non-league football, and with Roger Connell and John Leslie too, we had a wealth of attacking options. Meanwhile, Midget was now running the midfield, and would end up as a shoo-in for player of the season.

The unbeaten run came to an end at Huddersfield, but with Steve Perkins and Paul Haverson coming in from QPR, for £4,000 and £1,000 respectively, to strengthen our injury-hit side, we were soon back to winning ways, and back at the top of the table. Perkins was another whom Dario had worked with at Chelsea, where he captained the reserves.

There is a match report from that season, which makes for interesting reading regarding our tactics. We had beaten Bradford 2–1 at Plough Lane on 30 September 1978, with Knowles, on his birthday, having set up the equalizer for Paul Denny with a long throw, and then Steve Parsons scoring the winner direct from a free-kick. Dario was praised for his 'dead ball coaching'; he said that 'all we told Steve to do was drive free-kicks at goal and let someone else get on the end of them. He found the target as he was supposed to do and a second from another player this time was not needed.' Dario then, however, complained that: 'We haven't really played to our capabilities this season. We are struggling to build our game from the back, knocking too many long hopeful balls for the front three to chase. Currently, we lack width in our build-up, but that is something we are working on.'

Long hopeful balls, you say?

We ran First Division Southampton close in the Third Round of the FA Cup too – with a record crowd of 9,254 at Plough Lane there to see it. As seemed always to be the case in those days, we hardly played in January, games being called off with the weather – and it wasn't hard to waterlog Plough Lane, the pitch was that shit – but it really was fucking arctic that winter, the mud frozen solid. When we finally got a game on, beating Rochdale 3–2, Dario made the famous prediction that we would be in the First Division 'within ten years'. Not bad, Dario, my son, not bad . . .

Corky, sporting an impressive 'tache in those days, scored four as we battered Torquay 6–1 at their place, but we soon hit a rocky patch, failing to score in four straight games in March. That prompted Ron Noades to get the chequebook out, and ahead of the transfer deadline an unheard of £45,000 went to QPR to persuade Tommy Cunningham to swap W12 for SW19. You can say what you like about Ron – and most people have – but he would put his hand in his pocket when the situation required.

Tommy was a key signing, providing the solidity at the back we had been sorely lacking. He had lost his place to Glenn Roeder at QPR, but was a bona fide First Division player, and Dario and I paired him with another new face, Paul Bowgett, who had been attracting some attention in Spurs' reserves. The pair of them settled the ship.

We had slipped out of the promotion places but had games in hand, even if that meant a crazy schedule, playing every three days for months on end. But that was where the extra work that Dario and I had put in on the players' fitness paid off in dividends. It was the one key factor that had been missing from our first season in the Football League. We had to be full-time, and full-on, and it set the tone for what would be one of the Crazy Gang's greatest assets. If there was a harder-working team in the Fourth Division that year I'd like to have seen them.

We had three home games left over to finish the season. We couldn't catch Lawrie Sanchez's Reading, who would be deserving champions, but win one of those games and we would be promoted. It only took one, and that game, against York City on 11 May 1979, saw a place in the starting line-up, at centre-forward, for a 17-year-old called Wally Downes. Well, as I've always said, if you're good enough, you're old enough. And, as I knew he would, Wally didn't disappoint. We beat York 2–1, with Corky's winner five minutes from time – his 25th goal of the season – making Plough Lane erupt with joy.

There was still time for Wally to score his first goal for the club, as he never ceases to remind us (and to which I always respond that you should have scored a few fucking more!), in a 1–1 draw against Allan Clarke's Barnsley, who were also heading for promotion. I recall they brought down 16 coach-loads of supporters for the game. Well, Wally was wearing the number nine shirt, and was playing up front, so he was doing his bloody job! Fair dues, though. It was a decent strike, and he was up against that tough old war-horse Mick McCarthy and gave as good as he got!

Wally kept his place for the final league game against Darlington and, true to form, was booked – taking Wimbledon over the 150 disciplinary points for the season, which led to a hefty fine. That would set another pattern in the fabric of the club's history. The FA called the number of cards that we incurred 'reckless'. Bollocks!

5
Lurching Onwards

Wally

MAKING MY FIRST-TEAM debut, getting promoted and scoring my first Wimbledon goal in the space of a week – life hardly gets better than that. I managed to squeeze in a yellow card too, landing the club with the big fine and leaving my wage packet empty as usual. But if I thought I could walk into the starting line-up as the new season kicked off, I was mistaken. I'd only just turned 18, and there was stiff competition for places, even if Dario had released a lot of the older boys – Jeff Bryant, Roger Connell, Dave Donaldson and Dave Galvin – in the summer. I would have to bide my time, work on my game, and take my chances when they came.

It's funny now looking at the line-ups from some of those games in the Third Division. We weren't much changed, although Ray Lewington coming in from Vancouver Whitecaps of the NASL made some headlines when he joined in September 1979. Ray was another who had played under Dario as a kid at Chelsea, and that deal was a bit of a coup for us, seeing that we didn't pay a penny for him and that Ray was a natural leader on the field. There was also Steve Jones, signed from Walsall to play left-back, but otherwise we had the same basic team that had gained promotion the previous season, with an average age of just 23.

There were some good players in that league, some of whom went on to be really quite handy. Peter Beardsley at Carlisle; Ian Rush at Chester; Norman 'Bite Yer Legs' Hunter at Barnsley. Duncan McKenzie was a striker and Howard Kendall player-manager of Blackburn, who would go up with Grimsby and Sheffield Wednesday, who in turn had Big Jack Charlton in the dugout. Sheffield United were in the same league too, featuring one Alex Sabella, who coached Argentina to the 2014 World Cup final. Not that I was aware of many of them at the time. I had to go about doing my own thing.

But they were bigger names, bigger clubs than us. Some of our players were still, in Dario's words, 'struggling in the professional game'. Allied with a tendency to give away stupid penalties and to leak goals in any fucking fashion we could conjure, plus a regular supply of red and yellow cards to keep our reputation intact, it wasn't any great surprise to most in the game that we were rock bottom of the table come November and would finish 24th in May too. Dario wasn't happy, and let us know about it, believe me. I remember one game, a 0–0 draw against Brentford, when he went absolutely fucking ballistic at half-time. He then complained about our League Cup run – we got to the Fourth Round only to succumb to Swindon – distracting from our league form. I've no idea where he got that quiet man reputation . . .

Ray Lewington jumped ship for Fulham in the spring, with my old mate Steve Parsons opting for Leyton Orient, and Les Briley for Aldershot. After fourteen games without a win, we finally got two points off Hull after I scored a pen to put us in the lead. I scored in the next two games too, but it was all too little, too late. After just one year, we were straight back where we had started. I didn't think my performances had been that bad, despite being unceremoniously dropped in January before an FA Cup replay against Portsmouth, and of course I had my fun off the field, but truth be told, it was a depressing season, made worse by Dario then putting the entire squad up for sale. The fucking cheek!

Despite the meltdown, our less than stellar punt at a higher league, and our financial dirty laundry being aired in public, Ron Noades put a positive spin on the situation. The setback of relegation, he said, would only be a temporary one, and we had to wait for our youth policy to pay off and produce good young players, so that we would be better prepared the next time we made it into the Third Division. As one of those young players, I could heartily agree. Optimistic as ever, I knew the only way was up.

The new year had also seen Lurch turn out for

Wimbledon for the first time – unfortunately he made a terrible ricket and had an absolute fucking 'mare. He only played one more game that season, when Ray Goddard was suspended. Ray was a good keeper but he was getting on a bit, and he used to wear special padding on his hips for when he dived. He couldn't move much and looked a bit like an ice hockey keeper.

I'll never forget the impression Lurch made when he arrived at the club. He turned up to his first day – all 6 feet 4 inches of him – on a Honda 50 moped, dressed head to foot in black leathers. He made the mistake of leaving his crash helmet around. On his way home he put it on and was covered in talcum powder. Anyway, on Lurch's debut, against Blackpool, he let a pea-roller in, but that could happen to anyone back then. We were soon in the bar afterwards telling him and anyone else that cared to listen not to worry about it.

Lurch would, of course, go on to be a Wimbledon legend, and he was intrinsic to the changes that Harry would bring to the club. When Harry adopted our new style of play – very direct, attack-minded, high intensity – we had a massive advantage in our keeper. Brian Clough said a good goalkeeper saved you ten points a season. Well, our goalie not only saved us ten points, he earned us another ten with his distribution!

Playing the way we did meant both full-backs had to push on to engage the opposition as high up the pitch as possible, while the rest of the team pressurized the ball (it's called 'pressing' now) in order to win it back in the opposition's half and greatly increase the chance of scoring. Consequently this left the two centre-halves exposed two against two with the opposition centre-forwards (no teams played with one striker back then), so you had to have maximum confidence in their ability to cope in half an acre of the pitch.

But, in effect, because of our goalie, we were operating with an advantage of three against two. Any ball over the top into space was wasted because our goalie was as quick off the mark as any outfielder – a rare situation, but one he was all too pleased to prove in Friday morning sprint sessions. He was lightning!

This allowed our centre-halves to stay tight and win any ball in front of the strikers, making us always on the front foot and 'after' teams. As our goalie had to get to any ball over the top first, this meant that he constantly had to remain alert and monitor his starting position. If the ball had to be dispatched into the stand, well and good, but if he had time, he was comfortable enough to get it under control and start off a counter-attacking move.

This confidence used to frighten the life out of us on occasion, as Lurch had the ability to judge within inches how close he could let the centre-forward get to him before he released the ball. But at the same time he used to physically and mentally destroy the centre-forwards – they were knackered because their manager would be screaming at them to close down the keeper, and then screaming for them to get back onside when they failed to get the ball. In general, centre-forwards are lazy sods anyway (Corky, Evans!) and would be thoroughly pissed off with this after ten minutes and down tools in a lot of cases.

A manager called Colin Appleton had his goalkeeper taking the ball outside his area to gain a few yards when kicking, and Harry saw this and thought we could exploit it. And as well as being fast, our goalie also thought he was one of the best outfield players. To be fair, he was good, although he was a bit touchy if ever he got tackled! A tart in fact. But when Harry suggested bringing the ball out, he didn't need asking twice.

The keeper delivers the ball back into play at least forty to fifty times per game, so if you have a goalkeeper whose distribution is accurate, then that is a fabulous attacking weapon. Lurch's distribution was magnificent, easily the best in any division and the best I've ever seen since. He was accurate to within a yard over half the length of the pitch, and time after time created direct chances – if not a direct chance, then the pressure to create a chance. He could throw the ball to the halfway line, he could kick half-volleys like missiles and, if needs be, he could launch one skywards that would be up there for what seemed like minutes before hurtling towards earth like a meteor. Defenders hated this.

I haven't begun to tell you about his actual goal-keeping which, for me, was flawless. He had great reactions, superb hands – that sounds obvious for a keeper, I know, but he would catch things in the top corner that others would be happy to get a finger on, let alone punch away.

And there was no more comforting shout from a corner or free-kick than 'Heeeeeper's!' (which was a piss-take on the way goalies always shouted 'keeper's'): you knew Beasant was going to come and take it clean and get you on the attack. He'd be about to take the ball 'at its highest point' which is how keepers are coached; fortunately our goalie's highest point was his height – 6 foot 4 – plus his arms – 9 foot 4 – plus a jump – fucking 12 foot 4! The attackers had better have a bloody good jump to head one in above him from a set-play, or cross, for that matter.

Now I'm thinking about it, the only flaw I ever remember was one that made us all laugh. If Dave had taken a shot or cross and had gone to ground, he'd be so keen to get us on the attack that he'd get himself in a 'mucking fuddle' trying to get in good shape to kick quickly. In the meantime a centre-forward would be trying to stop him and Dave would inevitably balls up the kick, get a free-kick, go mad at the ref and want to kill the forward who'd impeded him!

There were very few goalkeeping coaches in those days so training for them would be shooting practice. This is frowned upon today but back then we'd just pound balls at Lurch all morning. It was the same in the warm-up – all it consisted of was smashing a few balls at him. This left the goalie apoplectic at times, especially if we chipped him. All the outfield players knew we could get him to lose his head in the right circumstances (Harry actively encouraged it at times) and invariably he did. I've seen Lurch chase a player while the rest of the squad rolled up. After 20 or 30 yards he'd realize he'd cracked and dissolve in laughter as well. It was so funny that I'm laughing now, writing it up more than thirty years later.

But from the day he came in, Lurch was such a big part of what we achieved. Our goalie was everything that was great about us lot and it was no surprise to me that he went on to have a great and long career culminating in being selected for England's World Cup squad. He was the best goalie I ever played with or coached. Oh, and he saved a penalty after I left . . .

Here's Lurch's memories.

Dave Beasant

Curly-haired and naïve, I joined Wimbledon in March during their first season in the league. But from the day I arrived to the day I left it was fun. I had played against Wimbledon for Edgware Town in the London Senior Cup. I've got a photograph of that day. I had never played at Plough Lane before and at one end the sun went down over Durnsford Road and I didn't have a cap. I couldn't see a thing. There was a reporter from the *Edgware Times* there and he had a flat cap so I asked the chap if I could wear it during the second half.

I was recommended to Wimbledon by Brian Hall. He

had spoken to Harry about me and they both turned up to watch and they went back and recommended me to Dario. I cost about £1,000. I was also playing Sunday morning football at that time, a 16-year-old against men of around 29 or 30. After one game our manager at the time, Dave Finn, said, 'Harry Bassett wants to talk to you.' Being a kid I wanted to talk to him right away, but I was told to have a bath first, clean myself up. Harry waited for me and invited me for a trial at the training ground against Cambridge.

We drew 0–0 and I thought I did all right. Harry liked me but Dario wasn't quite sure. He had a friend called Mike Kelly, a former top keeper and England goal-keeping coach, and he sent him to watch me play at Brighton in a reserve match, where Martin Chivers, the former Spurs and England centre-forward, was playing. We won 3–2 and on the way home we stopped at a pub and Harry took me into a corner and said, 'We like you. Mike thinks you're all right: big feet, big kicker.'

I was working as a silk-screen printer at the time and Harry asked me what I was earning. I told him £25 a week and he immediately said he'd match it. I was also earning £18 at Edgware Town, but I thought I always wanted to be a footballer and so joined, taking a wage cut. Working as a silk-screen printer wasn't a glamour job. I used to go home smelling like a fishmonger, and it wasn't something I wanted to do all my life.

There were the likes of Corky, Wally, Steve Parsons, the pilot Dave Donaldson there. All strong characters. I had liked the social life at the time and had gone out drinking with the Edgware boys, and I thought this was all going to change now I was at a pro club. Instead, it got better!

Even now when I go to clubs people ask me about the Crazy Gang. I wore pink shoes once, and Anton Ferdinand looked at me and said, 'You would not have got away with them in the Crazy Gang.' He was right. I always had the ability to kick long, and I think that also helped. Those were fun days, driving to reserve games in a minibus, stopping for a pint on the way home, getting home late, that was what the Crazy Gang was all about.

Wally *was* crazy. If he wasn't there then it was a normal day. Wally could be a bully. He always seemed to pick on me. He was all mouth and no trousers – hence his nickname, 'Trousers', although he tells some tall story about the name coming from 'trousers down'. He did me lots of times. I don't know how I survived. But there was nothing evil. For all his noise, bluster, trickery and mischievous ways, life would not have been the same without him. He was also a good footballer, and could have seriously been a contender but for his injuries. He fancied himself as the new Rodney Marsh.

The fact people still talk about the Crazy Gang makes me realize what an incredible story it was and what an incredible bunch of people made it so. But I thought my career was over after my first game. We were playing against Crystal Palace in pre-season when I went down for a save and fractured my scaphoid. The doctor said it was a really dodgy bone and I might suffer for it. Maybe not even play again. So the whole summer I worried if my career was over before it began, but come the next season I played every game and my fear was over.

Harry trusted me, and we all trusted him. He would tell tales of how he would beat people up, climb over barriers to fight with fans, but it helped us a lot. He was one of us. He was a cracking bloke. He made sure there were plenty of laughs. There was also a lot of hard work because we all knew the most important thing to him was winning. The basis of our success was the family atmosphere he helped create. This had already been in place before I arrived, but it grew and grew. It was all for one and one for all. Harry fostered this spirit and it's fair to say the success we enjoyed was a lot down to him. He was Wimbledon. He liked a joke and even overstepped the mark on a few occasions. Sometimes he knew when to end the joke and sometimes he didn't. Yet for a lot of the time the joke was on him. We'd roll him around in the mud, stop him from getting off trains and often threw his shoes out of the window so he had to walk home barefoot.

He was the perfect assistant to Dario and his move into the manager's seat was seamless, especially as we knew him as a player. We had our own language, our own ways, which at another club would have been regarded as silly. But it worked for us. Everyone had a terrific sense of humour, none more so than Gary Peters. We used to call him the worst right-back in football, and he would go along with it and often would tell us how he cleared two pigeons from the main stand when he was at Reading. But if you couldn't laugh at yourself then you'd be ridiculed. Stunts were commonplace. Eggs were pelted, trouser bottoms tied together and hotel rooms wrecked.

Going back to my debut against Blackpool. We were drawing 1–1 and I'd hardly had to make a save until their tiny winger Colin Morris cut in and hit a bobbler, a real bobbler. I got in line with it, but it went between my legs. It didn't even make the back of the net, stopping just over the line. I was thinking my career was finished.

I went upstairs to the executive bar for a drink. Wally was there, Parsons was there, and they got me absolutely rip-roaring drunk. I remember Ron Noades eventually coming over to me and saying, 'Don't worry about it, we have complete confidence in you.' So for me thinking my career is over and then having the chairman come over, wrap his arms round me and to say those words, sticking with me, that was what Wimbledon was all about. I drove home happy and steaming but that was what was normal in those days!

I was playing reserve games as well as first-team games. I remember I played a Division One game on a Saturday and a reserve game against Barnet on the Tuesday and I got stud marks up my leg and I could have missed the next game. But that was how Wimbledon was. You just wanted to play with your mates. I played one reserve game at Doncaster and at dinner beforehand someone got a roll and threw it, then it would get worse and worse with things splattered up the wall, and eventually I went to my room, but not before Harry – or was it Paul Denny? – emptied about 20 of those little cartons of milk into a jug and threw it over me. I smelled horrible.

Harry would always tell the same stories. We hated it when new players arrived because we knew he was going to tell them all again!

Wally and Parsons were the crackpots, but it was important we also had Lawrie 'Mr Sensible' Sanchez around. Lawrie and I forged a friendship that binds to this day. We shared rooms on trips together, but he has never forgiven me for taking his thunder when we won the FA Cup in 1988. He may have scored our winning goal against Liverpool but I was given the match ball because, in those days, it was always given to the winning captain – me!

I love Sanch. He had more A levels than the rest of the team put together. He knew the answer to everything. It took him a while to work out Wimbledon but when he did there was no more true man in yellow and blue.

Corky was another player you could not help but to love – even if he could be morose at times! He was there from the start, a quiet bloke from Derby whose dad worked for Rolls Royce. But even he, in the end, became simply mad like the rest of us.

Vinnie and Fash arrived later. Both were incredible characters, both easily moving into the way of things. Lots has been said about the both of them but, take it from me, Vinnie was a decent fella with a heart of gold. I remember him arriving for a trial and being noisy and Wally saying, 'He's loud', which I thought coming from Wally was a tribute.

Fash is a book on his own. He ruffled some feathers, but never mine. Sanch would always laugh at his clothes, his style, but Fash would reply, 'When you have a month, come walk round my wardrobe.' We had this rule at Wimbledon that it did not matter what you earned, what you did off the pitch, but as long as you did the business on the pitch and never let a pal down then you were one of us. Fash never let us down on the pitch. When people ask what I think of him I always reply, 'He never let us down.'

Those were magical days, with physio Derek French another larger than life character, and not a bad singer too. He once took over the mic at Frank McLintock's bar near King's Cross, after we won the Division Four Championship, and brought the house down with his version of 'High Heel Sneakers'.

I cherish those Wimbledon days. They made me the person I am. To me Harry wasn't just a manager but also a great friend. The same can be said of those who sailed through my life. When I sipped champagne after winning the FA Cup my thoughts drifted back to those days in Division Four – the minibuses to reserves games, the banter, the players and those who helped us get to where we were. There was a tear in my eye, that's for sure.

6
Leading from the Front

Harry

SAM HAMMAM'S PART in the Crazy Gang story has been well documented, but it's worth remembering what an odd story that was at the time. He was in a car with a chauffeur, the story goes, when he borrowed the chauffeur's tabloid and started reading about football. 'I got interested, and decided to buy shares in a club,' he said.

In the 'Down the Lanes' column of the weekly *Wimbledon News* in late February 1979, he appears for the first time under the headline SAM'S THE MAN. 'Dons have found themselves a colourful, rather rich and enormously enthusiastic new director,' it reads. 'Lebanese-born Sam Hamman [*sic*], a construction engineer who is based in Saudi Arabia, is football mad and decided it was time he became involved with a league soccer club. His wife originates from Wimbledon and one of his children was born in the local St Teresa's hospital, so Plough Lane seemed an obvious choice.

'And since his appointment to the board in early January, he has become increasingly popular with everyone. Two visits to the supporters' club shop resulted in an extravagant spending spree which went well into three figures. And, although coy to divulge by just how much, Wimbledon have benefited quite nicely due to his generosity and considerable wealth.

'He's so keen that he rings the ground from all over the world just to find out how the Dons have fared. "He's always phoning me and is a useful man to have around because of his practical knowledge of construction," said Dons chairman Ron Noades.'

By 1982, Sam was the majority shareholder and the rest is history – not all of it painting him in good light, owing to Wimbledon's controversial displacement and eventual rebirth as AFC Wimbledon, as well as the plentiful stories of him threatening the players with having to eat sheep's eyeballs in his favourite Lebanese restaurant. But with hindsight we can say that there weren't then, and aren't now, many money men behind football clubs who were so approachable and close, not just to the manager but to the players as well. It fostered a spirit of fun, but Sam is a businessman first and foremost, and the attributes he brought to the club were vital to our success.

Stanley Reed, Ron's successor as chairman, was always quick to pay credit to Sam's role at the club – in terms of administration, as well as putting his hand in his pocket. And even though the money was minimal (with the exception of the £125,000 we forked out for Fash), of course the club had to be well run behind the scenes for every penny to be used well, whether it was gate receipts or cash from the Sportsman and Nelson's, both of which had been bought and developed by money brought in from selling players on. Quite a lot of activity at the club went on in those two venues, as you can imagine.

I know this is all jumping forward in time a little, but I think it's important here as part of the Crazy Gang story to look at just what extraordinary obstacles we had to overcome to achieve what we did.

The lack of any real cash worth talking about from those gate receipts was the biggest problem we had to face, year after year after year. With the lowest gates, you have the lowest salaries, so have to find money from elsewhere or, of course, develop your own players. When we were promoted into the First Division, our chief executive Colin Hutchinson, a Yorkshireman who smoked like a chimney, made the bold proclamation that within five years the club would be able to break even before a single spectator walked through the turnstiles. As it happened, I made so much money for the club from transfers that wasn't so far from the truth. But even on minuscule budgets, we managed to make do, even making a profit, I see from the records, of £13,750 in my first five years as manager. Our finances were healthy because we didn't want to go into debt. Contrast that with the billions blown on rubbish in the modern game.

There was also a mini-gym, open to the public, and a sauna under the main North Stand at Plough Lane, which had been opened just before our first Football League season, under the initiative of Ron Noades, and which, believe it or not, was lauded at the time for being one of the best in the country. In the South Stand was the Dons' shop, also newly expanded in the summer of 1977 to deal with the demands of league football, and Ron had also given his blessing to a new tea bar and supporters' club office on the Plough Lane side of the ground. The car parks were used for storage by local dealers, or for car boot sales. Any unused space was available for rent, especially during Wimbledon tennis fortnight, not that our Wimbledon bore any resemblance to the venue frequented by the strawberry and Pimm's brigade.

There were savings elsewhere to be made that you wouldn't find at other clubs. I remember Midget expressing surprise that we had to travel back from matches on the milk train to London. 'We were supposed to be professionals but still played with amateur ideals,' he said. 'That first season, the club expected me to supply my own training kit.' Quite right too. Although eventually, with the advent of shirt sponsorship, we did manage to get to the stage where players didn't have to launder their own kit, after washing machines and dryers were donated to the club. That wasn't till about 1986 though, and I wasn't too happy, telling one reporter that I was all in favour of the old way to keep the players on the straight and narrow: 'It made them appreciate that other people go to work.'

Plough Lane, we were constantly being told, looked like a non-league ground. But that was because it was a fucking non-league ground, wasn't it? Or, as Sam said after we made the top flight, 'To be honest, we're ashamed of our ground. Our facilities are Fourth Division, at best.' Even when it was modernized, or just given a new lick of paint – we spent £350,000 the summer before that first season in the First Division on safety improvements – opposing players and fans hated Plough Lane. The players hated the claustrophobia of the pitch, the low stands, the intimidation. I remember one Liverpool fan asking me why they always got pissing wet in the rain when they came to Plough Lane: 'Why don't you have a fucking roof?'

This was an era of hooliganism, let's not forget – the Luton–Millwall riot was a particular blot on the football landscape, allied with some terrible disasters like Bradford and Heysel in 1985 alone – but apart from some idiots from Brentford and Burnley who tried to take the home end, there wasn't ever much trouble at Plough Lane. I was a firm believer, and still am, that what happens outside the grounds is society's problem, not football's. A club can only control what happens inside it. That's their only responsibility. As for players being role models . . .

Journalists couldn't believe that I held my press conferences in my office, with all my tactics sheets and everything pinned up on the boards. There would be up to twenty of them crammed in there at any one time, yet the office was only about 15 foot by 15. That was Wimbledon, though, and anything we could use as a weapon, we did.

I did once ask a reporter, Julie Welch of the *Observer*, to come and watch a match from the bench to see what the match-day experience was really like. I think the language took her aback a little, not to mention the volume generated by Alan Gillett and Sid Neale, our kit man. It was a Sunday morning derby against Crystal Palace, in November 1984, and she wrote a nice piece about the 'charm and warmth' of the club. Luckily, a substitution came off for us, with Andy Sayer scoring with his first touch after coming on for Steve Galliers, and we won 3–2. 'The crowd hardly existed for us, down there by the touchline, so close you could see the sweat drip off the centre-half's nose . . .' she wrote. Poetic. Not most people's impression of Plough Lane.

So Alan became my assistant manager when I took over from Dario Gradi in January 1981. Ron Noades had upped sticks, sold the club to Sam Hammam and taken over at Palace, taking his fellow directors Bernie Coleman and Jimmy Rose with him, as well as Dario, who he saw as the ideal manager to save the club from relegation from the First Division. That didn't quite happen, as it turned out. Ron also had ambitious plans for a merger of sorts between Palace and Wimbledon, which caused awful friction, and although it didn't seem so at the time, given all the turmoil, Ron and Dario's departure turned out to be the best thing that could have happened, at least from my personal perspective.

I was 36 at the time, which made me young for a manager, but that was also an advantage because I was able to mix with the players – I'd practically grown up at Wimbledon with people like Wally and Corky – and that's what created our fantastic team spirit. In fact, that is probably how the Crazy Gang really started – me in the dugout; Wally orchestrating things in the midfield or as a sweeper; and Corky on target in my first game as manager, a 3–2 win at Port Vale, sealed by a brilliant left-foot volley by Mick Smith, which was part of a 12-match unbeaten run in the league from December to mid-March that put us firmly in the frame for promotion. Some regular fans had stayed away from games after Dario's departure, even if the results hadn't been great under him, but they were soon coming back.

Despite having turned it down before, I had no doubts in accepting the manager's job on this occasion. There were plenty of voices of discontent about my appointment, though. As a player, my nickname had been 'the Mouth' (can't think where that came from), and there was an older contingent of supporters – a majority, in fact; perhaps around 80 per cent of the total support – who didn't want the likes of me at Wimbledon as a player, let alone as manager. The amateur roots of the club were still strong, and that genteel ethos didn't tally with what they thought of me – a thug. Younger fans liked the way we went about things, but the snobs at Plough Lane referred to this small group of oiks as The Bassett Fan Club.

I was thrilled to be in charge, because I knew behind me there were players who just needed the chance to tweak noses. I had seen talent with ambition in the reserves, and players who liked a laugh.

Another time when we stopped the minibus for fish and chips, Wally and Steve Parsons got out to get them. I immediately ordered the bus to drive on, leaving them stranded in east London. Next morning they were first in for training and demanded to see me for an explanation of why they were abandoned. I said it was nothing to do with me, but it was the younger players like Glyn Hodges, Paul Fishenden, Kevin Gage and Mark Morris who had made the driver move on. The next thing I heard was squeals from the dressing room as both Wally and Steve took revenge. I loved it. It was bonding, Bassett-style.

So when I took over I was confident we could achieve something. I had witnessed the youngsters fight the odds, listen to more senior players and be keen to learn. So before the Port Vale game I called the players together and told them I still believed we could get promotion. I asked them to buy into my dream and the 'them and us against the world' mentality – and because they knew me so well they came with me. Wide-eyed kids became men overnight, and my journey as a manager had begun.

I fostered the idea that we were real people, kids from dead-end streets, not prima donnas – more like hod carriers, plumbers, pub footballers, former barrow boys and the type of team everyone looked down on. We didn't dye our hair, make records or generally look like pop stars. We wound people up.

But behind all this was steely-eyed professionalism. I had excellent back-up from Vince Craven, Alan Fogarty and Neil Lanham. When Sam Hammam took over I persuaded him to fork out £11,000 to invest in computers to put into Vince's house in Old Windsor. Vince had a marvellous eye. He could analyze games better than anyone I had met then, or since. He would work out how games were won and lost. He would, in careful handwriting, spell out in simple English the strengths and weaknesses of the opposition. He would use old tapes, old-fashioned cassettes, of matches, both home and abroad, to bring world-class players into our dressing room. His knowledge was unsurpassed. He could explain tactics better than any man I have known.

Helping him was Neil, whose analysis of matches was also first class. He broke down the opposition in similar fashion, showing how they defended, where they lost the ball and what they did in the final third. In simple terms, their strengths and weaknesses. They were both ahead of their time. Only in recent years has football caught up with the likes of Opta and Prozone.

The 1980–81 season had actually started slowly, with Wally salvaging a point on the opening weekend against

Bradford after his penalty had been saved (I have to say that he didn't miss many). There were a few new faces in the team, Peter Brown, a teenage full-back who had been on the books of Chelsea, being one of them. There may not have been many changes, but the players were starting to show some confidence and self-belief. In September, another of the youth boys, 17-year-old Glyn Hodges, made his first-team debut, then his first start in a 5–0 drubbing of Hartlepool – his quality was shining through even at that tender age, and he could turn matches single-handedly when he was on his game. By this time Bez was firmly established as our first-choice keeper too, although that Hartlepool game was one of his few clean sheets at the time, and he was attracting plenty of envious glances from other clubs – he was named our player of the season come the end. What a great piece of business that was. At the risk of repeating myself, which my missus says I'm prone to do, he cost £1,000!

Our home form was rock solid – we even had new floodlights to play under, even if Ron was continuing to talk about the need to move away from Plough Lane that autumn, with fans' protests against any relocation or ground-sharing getting louder and louder. I could understand the reasoning – I'd make the mistake of moving to Selhurst Park myself before too long – but especially with hindsight, talk of mergers and buying out other clubs was bound to provoke a reaction. There's no football club without fans.

Despite the low attendances at Plough Lane, the Hartlepool game was followed by comfortable wins against York, Peterborough, Northampton and Aldershot. We were dire away from home, but did enough to stay in the promotion hunt, with Dario winning manager of the month in December, when Francis Joseph also made his debut after signing from Hillingdon. More from Joe later, but it was a landmark moment for the club, signing our first black player. Of course, he got a fair amount of stick: this was 1980, not 2015. As some idea of the madness of the time, we played at Torquay on Boxing Day and had to get back to beat Bournemouth at Plough Lane 24 hours later. What were the authorities thinking?

Dario took charge for the last time in a narrow FA Cup defeat at Second Division Wrexham, who had beaten West Ham in the Third Round after two replays; Dave Hubbick, on as a sub, should have scored late on and taken the tie back to Plough Lane. But then off Dario went with Ron to Selhurst and it was down to me, and then came that 12-match unbeaten run. The players were brilliant, especially given all the off-the-field shenanigans. They just got on with their jobs, gave their all, and churned out the results. With Ron and Dario having gone to Selhurst, the board eventually backed down on the idea of transporting the whole of Wimbledon there too – well, for then at least.

There's a brilliant book called *Wimbledon: From Southern League to Premiership, A Complete Record* by Clive

Leatherdale, published by Desert Island Books. It's full of facts and statistics, and I love to delve into it for a trip down memory lane. I know some of the players do too – Sanch has a copy, but then he has always been a scholarly type! Clive's work has been an invaluable aid in putting together this book too. And I thought it would be interesting to see what Clive wrote about me taking the helm in January 1981, so you can get an idea of how my appointment was received in some quarters:

> Nowadays, everyone with a passing interest in English football knows the name of Dave 'Harry' Bassett. In 1981 he was a thirty-something nobody of no great achievement. One season in League Division Four was all he had achieved in a playing career almost wholly played out at amateur or semi-professional level. But for being on the books at Wimbledon, he would surely never have sampled League football at all.
>
> Bassett had hung up his boots in 1978, following his appointment as Gradi's number two. Bassett was a hard man as a player, and remains a hard man as a manager. He is the quintessential man's man, a player's man, someone who thinks nothing of attending press conferences in his birthday suit, of calling a spade a bloody spade, and whose transparent honesty endears him to his players as much as to his employers.
>
> If Bassett possessed any tactical acumen – and there were those who doubted it – this was dwarfed by his

ability to communicate, on TV as well as in the dressing room. Bassett had charm, a roguish, boyish smile, an eloquence that belied the bluntness of his message. New fangled methods get short shrift with Dave Bassett. 'Get the ball up there and get bodies up there after it,' sums up his team talks, but none could deny the fighting spirit he instilled into those bodies. Bassett was tailor-made for Wimbledon, and the club for him. The Crazy Gang were on the march.

The unbeaten run came to an end with a 4–1 defeat at Darlington, with Midget and Tommy Cunningham both seeing red – Midget got a five-match ban for his part in proceedings. As Midget tells it though, our preparation wasn't ideal: 'We stayed in a plush hotel and Ketts and Wally started filling bins with water and flooding the rooms the night before the game. The ref was a nightmare, and I remember at the end of the game, Hodge was trying to knock the ref out with the ball, by kicking it at his head, and it all kicked off then.'

Here's Ketts' version of events: 'Darlington away always used to be a nightmare trip for us. We used to leave at silly a.m. – we might even have been driving up in cars because we couldn't afford a coach. Harry would name the team for the following day, and whoever you were playing alongside you roomed with. I was rooming with Wally and, as we shut our door, Paul Denny walked past so we done him with a pint of water, and then he was banging on the door for ages calling us bastards, threatening to kill us. Then there were gushes of water coming in the room and we were three floors up – the floor was flooded, then the room was flooded. Harry then called the room and said there was a meeting downstairs.

'Straight away he started shouting, "Who has been pouring water in Wally and Ketts' room?" No one owned up, then he threatened to fine us two weeks' wages. Still no one owned up and we then went and lost the game 4–1 and Galliers and Cunningham were sent off, and we drove home in a convoy of cars. We got home at 4 a.m. and Harry tells us we are in training that day as a punishment.'

Quite right too.

But after that defeat the players just dusted themselves down again and got up for the next fight. In fact, it was the following weekend, against Hereford, that I handed Wally the captain's armband for the first time. He may only have been 19, but I had no hesitation and knew he would do the job for me on the day. Hardly a punishment for his water antics!

At the end of March, a 1–0 win over Wigan (thanks to a Hodges header) saw us climb into the top four. Micky Quinn was up front for Wigan – what a difficult bastard he could be – but we kept him nice and quiet. As for our main striker, Corky had been on the transfer list but finally signed a new contract – and where would we have been without his 26 goals that season? As for the defence, we were rock solid, and that was the key to our promotion. 'One-nil to the Wimbledon' became a common refrain; as well as Wigan, York, my old Leeds adversary Billy Bremner's Doncaster (he even picked himself!), Bournemouth, with Wally's goal on the Easter weekend, and then Torquay were all dispatched by the same scoreline. The game plan was simple – take the lead in the first half, then defend it. Well executed, it was unbeatable.

Promotion back into the Third Division was secured with a 4–1 thumping of Rochdale at Plough Lane, and then the party started – again. We didn't have a bean to spend on new players, but we had a team of winners. This management lark was easy!

Having said that, certain players had a tendency to send me flying off my handle. Talented as he was, Glyn Hodges was one of them. There'll be a lot more of him to come but here's some Hodge for starters.

Glyn Hodges

Dario took me to Chelsea and then to Wimbledon. I was still in my last year of school and already playing in the reserves with Wally and Harry. After playing a bit for the reserves, I was offered an apprenticeship and then officially joined, and I said to Paul Fishenden, 'Come on, come with me.'

Me and Fish both turned our backs on Chelsea to go down to Wimbledon, and when you look back now it sounds crazy – but it worked out well in the end. I never gave another club a thought. Wimbledon at the time were taking people on trial who had been released from the likes of Chelsea and Tottenham and other top clubs. We were in the Fourth Division and we started thinking, 'Well, if we don't do well here, where else is there to go?' So almost immediately there was a sense of 'sink or swim'.

Dario didn't say anything in particular or anything profound to get me to go there, but having worked under him all the way through from being a kid I thought he would help my game, develop me as a player, more than anybody else. And then Harry threw it straight out the window when the long-ball game came in – but I still enjoyed it!

As soon as I was signed I was put straight into the first team. It was a steep learning curve but absolutely fantastic, and I knew even then that I wouldn't have got that at Chelsea.

I know Wally used to make out he was a barrow boy on his family's fruit and veg stall in Shepherd's Bush, but that was all bollocks. I was the one who did the two jobs on the markets. My family had a fish stall on Brixton Market and during the season when we were in the Second Division I used to finish training on Thursdays and Fridays and then go and get the takings and lock up so my old man could go home. In the summer I used to work there for two weeks so I could afford to go away on holiday. I'd have one stall and my brother would have the other, and I would be up Billingsgate Market at five o'clock in the morning. I would do the buying and the setting up until 7 a.m. and then go to training. I did that for a good few years until my brother joined and took it all over. It was hard work but I got my hands dirty, unlike Wally.

I played with Harry in the reserves and he was useless, absolutely useless. I could not believe how bad he was. He was obviously bright and intelligent, and he could talk about football and how it should be played . . . but he couldn't do it. When we were all apprentices, good young players who went on to play a lot in the first team – me, Fish, Guppy – we would travel to games with the reserves (places like Colchester away) and Harry would want to play to show us what he could do – he would pick himself ahead of us, and one of us would be left behind. He was switched on, and he helped bring us along with some of the antics he was getting up to.

We ended up signing Francis Joseph as a result of playing against Hillingdon, whom Joe was with at the time. Harry caused an absolute riot. He caused murders, got himself sent off, completely coated himself off in the dressing room in front of everyone and then fined himself a fiver for dissent. He used to cause such bollocks when he played. He used to have a great big gold ring on, like something off *Mr T*, and if anyone ever dared run past him he used to hit them with it and cut them to pieces. He never took it off.

Harry and Dario were totally different – from how they were as people right through to their coaching sessions. Dario would have all the cones lined up – all crop circles and drills – while Harry would have us playing a game called 'Harryball', where anything could go. But he was good at the tactical side. With Harry we were usually running or doing tactical work. Either way, when it came to training, it was work, work, work. Probably not as much fucking around as people think.

When we turned up as APs (Apprentice Professionals) we didn't have to clean boots but we were in charge of the kit. We only had two sets back then, so one set would be for Monday and Tuesday and the other was for Thursday and Friday. On Friday we would take it all down to the launderette. There were big drying racks that we used to hang it all out on to dry, but there were only ever three or four towels. So the first person would come in and have a lovely fresh dry towel and he'd dry himself from top to toe and probably use it to stand on to keep his feet dry – and when he was done he would have to hang it on the drier for the next bloke . . . then the same for the next bloke and the bloke after that. By the end the place would stink and the towels could have stood up on their own in the corner. If anyone was silly enough to bring in some soap or shampoo everyone else nicked it – there were no communal toiletries or anything like there is now. It was a tip. That was how it was. If it pissed down with rain you had to hope and pray it dried quickly, and you looked after your own boots – if they got wet and it rained overnight they were usually soaking for the next day as well.

Then Harry took over. Because he had trained and played with us in the reserves, he knew we could play – he knew there were no mugs and he knew we were all right. It wasn't as if we had the current 25-man squad. We would have been lucky to have had 20 – and that would have included the apprentices, who would have been 16 or 17. You knew if there were any injuries in the first team that you would get a chance – beggars couldn't be choosers – so it kept us on our toes and made us work hard because we knew the chance was never far away. Thankfully we almost all stepped up to the plate and produced.

It was unbelievable going into the first-team environment. You went in straight from school. One minute you're mooching about doing what you like, and the next you're running round Richmond Park doing six-and-a-half miles in the boiling pre-season summer with nothing but a slither of watermelon to keep you alive – even now when I see or taste a watermelon it reminds me of those runs. After that you were training with them. There was no messing around. Now, if you're a first-year scholar, clubs are wary of playing you in the under-21s because you might be too small; but we went in and trained with and against blokes. When you finally got in the first team, it was even more unbelievable with people like Wally, Roy Davies, Steve Perkins . . . there were real,

real characters. There was never a dull moment, always something going on.

We feared failure. We never wanted to lose and let the boys down. We were going in as young Herberts, and we didn't want to let the older blokes down. The bonuses played a big part; money was tight. It was massive, we needed a win bonus. Players now can lose but still be cotchelled up with £80k a week. With the goal and clean-sheet bonuses we used to get we gave it everything we had. We never wanted to let anyone down, and if you did you got slaughtered by absolutely everyone. But after that they would teach you as well. Players would pull you aside and tell you what you had to do, what you needed to improve, and things like that. They would talk to you, and that was where you learned the game. What doesn't get picked up now is that back then players were naturally bright enough to learn what they needed to do to improve. There are loads of hugely talented lads around now who haven't got enough of that to understand that they need to learn more, or other things. We were all picking up as much as we possibly could. There were some very bright people in the team – not only was Harry shrewd, there were plenty of players who were bright as buttons as well, like Wally and Corky – but even the thick ones wanted to learn about football. Very early on we were taught what it took to get a result, what we had to do to beat a team.

When Dario left, he left behind a style that was all about getting hold of the ball and playing and trying to express yourself. He wanted the midfield to get on the ball, and it was enjoyable playing that way. When Harry took over I think he tried to carry that on, but ultimately the results weren't good enough. The transition went so sweet: Harry came in, put his stamp on it, and we got promoted.

One thing I think I realize now, through doing the job I'm doing, as development coach at Stoke City, is that you can sometimes sit on the sidelines and watch a player and think 'brilliant' but the absolute best way to know is to join in the training session, because then you can see up close what they're doing – and you can link up with them and really get a feel for them and what they're doing. And I really believe there was an element of that with Harry. Because he not only knew us as a coach but also as a teammate – he knew our attributes and he knew he could trust us. That's why we did so well.

You have to be as physical as the level of football you are playing at demands. So when we were playing for the reserves of a Fourth Division side we had to be able to look after ourselves, and I suppose that does get ingrained in you – it's not something you can suddenly shake off just because you go up a division or two or three. Anyone that was successful in that era of football was tough. It was drummed into us from the experiences of playing against Wealdstone and Barnet and Hillingdon. When a professional team plays a non-league team the non-league team are always keen to have a pop, and we were only young. It was serious and it was hard; you didn't want to back down and you didn't cower, but if you did you got a bollocking. You had to look after yourselves, and if you got a dig then you were expected to give one back. You were encouraged to constantly win your own personal battle. If we couldn't outplay a side then we would outrun them, and if we couldn't outrun them then we would outfight them. One of those three we would win – especially the fight.

We got on top that way. They were things you had to do. To say we had to do things to survive is too strong, but if we were to have any chance of competing, let alone winning, we had to take it on and carry it forward. We were big strong boys and we could play. We could have a team beaten before the whistle blew. We were not bullies, but they knew they would have to have the game of their lives to beat us, and they knew they couldn't sustain it. They knew that the barrage of running, shouting, crosses, shots and tackles would eventually overawe them – and that was without us starting to play our football. There were so many things we could throw at teams: we could all create, and people just could not deal with us. More often than not we could tell from very early on that teams didn't fancy it with us.

I know Harry liked a tearaway. These days you don't see many characters in dressing rooms, but it's nice to have boys who have got a bit of an edge, or a different personality, or are maybe hard to handle. Harry did like boys who were hard to handle, had a reputation or were just different. Harry was happy for lads to be themselves and cause a bit of bollocks – as long as they didn't cause too much trouble. If you were part of the team and you performed in the game he let it go, and probably encouraged it. That is why he let all the off-field antics go on, because it didn't stop us winning matches. Believe me, if he had an inkling that was the case he would have changed it. He encouraged us to all go out together and enjoy each other's company – it was a fantastic time to be there. Harry probably encouraged the loonies because they were the ones who got the other ones going.

I never had any problems with anyone because I came through the youth team with almost everyone, and then the reserves with them too. You all came through together. I think if you were respected as a player then you were respected. Looking back there probably were players who came in and didn't buy into it – or certainly not enough – and they found it really hard. Sometimes we were out of order – we were such a tight group and sometimes we didn't let people in. That was a mistake. It was a hard team to break into, but that was what got us success.

Harry, however, always used to get his words muddled up, especially if he had the hump and was trying to bollock you. One week I was playing for the reserves on a Tuesday, then we had the debrief on the Wednesday or Thursday. I had either got booked or sent off, and as he went through the whole team, speaking to whoever was there – saying things like, 'Well done, Fish; liven yourself up, Guppy' – he finally got to me. He would always call me a 'fat petulant cunt', only this time he got the words mixed up and just called me a 'petulant cake'. So for about six months my nickname was 'the Cake'.

7

Football in Perspective

Wally

DARIO MAY HAVE a reputation for his sides, most notably at Crewe, playing lovely passing football, and developing young players, but he wasn't afraid to mix it up. 'Cut out the football!' I once heard him shout when someone tried something fancy. We were quite capable of playing passing football ourselves, of course – we were professional footballers! The key to it was not to lose possession in bad places, not to dwell on the ball. No one was allowed to stay still for a moment. It was constant movement, constant pressing.

To survive in the Third Division this time, we were going to have to use all our wiles, all our effort, and mix it up with the better-funded teams. Harry had experienced success as manager at the first time of asking, and wouldn't settle for anything less than 100 per cent commitment and the highest of standards. What happened was about as far from the script as could be imagined, and Harry gave us hell.

Our defending was woeful, to be fair, although apart from a 3–1 drubbing by Fulham at Plough Lane – they would go on to be promoted with Carlisle and champions Burnley – we were never really outclassed. But that Fulham defeat was one of nine winless games at the start of the season. Two points from 27? The writing was on the wall from the off. Fucking curtains. Especially given that it was now three points for a win, something which we clearly hadn't fully understood the importance of. And all that was after we'd had a great pre-season in something called the Group Cup, beating Gillingham, Orient and Southend (we would go on to make the final, narrowly losing to Grimsby) to go into the league campaign full of optimism. But even dominating possession in the league opener against Swindon, hitting the post twice and forcing 14 corners to their five, couldn't help us from going down to a 4–1 defeat.

Injuries, bad luck and a tragic loss all had a part to play in our downfall. For once the injury problems were not mine, as I only missed four games all season – the only ever-present was Lurch – but you could sometimes sense that the fans thought it was a lost cause. The club's new chairman, Beau Reynolds, who was quite a character (he liked his bling), tried to talk a good game about the fans' vocal inspiration. 'It is when things are not going so well that encouragement from our supporters is most needed, and you have not let us down,' he said. But remember this was the early Eighties and there was fighting on the terraces that sometimes spilled over on to the pitch. All in all, Wimbledon's fifth season of league football was the most depressing one of all for Harry, the players, officials and fans – anyone connected to the club.

September was particularly shit. Tommy Cunningham left to sign for Orient, and then Corky managed to miss two vital penalties, get sent off and then stretchered off with a broken leg at Walsall after colliding with their keeper Ron Green. One of his red cards came in a particularly nasty game at Plough Lane, against Doncaster Rovers, for whom Ian Nimmo was also red-carded for fighting Midget. Corky had lamped the opposition's Richard Dawson, who had a bloody nose for his troubles. There was a brawl in the tunnel after the game, involving the Donny manager Billy Bremner, whose assistant locked himself in the ref's room! There was an FA inquiry, one of a long line of them down the years, which summoned me and 'a man in a black leather coat'! Harry also had to attend as manager. Joe hadn't been playing that afternoon, so had his black John Shaft leather coat on. He certainly came in handy: he'd seen me run down the tunnel and got in there with me! He was throwing Doncaster players about while I took revenge on the bloke who'd got Corky sent off . . . handbags it wasn't! And there was history between the clubs – the Dons' directors had had abuse and beer hurled at them at Belle Vue the previous season, but it was all harmless, really. Throw in the League Cup shambles against Fourth

Division Aldershot, which also took place during that nightmare month, and, as I said, it was shit piled upon more shit.

At the tenth time of asking, and after losing our first five games of the season in league and cup at Plough Lane, we finally got the monkey off our backs with a 1–0 win against Chester in front of just 1,659 (Paul Lazarus netting), only to lose Steve Jones for the season three days later. There were more missed pens and red cards – Hodge and Ketts respectively against a Gillingham team featuring Steve Bruce – and then Midget left, following the gravy train to Palace. It was 70 grand or so they paid for him, so good money for the club, but you can imagine how the fans felt, not to mention the players. Personally speaking, I was gutted.

Mick Smith was stretchered off against Exeter, in a game when Mark Morris made his debut – Harry had no option but to promote more boys from the youth set-up. We called him Guppy from the start, because he had a habit of opening and closing his mouth like a fish. Then again, we also called him Wilf, from Wear 'em out Wilf in the comic. And Smithy, incidentally, became Ralph, along with Steve Hatter as Potsie, from *Happy Days*, an ironic naming for the pair bearing in mind their ferocity compared to the TV characters.

Paul Geddes and Paul Fishenden were drafted in for their debuts in the following game against Portsmouth, but even when we did manage a win, against Preston, Ketts was sent off again for a rumble with Gary Buckley.

As for me, I blew my fuse at Chesterfield, when a perfectly good goal was disallowed by a particularly blind fucking ref who claimed not to have seen the fucking ball ACTUALLY GO INTO THE FUCKING NET!

We were certainly on the end of some dodgy decisions, but we probably didn't help our cause with some, shall we say, over-zealous tackling. But along with our defensive problems, the string of suspensions hung around our neck, the good that our physical approach brought us was undermined by the lamentable disciplinary record – not least in leaving the players out of pocket, and therefore even more thoroughly pissed off.

We hardly played a game in December – the poxy weather contributing to the general shit atmosphere – but the only game that did actually beat the postponements was in the FA Cup – it had originally been scheduled for the Saturday, but was moved to a Tuesday. It was a snowy night, on a frozen pitch, and proving that you will win nothing with fucking kids, we were battered 4–1 by non-league Enfield, despite taking the lead. The match suited the weather. They say history doesn't repeat itself but don't mention fucking Enfield and the fucking FA Cup to me, or to Harry. What was it he said after the game? 'It was men against boys. They had men.' And it's true, they were older and just more physical than us, shoving us all over the place at free-kicks and corners. A fucking embarrassment it was.

We actually managed to win away from home, as 1982 promised something rosier – 3–1 at Bristol City, whose caretaker manager went by the name of Roy Hodgson. At the end of January, however, there was another broken leg – for Dave Clement at Doncaster. And worse was to follow, a tragedy that put our shit football results into context.

Dave had arrived from QPR after 17 years with the Rs – one of their all-time greats; 476 games no less – and, as a former England full-back, was quickly installed as skipper by Harry. He only played 11 games for us, scoring a couple of goals, but was a steadying influence in the dressing room when everything else was falling apart.

By all accounts, Dave just couldn't cope with the injury and the possible end of his football career, although we were hardly aware of what must have been going through his head. Harry says he feels guilty that he didn't read the signs about how the injury had affected him, even when Dave told him how he was worried about his future. Harry had asked Dave to do some scouting with Geoff Taylor, but that didn't help.

Dave took his own life on 31 March 1982, at his father-in-law's flat in Battersea. There was a memorial match in his honour that May before QPR's FA Cup final against Spurs, with the likes of Phil Parkes, Frank McLintock, Stan Bowles and Gerry Francis all turning out for a Dave Clement XI. RIP, Dave.

The effect on the club of Dave's death was devastating. We had a game at Chester the day Dave died, and the club's intention apparently was to keep the news from the players until after the final whistle. But it was always going to come out, and we heard it during our pre-match meal. I can't say if it was a factor in my getting sent off, and Peter Brown too, but it can hardly have helped. We lost five of the next six games too. Even after a comeback 3–2 win at Brentford, for whom Stan Bowles scored a peach of a free-kick, Harry was saying that he would personally welcome the end of the season.

He was in an even fouler mood the following weekend, when we succumbed to a 2–1 defeat at Carlisle, despite Hodge having given us a first-half lead by scuffing a shot in from 25 yards. They equalized and then, in the 75th minute, I was penalized for an incredibly overenthusiastic tackle, and from the resulting free-kick John Leslie and Lurch hesitated and the ball trickled in off our makeshift right-back.

Harry accused us of lack of effort. 'I felt some of them didn't die for the cause,' he told the press. 'At 1–0 up against the league leaders the game was ours. But we panicked, and surrendered on the edge of our box. We just didn't push on as strongly as we should have done. Those three points, and a few from the Easter programme when we showed no confidence, would have made all the difference. We've still got a glimmer of hope, but it's a tall order. We could have been in with a shot, if only the spirit had moved them.'

That flicker of hope of survival was given oxygen by four wins in our last five games, but relegation on goal difference was confirmed on the final weekend, with a few more fans at least turning out to see us beat Portsmouth 3–2, although we had to win by eleven clear goals to stay up. 'I have nightmares about the early part of the season,' Harry said, as we accepted our fate. 'Penalties missed, goals given away, good chances wasted. If only . . .'

In fact, had we not drawn 0–0 against Bristol City in the only one of those last five games we didn't win, we would have stayed up. Harry hauled us in for Sunday training after that match. But it wasn't to be, and the consolation was that the team had taken shape during those final weeks of the campaign – even though we missed out on staying up, the framework was in place to start rebuilding the following season.

Francis Joseph had been banging in the goals during those last few games, taking his tally to 13 for the season (including two against the Bees at Griffin Park), and he caused opponents no end of problems with his pace. Joe's goals certainly helped to plug the gap left by Corky's broken leg, and he was ably abetted by Stewart Evans, who had joined from Sheffield United in the spring. That was another sign of things to come – I lost count of the number of headers the man soon christened 'Good Evans' scored from our crosses and set-pieces. Stewart, who had been recommended by our northern scout, Alan Fogarty, took time to settle but came good.

As for Joe, he may have been our player of the season but he would soon skedaddle away from Plough Lane, as would Gary Armstrong, runner-up in the player of the year stakes, for which he was photographed sporting a quite spectacular blond mullet.

I'll let Joe take up the story. And remember that these were different, slightly less politically correct times . . .

Francis Joseph

I made my debut under Dario, and when he told me I was going on, I thought, 'Fucking hell, I'm going to get slaughtered here.' Not by my teammates, but by the supporters, because I was black. But I remember even before the match, when we were doing our warm-up, some white kids came up and asked for my autograph and I thought, 'What the fuck?' and that set me at ease.

Intimidation is a strong word, but everyone was hungry; what was dished out was normal – you get it today in some places, maybe not as much. I think today, if you had a go at a foreign player, say, for not passing you the ball then they might go into their shell. Whereas when we were playing, it would have been: 'Oi, you fucking idiot, give me the ball!' But because you knew that everyone in the dressing room would be doing it, it never felt spiteful.

If you gave the ball away, you got slaughtered; if you missed a sitter, slaughtered; if you pulled out of a tackle, you got fucking slaughtered. Because it was people forgetting what we worked so hard on in training. That's how and why Wimbledon had such an ascendance, because of what we were doing in training every single day and taking that into matches – and the minute anyone forgot that you reminded them. It wasn't, 'You cunt, I'm going to kill you.' It was probably, 'Oi, you cunt, we don't do that, we do this.' You would get a running commentary from every single player, even the quiet ones off the pitch. It was a hard school to learn in, and if you couldn't cut it you went.

I was asked to contribute to a book about Brentford after my time there, and I explained to them that being at Wimbledon and then going back there taught me how to be a professional footballer and how to be a coach, and that will never leave me at all. The camaraderie was always there. I would have shooting practice with Fish and kick his arse – the loser was always supposed to buy the winner lunch, but he only did it once. He would lie and cheat, but it wasn't nasty – there were nasty incidents but that wasn't nasty.

I was called Black Joe to differentiate me from a player we signed called Joe Blochel – Harry got him on loan from Southampton, and he was fucking terrible. One day we're doing set-pieces and Harry shouts, 'Joe, I want you on the front post.' So I walked to the front post but so did this Blochel geezer. Harry then shouted, 'No, no, no, I meant Black Joe.' I said, 'Hold on, Harry, I was here first. Why don't we call him White Joe and me Joe?' That was a big mistake because then it stuck for ever. Did it hurt or annoy me? No, absolutely not. That never annoyed me, but if anything else did manage to annoy me then we would just have a wrestle over it. We were always wrestling.

When Ian Holloway came to Wimbledon he couldn't cut it, and then he followed me to Brentford and he was a diamond. I was a centre-forward and I wanted goals. He created them for me. Loads of things came into play, but for me the thing that changed and made him the player he went on to be was when they switched him from out wide into centre midfield and that's when he kicked on. The same happened with Dennis Wise – he used to play out wide for us and did OK, then he moved into the middle and he was the absolute man. Same thing with Colin Gordon – he was fucking shit, I wanted to kill him – but he improved when he moved position. After we went down following the last match against Portsmouth I left for Brentford, but I didn't want to go.

I came back from Finland after playing for a bit on loan over there, and I was promised all sorts – double my wages, a signing-on fee – and then Harry wouldn't give them to me. I honestly could not believe it, I was stunned. He said he would put me on a par with the rest of the players; I was top goalscorer and player of the year. We walked round the Plough Lane pitch a dozen times rowing about it all, but Harry didn't know that Brentford had already tapped me up. So I turned down Harry's offer. He went berserk, jumping up and down on the pitch saying, 'If you don't want to play for me then you can fuck off!'

I said, 'All right.' I was walking out of Plough Lane, up

to Wimbledon Park, wondering if Harry would say sorry and ask me to stay. Suddenly his car pulled up and Harry was there shouting, 'Joe, Joe, Joe.' Sadly he wasn't back to plead with me; there were certain signing-on and release forms you had to sign when you went abroad to play, and I hadn't signed mine since coming back from Finland. So I had to go back and sign the forms, and finally he did try to convince me to stay but I told him no, unless he gave me what I had been promised.

Harry had aggression like I have never known – he was a pocket rocket. If you didn't go out on the pitch and look after yourself and your teammates you were bombed. You could be fucking shit and shank your passes, but as long as you competed and put yourself about you were OK. Because the rest, for young people, is easy to learn – but if you are not a natural competitor or fighter you will fail. Fifty-fifties you had to make 60–40s. 'Fuck them,' that was the bottom line. I felt like I was going into a fight when we walked out of the tunnel.

Long before the Crazy Gang there was the white gang and the black gang at Wimbledon – which was tricky, because I was the only black player. But I got in four recruits for my gang and we all terrorized each other. Mick Smith was on my team, Fish, and a few others. We would have competitions and wrestles and all sorts. The changing rooms were tiny so we would split up, and one day I walked into the wrong changing room and Wally and Ketts were there and pounced on me. They thought I would run but I locked the door and started the wrestle, no punches or anything silly. In the end I had them both begging for forgiveness.

I came back to Wimbledon on loan from Brentford and played for them in the First Division in 1987. You wouldn't have thought that when we were relegated in 1982! And with Fash and Fairweather there I wasn't the only black player any more. Harry had told me that Millwall were interested and asked if I wanted to go there. I said, 'I wouldn't have thought so, not with my skin tone.'

8
Time for a Rethink

Harry

THESE DAYS, RELEGATION would result in the tin-tack and a P45, but luckily that was not the way then, at least not the Wimbledon way. But after promotion, relegation, promotion and relegation in the previous four seasons, it was clear that we had a bit of a fucking problem at the club. I laid my thoughts bare about the season that had just passed in the 1982–83 *Wimbledon Football Supporters' Club Handbook* – the front cover of which proclaimed DOWN – BUT NOT DOWNHEARTED! – in an article entitled 'Our Yo-Yo Image'.

I hope you will bear with me as I reproduce it in full and forgive the occasional ramblings. I think it's quite a revealing slice of what life was like as Wimbledon manager at the time (as well as the language of the day!) – indeed of what the football world was like in that period.

The pre-season was one of turmoil as the club was completely unaware of its destiny at that time. There were certainly 'behind the scenes' problems and financial implications that were causing the club enormous difficulties in being able to trade. Fortunately, Sam Hammam became the majority shareholder just before the start of the season and it was, therefore, a necessity to reorganize the 'behind the scenes' attitude and work force. There have been many changes during the last season that have seen people go, to be replaced by new faces. In my opinion, this will be for Wimbledon's long term benefit.

Unfortunately, it is disappointing to report that we have been relegated back into the Fourth Division after what promised to be a season of consolidation. During the pre-season, which was full of sunshine and hope, I felt, given a little luck, we would survive in the Third Division. Our results in the Group Cup augured well. Unfortunately, from the first game where we did not play with any confidence and conviction we seemed to go downhill badly.

As I was aware that money had to be raised to ensure the club's future, it was not surprising after three games that Tommy Cunningham left us for Orient F.C. Although it is easy to appreciate the club's overall picture, I was disappointed to see Tommy go from the football side as he was a skipper who led by example and helped me enormously when I took over as manager. Players of this calibre are not easily replaced. Worse was to follow as in our sixth league game of the season at Walsall, Alan Cork broke his leg and was not able to play again during the season. Alan was a great loss to the side and, looking back, we never replaced him in any shape or form until Stewart Evans arrived from Sheffield United towards the end of the season. It is a priority, I feel, in the Third and Fourth Divisions, that it is necessary to have a big centre-half and a big centre-forward. In this respect, Corky's absence was the most significant during the season.

At the time our eleventh game of the season had finished against Plymouth Argyle, Steve Galliers was joining Crystal Palace in a transfer deal that was necessary, plus I had the additional problem of Steve Jones being injured, which resulted in a cartilage operation. Once again, this player has not represented the club during the remainder of the season. In the thirteenth game, Mick Smith received a knee ligament injury which put him out until 2nd January. Fortunately, this meant he only missed five games due to the weather. Had the weather not been kind to us we would have been without his services for a minimum of 12 games.

These problems, coupled with normal injuries received by all players during the season, left me in a position on many occasions where I had 11 or 12 players to select from. On a couple of occasions it was necessary to play trialists in the team, which is

Above: Wimbledon Football Club. My home for 14 years.

Left: Allen Batsford was my manager, and mentor.

Below: I took over from Dario Gradi when he went to Palace in January 1981.

Above: Squaring up to Billy Bremner. Tough opponent? Nah.

Below: Wimbledon were Southern League champions every year I was there.

Right: This time the celebrations would last even longer.

Below: Jeff Bryant scores the first Dons league goal, against Halifax on 20 August 1977.

Bottom: January postponements at Plough Lane were common. Winters were worse then.

Above: I soon got an appetite for life on the bench.

Below: Away games were a riot, and Wally usually started it. Ron Noades is front far left.

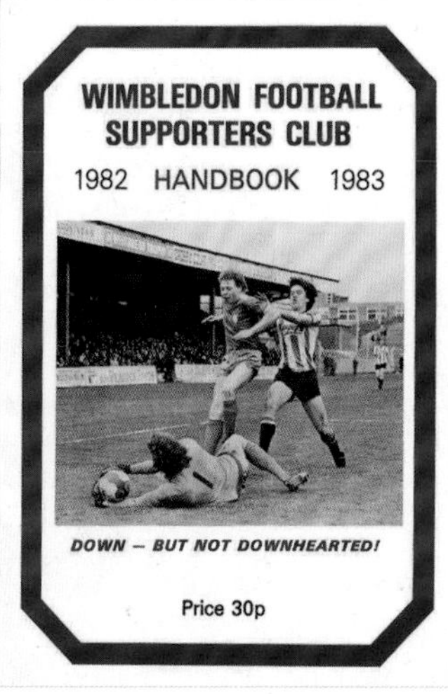

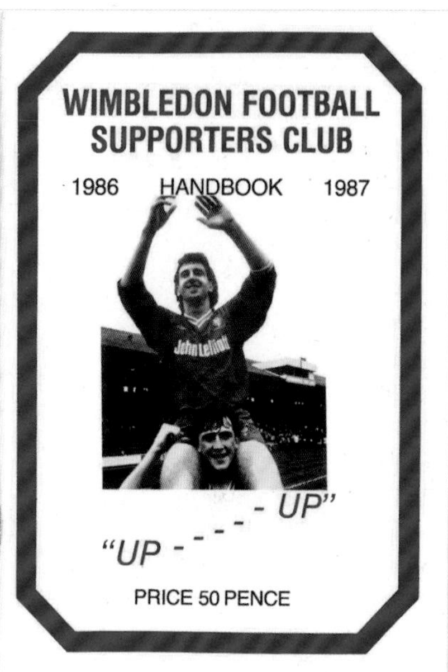

Above and right: Wimbledon was a roller-coaster ride, but we made it up in the end.

Below: Celebrating getting Forest in the Cup. I had Cloughie's number.

Above and below: The personnel – and the haircuts – changed over the years, but not the winning ethos.

I collected my fair share of awards over the years, and yes, the whisky bottles were bigger in those days too!

Above: Promotion to the top flight was sealed at Huddersfield on 3 May 1986. Lawrie Sanchez, to everyone's astonishment, rifled home the free-kick, the players celebrated (**below**), and then the party started.

Our keeper was at the centre of it all...

ridiculous when one is trying to survive in the Third Division. This is not a criticism of the club, as we had sufficient players, but our injury list was enormous. To say the early part of the season was traumatic is an understatement.

With the advent of 1982, our fortunes improved partly due to the fact that several of our young players – namely Morris, Joseph, Hodges and Gage – began to come to terms with the Third Division. These players acquitted themselves extremely well considering they were asked to do a job which they were not quite ready to accomplish, due to inexperience and age. David Beasant looked a totally different goalkeeper in the second half of the season and started to perform in the way which we have all come to accept.

Without doubt, had we been able to cope moderately in the early first half of the season, namely September to January, I am convinced that we would still be in the Third Division. Our fight to the end, I feel, is a credit to the players who competed magnificently to try to retrieve the position. At no time did I feel that anybody on the football side gave up the battle as a lost cause, and this was epitomized in our later performance. Whilst it is very little compensation, many managers in the Third Division have complimented me on the way that the team have played and battled and cannot understand how we were in such a low position. It is the problems in the early games that account for this, as I felt at the start we had a squad that could survive.

Our exploits in the Cups were unfortunately dismal, except for the Group Cup where we reached the final and played extremely well throughout. The final itself was tremendously entertaining and one of the best type of Cup finals I have seen in many a long day. The football played on both sides was entertaining. In the League Cup we played Aldershot for the third year on the trot and played extremely well, but only gained a draw. I felt that the stage was set for another home victory in our home game. This did not materialize and we played very poorly on the night. In the FA Cup we travelled to Bedford and won quite comfortably before meeting Enfield, who were a totally different cup of tea. On this night we were well beaten and this was probably as low as I have felt since becoming a football manager. Whilst I appreciate our side played abysmally, I was asking several members to play in a game for which they were not ready at this stage of their careers. There was only Beasant, Ketteridge, Leslie and Downes playing out of the side who gained us promotion the previous season. To rip a side to shreds in such a way and expect to be successful is asking for the eighth wonder of the world!

The 1981–82 season is now history, and it is the following season that is now of paramount importance. Several players have left the club and will be replaced by others who, I hope, will prove to be an improvement. Our intention will be to get back in the Third Division as quickly as possible, and we shall not be able to do this without the full commitment and enthusiasm of the players, plus the back-up of the staff, as well as our supporters. I am totally ambitious for the club and whilst we may have taken a step backwards, I am convinced our foundation is stronger on which to build for the future. Naturally, I shall also be looking for an improvement in our performance in the Cup ties so that we may have one or two glamour games for everybody's enjoyment.

Finally, I feel it is necessary to say that I feel that Wimbledon's football is developing satisfactorily in that we have so many young players who have established themselves in the team, as well as many excellent schoolboys who are potential Wimbledon players. As we will never be in a position to purchase our own players at any high fees, it is essential that our local youth is developed. In this respect we have one or two outstanding players who, in my opinion, will go the whole way in the game. Therefore, I do feel that the following season should be treated by everybody as one of potential and hope.

So I felt under pressure to deliver, and the only way I could survive was to get promotion once more. The players were still confident, and around this time another major part of the Wimbledon jigsaw was nicely settling in.

Following relegation in 1982, we were joined by our new physio, Derek French, a former cabbie and part-time sponge man at Barnet. Our gates were poor, there was little money, and we told him not to stop his taxi driving just in case it all went pear-shaped. Frenchie, as he was to be known, settled into the club as if he had been waiting for it all his life. He quickly became part of the fabric of life in SW19. He was quick-witted and could handle himself verbally. The boys loved him. Stevie Galliers told me that when his daughter decided to do her physio training, she saw it was a five-year course, but Frenchie spent five minutes learning it. He was a right laugh, especially when he had had a drink. There was a story that he let his dog out for a piss on a cold night once, and when he opened the door again to let it in the dog had frozen solid. (The dog did die, but not in this way. It was Frenchie's way of dealing with it. I decided to call the players together before training and to put black armbands on and hold a minute's silence in Scamp's memory.)

Frenchie wasn't too happy, however, when Wally and some others almost drowned him on a pre-season tour of Finland by holding him upside down in a lake. Wally wanted to see how long he could remain underwater and took him to the limit. Then, a few days later, some of the boys tried it again. One minute Frenchie was having a relaxing afternoon with a few beers, the next he was dangling over the side of a boat by his ankles. The weather was foul that day, the water black and murky, and all I could hear were screams as he fought for his life – his money and personal belongings tumbling from his pocket.

New boys were always considered fair game and a target for initiation pranks, but even Frenchie baulked when players defecated into a teammate's footwear. Blame me, I suppose, because I had always been in favour of high jinks. I invented 'Harry's Ball', where a player was asked to dribble through several grids with the ball and the rules were there were no rules. That caused a few skirmishes.

I allowed them a lot of scope, but came down heavily on anyone who allowed complacency to creep into his game. They knew when I got the hump. I was told I walked and talked quicker – Frenchie called it the Bassett gasket blow – and if they didn't match my standards I would often call them in for Sunday training. We had laughs, but when we were working we were fucking working. If anyone buggered about, it was off round the run from the A3 to the windmill on Wimbledon Common, or out of the club's door.

But as I had intimated in those pre-season musings, these young players were going to be key to the future of the club. That meant that the role of our youth team manager, Geoff Taylor – and development officer, Peter Prentice – in looking after and developing them, was going to be crucial. Peter had proudly stated in that *Supporters' Club Handbook* that the total of eight apprentices (plus 17 associate schoolboys) was the most the club had ever taken on. 'Once again,' he wrote, 'this proves the club's youth policy is being taken seriously at a time when a lot of clubs are looking to this area to cut back on finances.'

As well as a long-time associate, Geoff is a long-time friend of mine. Over to you, Geoff.

Geoff Taylor

I first met Dave Bassett around 1964 when we played for Hayes in the Athenian League, when you were charged tuppence for a programme. I wasn't a very good player and played all over the shop, from right-back to centre-back, but was very fit and enthusiastic. Dave had been bombed out by Chelsea. He arrived as a stroppy young forward who could look after himself mentally and physically – a strong player with a strong personality. I never thought he would be a manager. He left us for Wycombe Wanderers for a short period, before returning to Hayes, but a future manager? Never.

Throughout this time we'd go training together over at Manor Park. We'd also go to games together, particularly QPR, where I coached schoolboys in the evenings under their manager Gordon Jago and his assistant Dave Sexton. We also played a few Sunday League games together. Later, I was manager of Ruislip Manor when Dave phoned and asked if I fancied taking over at Southall under their new chairman Ron Noades.

Dave had his own insurance brokerage and his offices were in a building Ron owned, of course. They knew each other well. I was still working at QPR at the time but Southall was a challenge. We had a good side, with several decent players in Alan Devonshire, who I sold to West Ham, and also Chris Hutchings, who went to Chelsea.

The years rolled by, we kept in touch and when Dave became Wimbledon manager he upgraded Alan Gillett from youth team coach to his assistant and asked me to replace him. So the journey began.

We toured the area, scouting for youngsters, those who had been ignored by bigger clubs or were just hungry for a chance. We told those who had been approached by the likes of Fulham and Chelsea that by joining us they would get their chance and not just be a number. It worked: Brian Gayle, Andy Clement, Vaughan Ryan, Simon Tracey, John Gannon, Andy Sayer and Andy Thorn arrived, followed by Dennis Wise, who had been released by Southampton. Further down the line was Neal Ardley, Neil Sullivan, Chris Perry and Stewart Castledine, who would make their mark.

We welcomed all-comers, and many others were to follow. Not that it was easy persuading Brian Gayle. His dad was a brickie and he had set his mind on joining him! Andy Thorn went into the first team at 18 and stayed there. If youngsters needed proof they would get their chance then Andy was the shining light.

I was called 'Ball Bag', and you can probably guess

who gave that nickname to me. I knew the first team were a lively lot, and I knew there were going to be shenanigans, with the occasional punch-up. I would get the lads organized and then go out and join the first team. I would get them into a wedge because I knew once the first team saw the youngsters they would strip them off and throw their clothes into trees. Sounds gruesome, but it was all in good fun.

The senior pros loved the bonding and loved nothing better than joking around. The kids had to collect the balls and cones after training, but often had to fish them out of nettles or the nearby stream.

The first team would also force the kids to run naked to the dressing room. But it wasn't just the kids. I remember Lawrie Sanchez arriving and being stripped off in the middle of the field. He was stark naked and had to flee back to the changing room with his hands over his unmentionables with the old dears out walking their dogs shouting, 'Disgusting, look at that.' But they continued to keep looking.

Having said all that, the pros would protect the youngsters like elder brothers. There rarely wasn't a youth or reserve game they didn't support. There was never anything sinister or evil. I would never have tolerated it, and I know Dave would never have allowed anything overboard.

We also encouraged mums and dads, brothers and sisters to watch us train in the evening. These kids were around 14, and you had to sign them at that age. One of our youngsters got lured to Arsenal. His name was Michael Thomas, and he went on to have a great career there. We accepted things like that would happen. At virtually every one of our youth-team games there was a corner of scouts from other clubs seeing who they could nick.

But few had their heads turned by approaches. They liked what we had created: the comradeship, our work ethic and the prize that if they did well then they would get their chance. It was a rough and ready place, but also a fun place.

There was one occasion when the senior players were in a circle with two in the middle trying to intercept passes. They were on the far side of the pitch when, out of the corner of my eye, I noticed a woman get out of a car, collect a baby from her back seat and start walking across the pitch. I turned to our physio Derek French and told him to check it out. He said, 'Crumbs, that's Alan Cork's wife.' Some of the players saw her approaching and started to laugh. With that Corky noticed who it was and started running towards her. Then, from a few yards, she threw the baby into his arms, belted him and stormed off. By this time the first team collapsed, laughing on the ground while Corky was left holding the baby. Eventually, Dave had to come out of his office and sort it out.

It was one of many things that happened on a daily basis. I remember John Fashanu arriving and, even though the lads were a bit wary of him, he was told not to leave anything about in the dressing room, mainly because it was a public place too. But he made the mistake of leaving his car keys on a bench. They were eventually found in the middle of a patch of nettles. He got initiated quite early.

It wasn't always sweetness and light. I fell out with Alan Gillett – in fact, that was a big row. The first team were struggling for a centre-back and I said, 'Go for Thorny.' Alan was a bit negative. Andy wasn't the quickest in the world, but he had a brain on him. Harry backed my judgement. That row with Alan went on for quite a while, I might add.

I would like to clear up all the bollocks from this TV programme *The Crazy Gang*. I never witnessed anything that was expressed on that show, and I was there a long time. There was no burning of clothes, no vicious punch-ups. It was a happy environment. I looked forward to going into training and I am sure the players did, to a certain degree. Sure, there were mock battles, but the senior pros like Wally Downes, Mark Morris and Glyn Hodges, former apprentices themselves, would look out for the kids. They never abused them. The kids had to clean the boots, collect the kit and dig the ice off pitches – sometimes at 6.30 in the morning – but come Christmas time they were looked after well by senior pros, who would give them welcome cash gifts.

We would all dig in. The groundsman would have tidied the ground but we – Dave, Alan, the youngsters and me – would have to do the donkey work. We didn't have the money to bring someone in. We had many managers coming down to our training ground because Harry was doing something different and they wanted to know his secret.

No day was the same. I recall one long run that I led them on down the A3, away from London. Eventually we turned back on to Wimbledon Common and there, sitting in the woods with a fold-up table and two chairs, were Wally Downes and Mick Smith with a bottle of wine and two glasses!

Then there were those who would cut through the woods on runs, wait until the leader came through five minutes before anyone else – that was Dennis Wise, usually – and then fall in behind him. Wise had an engine and a half. Simon Tracey and Neil Sullivan, both keepers, Wally Downes and Glyn Hodges were not the best of runners.

Dave had his nutty periods, and Alan and I were his voice of reason. I would try to calm him down with my thoughts on life. I knew his moods well. I knew when he had his 'head on'. If Harry came in in one of these moods, Alan would spot it immediately and he would come out to me and say, 'He's got his nutty head on so don't start messing around in training today.' I always used to say he had many hats: the bad hat when he trained the players and gave 'em some; then the hat he wore when he went out socially; and also his sacking hat. Many hats. I knew. So I would go out and mention to Wally or Corky, 'Don't mess around today or you could be on the six-mile

Richmond run.' That always guaranteed a quiet morning. Corky and running were in daily conflict.

I've known Dave now for over 50 years. I wouldn't say we socialized much because we are different types of people, but I was not surprised at his success. I mentioned I never thought he would be a manager when we first met, but all that changed when we got to know each other. I could see in him a burning desire to succeed. He was a hard man at times, demanding success. His greatest gift was his motivation. He inspired others. He led. Only the foolish didn't follow him.

9

Up, Down, Up, Down, Up

Wally

As Harry said, after showing so much fight to try to stay in the Third Division, we started the 1982–83 season determined to bounce straight back. As usual, though, we were incapable of winning our first match of the campaign, drawing 1–1 with a piss-poor Northampton team who'd had to apply for re-election at the end of the previous season. Luckily there were only 1,703 at Plough Lane to witness it. But as the season developed, it did seem that we had learned our lessons from past mistakes and that there was an air of absolute professionalism that permeated the whole club, both on the park and off it.

Because of having to throw the young boys in at the deep end, it really was the pivotal season in Wimbledon's rise to the top of the football world. I was the first apprentice to become a first-team regular, and with Hodge now firmly established, of course, the likes of Mark Elliott on the wing, Dean Thomas and Gagey had also now been given their chance. Brian Gayle and Andy Sayer (inevitably soon to be nicknamed 'Leo') were among the next crop of youth team players to show promise – Sayer had scored 26 goals for the youth team in 1981–82.

Guppy was another who had really made the breakthrough in 1981–82. He may have been quiet, and only 19, but he was composed, and his partnership with Mick Smith at the back would be one of the key factors in a season when we finally worked out how to defend. I include myself in that number, having learned a few lessons the previous season and polished my game a little, since I had mostly been used by Harry at the back in the Third Division, before stepping forward into the midfield role I preferred.

Furthermore, we were scoring goals for fun, none more so than John Leslie, the last link to Wimbledon's Southern League days, who had been drafted in at right-back for the closing months of the previous campaign, but whose 25 in all competitions would make him a shoo-in for player of the season in 1982–83.

We also had a new skipper, Gary Peters, signed on a free transfer from Fulham. Gary thoroughly relished his role. Perhaps we had become a bit chummy as a group, having grown up together, and the captain certainly showed no qualms in digging out any of us who were drifting off-message! Gary joined in superbly and, as he was a bit older, we respected the fact that he had paid his dues but wasn't a busy bastard who wouldn't enjoy the training ground and environment that we had working. His was a great appointment by Harry – he was a perfect signing for us and was an enormous part of our success.

I played in front of him on the wing, and I'd like to think we didn't give a lot away down our side for a few years – and although he wasn't overly inclined to pass me the ball on a regular basis, we created a few goals between us. Gary loved a night out with all the boys – I'd say he was the player who embraced what we were about more than any other who hadn't grown up with it.

He did, however, make the fatal mistake of arriving at the club sporting a slug on his top lip, as he will now reveal as he describes his two seasons with the Crazy Gang.

Gary Peters

I arrived at Wimbledon after falling out with the Fulham manager, Malcolm Macdonald, when I still had three years left on my contract. We clashed immediately when he was appointed. I found him quite flash, the opposite to me, really, and to Bobby Campbell, the previous manager. Mac basically told me I would be stuck training with the reserves.

I think I agreed to take a third of my current wages and drop down two divisions because of what Harry told me. He would come and watch me play for Fulham reserves and he said he would make me Wimbledon captain and explained that he felt the club were going to do something.

I remember my first meeting with the squad. Harry walked me in and said, 'Fellas, this is Gary and he is going to be your new captain.' Now this was a team already with six or seven big characters who had been with the club a long time, and I could see that they weren't happy about this stranger coming in and taking the top job. There were a few hisses and dropped eyes, but I could understand it.

We were going on a pre-season trip straight away so there was a chance to bond, and after the introduction Harry gave out the rooms. Everyone was paired off, and right at the very end Harry said I would be sharing with Wally Downes. Suddenly everyone started giggling, and I had absolutely no idea why.

I found out the hard way. Around 1 a.m. the night before our first game, I was woken from my sleep to find him sitting on my chest trying to silently shave off my moustache! Apparently the players were refusing to have 'a 'tache captain' in their team. But I got on with everyone straight away. I liked a drink and a laugh, and I was a bit older than a lot of them. I think I was 29 when I arrived. I could never do what Wally or Glyn Hodges did because they were far more skilful than I was, but every single player in the team and in the reserves or youth team knew the jobs of every other player, and how the team played.

It didn't work from day one. When I went in we weren't playing that Wimbledon way, we were playing like everyone else, and not doing too well. After a few games in Division Four, Harry came up with the change. He got all the lads together and explained that we were now going to play like Watford and Sheffield Wednesday – but do it better than them.

It was hard for Harry because he, as the manager, didn't change – it was the style that changed completely. It was something many didn't want. The likes of Wally and Hodges were the biggest critics because they were talented players. If we hadn't gone on and won our next few games then it might never have started, and this book wouldn't exist. When it worked, instantly everyone bought into it. I could see at times that some lads were slipping back into their old routines. Wally could often be the world's worst moaner, and so could Hodges, because they had so much ability, far more than was required for them to play the way we were playing. Trying to get what was required wasn't easy.

Every single player knew exactly what to do at each point. They knew where the ball was going. You had to be ready. People think we were 4–4–2, but I am telling you we were 2–4–4. And no one had ever played like that. We had two centre-halves marking two centre-forwards, and if they couldn't deal with it they were dropped. The full-backs marked their wingers, and our wingers would pin their full-backs; we pinned everyone on the pitch, so as soon as we launched it there was no one free on their team, there was never a free header. We all had our man who we were going to mark and have our battle with.

I would do my job as a cog in a machine and, as I was captain, I had to make sure all the other cogs did their jobs. If people didn't pull their weight on the pitch then it would be my job to pull them up or have a dig. I had to gee them up to make sure they performed. I was trying to make sure that whatever Harry wanted to happen on the pitch happened. And I fell out with a few of the players. You had to mean business, and you might have a wrestle, but it wasn't nasty. The same two people fighting would be cuddling later.

It was a hard club to join, but it wasn't all that bollocks that was painted later. When Vinnie first joined he was a young boy, so he didn't have a way with him – he was an impressionable young lad. I didn't see nastiness. It was tough in the changing room, but nothing like what Fash went on about. The changing room was a tough place, but there was no physical violence. You went out and did as much as you could to the opposition.

I played with some complete lunatics in my career. I played with Robin Friday at Reading and I used to go out with him – he was a total loon. We also had a fella called Roy Davies, who was another nutter. Every team had at least one character, and ours was Wally.

Harry's management style was different to anyone's I ever experienced: he was strict and strong, but he was one of us. One day the players started throwing things around on the train home from a game. On Monday, Harry and Sam were lecturing me about the mess, and I pointed out they had started it. They were part of the Crazy Gang, it wasn't just the players, and it couldn't have worked without that flexibility. Harry could be the hardest person in the world when he needed to be, but I loved him.

We won the league and everyone got a tenner rise – well, the majority did, some got a fiver if they hadn't played many games. But Micky Smith and Corky didn't get any rise because they had been injured during that season – they were lucky to get contracts. We had a players' meeting and they were all arguing about the rises, saying everyone deserved one. I went to see Harry and tried to get Smithy and Corky their money. Harry said he would give them the rise but only if they would each work one night a week in the Sportsman. I went to Smithy and told him and in his thick north-east accent he said, 'Fuck off!' The lads then unionized and threatened not to play the first pre-season game. I never even tried with Corky, I just went back to Harry and said it was sorted and to give them their rise.

I ended up doing their two nights a week, working behind the bar myself! But that inspired me to buy a pub in Bracknell, Berkshire, and it changed my life completely, because the pub did well – and then I bought another one that did just as well. That fiver a night in the Sportsman helped me get a whole second career.

I played with a lot of teams before and after Wimbledon,

and I can safely say that we trained harder than anybody else, anywhere. We trained physically harder and longer than anyone else. And sometimes, after a game, we would go out and do an hour of set-pieces – people would be amazed at how come we were so good at dead-balls, but it was because we practised harder than anyone else. We didn't get to where we got through luck. We got there by taking it more seriously than anyone else and working harder than anyone else around us. It was almost as if we were running a business.

When I look back the only thing I can compare it to is the film *The Dirty Dozen*. They needed a job doing, they didn't have the money to do it, so they broke highly skilled people out of prison to do the jobs they needed. Once it was all in place everything took care of itself. As I said, the changing room was tough; if you went in being Billy Big Bollocks you were brought down. But when it worked, it worked.

Beating Bury away when we won the league is the game that stands out for me. It was on the TV and I have watched it so many times since. The ball came to me and I smashed it up and Fish flicked it on for a goal. We turned defence into attack quickly. We could do that because we were the fittest team – when the ball travels 50 yards in five seconds you need to get after it.

I enjoyed studying and learning what we were doing because it suited me down to the ground. I wasn't a good footballer; I couldn't pass and dribble. My nickname was 'Bosh'em'. Fulham fans said I should have played rugby. It took two seasons for me to pass it to Wally, and when I did he got smashed from behind and broke his ankle.

You never got an easy time off Harry, even if you had won. He didn't want us to get carried away. As we did get on a roll and started winning most weeks, I think there were times when we drifted away from the things that had got us there and got over-confident. That was my job on the pitch: to ensure we carried on according to the plan.

We went to Gravelines in France for an end-of-season once and had a whole week playing and eating in a little village on an estuary. There was a bar, but it was the same two old people in there every night and it was useless. On the other side of the river there was another bar that had flashing lights. It was about 12 miles to the nearest bridge and we couldn't afford a taxi, so me, Dave Beasant, Steve Hatter and Micky Smith decided to borrow a rowing boat and row across – this was long before Freddie Flintoff – but we only had one paddle. We got over the river fine and tied the boat to the side. But the other bar was exactly the same, useless, empty, but with flashing lights.

When we came out to go back, the rowing boat was hanging in mid-air because the tide had gone out. We managed to get it into the water, but the tide then started taking us further and further out to sea. Luckily Harry saw us. In the end we had to capsize the boat and carry it back to the hostel we were staying in. Wimbledon was not a normal club!

I understood when I was released. I was a lower division player; I could do Divisions Three and Four. Harry saw he needed to improve as we went up, and it was for that reason that the success continued. I went to Reading and got promoted all over again, getting up to what is the Championship now. Ian Branfoot took me there because of what I had done at Wimbledon, and we copied it – they wanted my knowledge from working with Harry. Then John Beck took me to Cambridge and Preston where we did the same things, and it worked. My two years was a wonderful experience – an education, plus tremendous enjoyment.

10

The Turning Point

Harry

BLACK JOE JUMPING ship, and to Brentford of all places, was a blow, but one that was more than cushioned by the return of Midget, less than a year after he'd gone to Palace. Sam was happy too – Midget only cost us £15,000, a fraction of what we'd sold him for. More good business for the club. I also brought in Tony Tagg and Chris Dibble on frees from Millwall, and both went straight into the starting eleven, along with Dean Thomas at left-back, who was only 20 but proving more than capable of filling Gary Armstrong's boots. He scored some cracking goals that season too, Dean; he had a peach of a left peg.

Continuing our habit of putting together runs, we went unbeaten for the first eleven league games of the season. At first, there was a glut of meek draws, but we then hit prime form, winning six on the spin, scoring 20 goals in those six games, to go top of the table. In fact, we were the only unbeaten team in the country, although that's ignoring a dismal performance in the League Cup, losing to a Brentford side featuring Paddy Roche, Terry Hurlock, Chris Kamara and Stan Bowles, along with Black Joe.

But in the league we were direct, getting the ball up to the front men as quickly as possible, and the results came with it. As I said after one game, 'This is the Fourth Division. When we play at 100 m.p.h. everyone else has to do the same.' It won me the Bell's Manager of the Month award, and believe me, the bottles were bigger back in those days.

The whisky caused a hangover. On 23 October, we were away at Bristol City, who had been relegated in each of their previous three seasons and had started this campaign in similar dismal fashion. They played host to us one place off the foot of the table with just one win to their name. But City started the match superbly and were all over us – 3–0 up by the interval and it could have been more. John Leslie and Dean Thomas pulled goals back late on to make the score slightly more respectable at 4–2, but Midget tarnished it with a red card. He certainly knew how to get himself sent off. The first yellow came for a stamp on Jon Economou, before he aimed a kick at Alan Crawford after being prevented from taking a quick free-kick.

The wheels came completely off in November, with three limp defeats in the league, and an early exit from the FA Cup at the hands of Northampton in the First

Round. I had already dropped Hodge for that one – all the praise was going to his head, Luton's David Pleat was rumoured to be interested in him, and he needed a kick up the arse, as well as some splinters from the bench – and now it was time to swing the axe too. As Clive Leatherdale puts it in his book, 'Bassett does not just tinker with the team, he dismembers it, bringing in six fresh faces.' Yes, I completely blew my Bassett gasket that time.

Hodges' memories of the third of those league defeats – 4–2 at home to Halifax, with Bobby Davison scoring a hat-trick – are interesting. He says that all the players went in on the Monday for the post-match analysis expecting the mother of all bollockings and to be run all over Richmond Park but instead I said, 'Well done, you played really well.' They couldn't believe it, they thought I'd gone mad. But I went through a list of how many shots and crosses, how many second balls we won, how much possession we had – and told them that if they carried on playing like that we would go up. They thought I was joking, because that wasn't the reaction they expected. But I knew I had to encourage them, even if collectively we were nowhere near good enough.

The Northampton game was the turning point in more ways than one. The initial Cup match at their place had ended 2–2 after a respectable comeback. We were two down with 40 minutes left to play and could have won the match only for a late and glaring miss from

Chris Dibble following a cross from Kevin Gage. But we were fucking dreadful in the replay, losing 2–0 at Plough Lane, Peter Coffill scoring a brace for the visitors. 'I can't repeat what I said to them afterwards,' I told the press. 'But it seemed to me we didn't have the imagination or alertness to succeed. If we were playing now and Northampton had gone home we'd still be struggling to find the net.'

To put it bluntly, what I then did was to rip up my tactics book, axing the sweeper system that had at one time worked so well for us. We had a meeting and implemented total change – for everyone in the club. From now on we would be considerably more direct, getting the ball in the opposition penalty area. It wasn't music to their ears at first, especially the midfielders, players like Downes and Hodges, but it was reluctantly accepted. As it started to work they all started to enjoy the success it brought them. It wasn't a flash-in-the-pan thing that hadn't been thought out. We knew what we were doing. There was very little time for the players to adapt and mould into it; the line had been drawn in the sand and it was – bang – this is how we are doing it from now.

So, the tactics were changed, and it was the turning point. Going out of both Cups early also left us to focus on the league, and the side became settled. Two of the new faces, whose debuts came in the pissing rain at Darlington, a game we won 2–0, with John Leslie getting us off to a flying start, were in on loan – Phil Ferns from Charlton and Steve Hatter from Fulham – but even more important was the return of Mick Smith at the back. That was the end of Tony Tagg's time in a Wimbledon shirt – due to injury. And a good festive season saw us back in the promotion places by New Year, only to have a sickener against Hull, the new league leaders, conceding a last-minute goal.

But that was the last time we lost that season.

Our unbeaten run of 22 games to end the 1982–83 season to clinch the Fourth Division Championship is one of my proudest memories of a long life in football. Tactically, we got it spot on – it may have been called direct, but it was bloody effective. Two from Morris, Smith and Hatter would play as centre-halves, with Peters and Brian Sparrow, on loan from Arsenal, at full-back. They would get it up to the front men – Evans and Leslie, then Corky when he finally came back from his broken leg in April – as fast as they could. We had to weather a few storms, but we were tenacious, determined and dogged in all departments.

We even had to deal with a bizarre incident in the game at Mansfield in April 1983 in which Corky made his comeback. It was 1–1, just after half-time, when Guppy brought one of their forwards down in the box. Sparrow thought he heard the ref's whistle so dived full length to get the ball and stuck it under his arm, before facing off with the ref in disgust. It turned out that the ref hadn't given the penalty at all, but now had no option but to. We were happy to leave with a 2–2 draw.

With the boost of having Corky back after injury, as

well as Wally in midfield, we were even harder to beat than usual. In fact, eight wins in our last nine games meant we were busy rewriting the record books. We won £25,000 from Capital Radio for becoming the first London club to score 80 league goals in a season – ending up with 96, and a record points tally of 98. The crowds weren't exactly flocking back to Plough Lane, but we got more than 4,000 for the visit of promotion rivals Port Vale in late April, which was a step in the right direction.

Wally's first league goal in two years took us back to the top of the table at Crewe on Easter Saturday and secured promotion with four matches to spare, even if the Dons fans on their way to Gresty Road had to run the gauntlet of Port Vale supporters who'd nipped up the road from Stoke to hurl bricks, bottles and iron bars at them. They obviously couldn't catch enough of us, those so-called fans – they'd been nasty bastards at Plough Lane the previous weekend too.

The title was in the bag too before we closed the campaign with a 3–1 win at Bury. The home side could have gone up too with a win, so the TV cameras were at Gigg Lane for what would hopefully be a formality. Evans gave us the lead in the ninth minute. Bury manager Jim Iley was mic'ed up by the TV crew for the match and when that first goal went in, the viewers watching at home heard him grumble: 'Well, we didn't need that. Not at this stage of the game . . . no way!!' This made us roar at the telly the next day when we watched it together, and we would use it for years to come. Bad idea, mics in dugouts. Wally then scored the second just before half-time, drilling in an attempted Bury clearance, and celebrated by doing the Magaluf shuffle for the first time. It was to become a famous Wimbledon move, but the fans were stunned as dancing was not the done thing at the time in terms of goal celebrations. But the players had been promised a trip to Magaluf if they won promotion, and this set it off. Bez then saved a penalty, diving the right way to foil Tommy Gore and push the ball over the bar – and although Bury pulled one back, Fish crowned the win with a third. We were champions. I hadn't heard that word since the Southern League days, and it had a nice ring to it.

It was actually Stevie Hatter and Mick Smith who invented the Magaluf shuffle a few days before the Bury game when we had already sealed promotion. Wally tells me that I was coaching up the other end of an 11 v 11 game and turned round to see my big two centre-halves dancing during my training session instead of concentrating. I went nuts: 'What the fucking hell do you two think you're doing?' I screamed, storming towards them. The rest of the players had seen what was happening and were pissing themselves. After a couple of seconds, Hatter and Smith both said, 'The Magaluf shuffle, Harry.' Everybody dissolved at that and they vowed to do it on the TV at the weekend – whoever scored the first goal at Bury had to do the shuffle. So Wally, as he puts it, 'spanked one in the top bin and the shuffle was born!'

The journey back from Bury was predictably raucous, and the players weren't going to let me get off lightly. I was already feeling edgy, as I had seen Wally and a few of the others whispering to each other and pointing towards my seat. My fears were confirmed somewhere just outside of Hemel Hempstead when the lads stormed over and stripped me – out of the Inter-City train's window went my jacket, shoes, trousers, any items of clothing they could lay their hands on. I was left with just a shirt, pants and pair of socks. They also blocked me and Derek French from getting off at our stop at Watford and we eventually ended up in Frank McLintock's pub. I eventually got home, still in shirt, socks and pants, and had to knock at the door to ask my wife Christine to pay for the waiting taxi. Mrs B wasn't pleased, and it was the sofa that night for me. It was one way to celebrate promotion.

Four years later, when we were riding high in the First Division, I remember playing a round at Surbiton Golf Club with Martin Hardy, the *Express* golf writer, as part of a series he was doing, and we were joking about how much had changed – but how little I had – since that memorable journey. 'If somebody had said after that match at Bury that Dave Bassett had been seen at Euston in his underpants,' I said, 'people would have replied: "Who's Dave Bassett? Who cares?" But I couldn't get away with that kind of thing now. It would be front page news! We certainly had some great laughs in the lower divisions . . .'

Although we wouldn't be staying in those lower divisions much longer – it's a cliché, I know, but the only way was up.

I'll hand over to Steve Hatter here. It was a great pleasure when he showed up for one of our reunions during the writing of this book. He may have been a Don for only a short while, but it was testament to the tight-knit nature of the group that he was there. Hatter has a special place in Crazy Gang history too: along with Gary Peters, who never missed a game all that 1982–83 season, the pair never experienced anything other than promotion in a Wimbledon shirt.

Steve Hatter

They signed me for £15,000 from Fulham. I arrived in the Fourth Division and we got promoted and then we got promoted from the Third to the Second, and then halfway through the season I had a barney with Harry and the next thing I knew I was at Southend.

It was a row after a match at Leeds, where we got hammered. Harry started having a go at one or two of the young players and I reared up. We had the barney and he said, 'If you don't shut your mouth, you'll be off.' At the time I still had plenty to say, and then on Monday morning I got a phone call from Bobby Moore, who said, 'I understand you're up for sale?' And that was it – two days later I was gone.

These things happen. But how could you fall out with Dave? You can't!

People have a go at our way of playing, but it worked. People think it was all long ball, but we just used to get it forward quickly and then we played in their half. Players like Hodge and Corky could play in their half. I think we were hard done by, people used to slag us off, but they had no idea what we were doing – we were doing some good stuff.

I remember when we used to go down to Plymouth to do the SAS training, and one day me, Ketts, Smithy and Lurch went down in a Morris Minor. We stopped off on the way down and had eight or ten pints, thinking that when we arrived we would have a rest and start training the next day. But the minute we arrived Harry sent us for a run.

Harry smashed his head on an assault course once. We were supposed to push him through a tunnel underwater, but we didn't push him hard enough, so he smashed his head open and the water turned claret. We trained three times a day and the soldiers there couldn't believe how fit we were. They felt a bit sorry for us – and they had just come back from the Falklands.

I was bought by the fans. I made my debut and wondered what was going on, because I saw fans handing around a blanket and throwing money into it. I was told after they had to buy me because the club was skint!

After I left, there was never a club like Wimbledon for me – I don't think there will ever be another club like

Wimbledon for anyone. The games I remember best are the games against Forest when we mullered them in the Cup – we played so well.

11

The Numbers Game

Harry

CHANGING OUR TACTICS in the 1982–83 season had been pivotal to our becoming champions, so I think this is a good place for me to spell out exactly how I saw the game then.

As I said earlier, altering Wimbledon's tactical approach to what was labelled long-ball football was not initially popular with the players, but I sold the idea to the team, and they bought it. I just knew it was right, like telling your kids the right way to go even though you know they hate the idea.

The only one who loved it straight off was Alan Cork who, as a striker, couldn't wait for the ball to be pumped his way. But the players proved to be open-minded and flexible enough to give it a go. They trusted me and I trusted them to adapt.

I took my FA preliminary coaching badge at 21 and passed my full coaching badge at the age of 30. I had always tried a variety of systems, but this was the way I had always wanted to play. Allen Batsford had taught a similar style, and I picked up more ideas under Charlie Hughes, the FA coach and manager of England's amateur international side. They impressed on me the importance of shape and the set-plays that were required to win matches. They were in the results business, not just the entertainment business. They preached that if a play in the West End was a flop it would soon be taken off and dumped. Entertaining is fine, but winning is better.

They showed me the areas where games were won and lost, the importance of where the opposition loses the ball, the value of corners, throw-ins and set-pieces, etc., etc. Together with Vince Craven and Neil Lanham, we devised what I call our mantra: what are the key factors, we asked ourselves, responsible for successful performance in a football match? I realize the tone of the following section might seem a bit at odds with the rest of the book, and I am sure I will get some stick from some of the boys as a result! Funny, though, they didn't give me too much stick when I was handing out their win bonuses as a result of it!

Soccer has a certain amount of organization: events follow one another in a fairly predictable and sequentially dependent manner. The rules of competition also lay out quite succinctly the objectives of the system. Possession of the ball becomes the critical feature of this structure. That is not to say 'keeping ball possession' is important, but by using possession as a critical element of analysis, all other events can be included and accounted for. During any game either one of the two teams has possession of the ball. The objective of the team with possession is to score goals and the opposing team's objective is, therefore, to prevent the other team from scoring goals. Tactics and strategy are devoted to fulfilling these objectives. Possession can be lost in three areas of the field: the defending third, the midfield area or the attacking third. For example, most shots at goal result in possession being lost. Or a loss can occur in the defending third, for instance a pass that is intercepted by the opposing team (like Steven Gerrard's infamous slip against Chelsea). You have to make decisions about what is acceptable lost possession.

Obviously, players need to get the ball into the attacking third, from where shots and goals can be scored. If possession is continuously lost in this third, the problem for the coach is less formidable than if the ball is lost in the other two thirds. Possession losses that occur in the defending third are dangerous and account for approximately 65 per cent of shots at goal. If possession is lost in the midfield third the chance of a shot at goal is reduced to 25 per cent, whereas this drops to 10 per cent in the attacking third. The conclusion is obvious. Do not increase the probability of losing the ball in your own half of the pitch!

How are Goals Scored?

The shot-to-goal ratio is around 10 shots for 1 goal, and

has been like this since the 1960s. If you can get your team to increase the number of shots at goal there will be a higher probability of scoring more goals and hence winning more games. The priority is therefore to get players to take all shooting opportunities that are presented. You have to realize that not all shots will be on goal; some will be wide, others high and some blocked or deflected. However, with the exception of high shots, shooting at goal either on or off target will produce situations from which other shots can arise. As a coach it is imperative that shooting practice is a major session throughout the week. One fundamental problem in coaching players the technique of shooting is to ensure that they keep their shots below the goal height.

It was also found that dribbling into congested areas around the penalty area yielded free-kicks or opened up shooting situations, and could free other marked attacking players. However, passing in this shooting area has been shown to be the least productive system in terms of creating shooting opportunities. In my view this is considerably over-exaggerated with the misconception that top teams try this technique most frequently to score goals.

What Leads to the Scoring of Goals?

Our conclusion was that direct play leads to goals being scored. This is behind the principle of 'penetration passes', whereby the ball bypasses as many defensive players as possible. It is vital that passes are made, runs with the ball are made and shots taken that go behind and between defenders. Having attacking players deployed high up the pitch as much as possible, and having the ball delivered from the defensive or midfield thirds, would require that the rearmost players move forward and keep the team compact. That equates to ten outfield players playing in an area that spans, at most, one half of the field. Maintaining compactness here as a team unit helps to win the ball back in the opposing team's defending third. In addition, compact team play leads to good supporting play and an improved percentage of completed passes. This means that the game will be played at a fairly fast pace, requiring a high level of fitness for all the team. Playing direct soccer and being fit leads to scoring goals late in the game. This style of play dictates certain other qualities, where all members of the team have to be able to defend as an individual and as a team unit. In addition all players are required to involve themselves in physical challenges for the ball. Full-backs and midfield players have to be technically proficient at playing high lofted passes accurately, and midfield players have to be skilled at predicting where defensive clearances (knockdowns) will go in order to challenge for the ball in the middle third of the pitch.

The middle third sees more action than any other part of the pitch. Therefore players operating in that area are required to be extremely fit, both physically and mentally. Front players need to be athletic and create space and arrive in that space at the right time. One other personal quality that is essential, for attacking players who operate in and around the penalty area, is that of courage. Players who will go into areas of physical danger are few, and so this quality must be nurtured in all your players.

The simple statement of 'direct play' brings with it many other essential features. There is a lot more detail involved for a coach to read into descriptive statements of analysis concerning how goals are scored. The fact that lone high balls should be kicked into the opponents' goal area and chased by one or two players will produce unsuccessful performance and also give a false impression of the benefits of direct play. A complete understanding of all the ramifications of this style, including the selection of players, must be thought through carefully and with the facts of analysis available to guide the thinking process.

The Importance of Set-Plays

Approximately 40 per cent of goals are scored from attacking set-plays. For Wimbledon in 1982–83, this figure was around 44 per cent, and continued to be each season thereafter. Corners are an excellent source of goals, and inswinging balls are more dangerous than out-swinging balls. It is the same for free-kicks from wide. Goals also originate from long throws that are delivered close to the goal, where shooting opportunities will occur, as no attacking players can be offside from a direct throw. Certainly this is a good attacking weapon that seems to strike fear into the defending team. Rory

Delap's success in these set-plays depended mainly on good team planning, organization and discipline to get the best out of such situations.

Practice is paramount. Downes, Wise, Hodges, Gage and Winterburn would practise set-pieces two to three times a week; Winterburn, Gary Peters and Vinnie Jones would work on long throws nearly every day. Wimbledon didn't score so many goals from set-plays by luck! It was practice and attention to detail.

Set-plays are difficult to defend for two reasons. First, the opposition can pack large numbers of players into pre-planned attacking positions. Secondly, it is impossible to exert a high degree of pressure on the service since, with the exception of a throw-in, the defending players always have to be ten yards away from the ball. The fact is that defending set-plays requires the most careful planning, organization and concentration. The basic problem is twofold:

1. Marking players
2. Zonal marking-space.

At Wimbledon we had a good record at defending set-plays due to the fine detail of each individual's jobs, plus a great desire to defend with our lives! Plus, this was regularly practised in a realistic setting.

This is not intended to be a coaching manual, which would be a book in itself, but an explanation of how the

Crazy Game evolved after Lanham, Craven, Taylor and I spent hours studying videos of football throughout the world to digest and analyze how games are won. Ultimately, we didn't get the credit we deserved from other teams and certain sections of the media, but I am of the opinion we got it right on how to win football matches: Fourth Division to 6th in Division One in five years on a pittance of a wage bill is no mean feat! Every player always knew their task as an individual and team member. They combined this with enthusiasm, aggression and confidence – which all equals what I call mental fitness.

Early on I found it baffling that our players were regarded as not good enough – not technically proficient enough – for the top clubs, due to the way we played. Yet when Kevin Gage went to Aston Villa, Mark Morris to Watford, Winterburn to Arsenal and, a year later, Beasant and Thorn to Newcastle and Gayle to Man City – which virtually signalled the end of the Crazy Gang – this was obviously proved to be rubbish. The techniques required of players to operate within a team playing in a direct manner are no different to those demanded of all players. The first and most important technique is that of receiving the ball. Players must be able to bring the ball under control from all possible positions, especially balls that arrive at head or chest height. Allied to this, players must understand under what conditions they should bring the ball under control with their first touch, and under what conditions they should play the ball away first time.

We had practice sessions that were realistic, designed to allow players the opportunity to experience many varied situations. These sessions enabled the player to provide himself with the time to select the appropriate skill (shot, dribble or pass). What was evident was that we had to detect and analyze game performance on a continuous scale, as it was obvious that some records of performance, other than subjective opinions, are gained from just observation. Human memory is extremely fallible and easily distorted by personal expectations. So Vince Craven was able to cut up video clips of all games to illustrate salient points about strategy, tactics or technique. In addition we used the same system for showing what other teams were doing. This was a long and painstaking chore as technology was in its infancy. At the same time Neil Lanham was at all games analyzing and marking out possession – how it was won and lost and where. Players would get feedback in the middle of the week as to how good or bad the results were. Based on this information, which I had by Sunday evening, the training schedule for the week could be formulated.

Of course, the players had to buy into this to make it work, so here's the perspective of the two for whom it was probably hardest, as creative midfielders – Hodges and, of course, Wally.

Glyn Hodges

Harry had a statistician, who was probably the most important person at the club at the time. Vince Craven was doing video clips before anyone else was doing them. He would help out when we went through a stage of doing POMO – position of maximum opportunity. We would be doing it for hours and hours. The ball would be coming across and it was usually down to me or Wally to get there, which we were not great at doing, so it used to lead to fights and bollockings because we couldn't get there. Sometimes we just refused to get there, which didn't go down well.

One day Harry had a bloke come down – a wing commander or something – and actually worked out all the reaches, so your first target would be a long ball from your final third to their final third, and you had to hit that 100 times. If out of that 100 the winger collected it 40 times you would get 12 crosses and, statistically, that would result in two goals and so you would win 2–0. I don't think they are the right figures but it was that methodical, that's how it was sold to us. It was a science that made sense and worked. We had to play that way, and that is how we won games.

At first it was a pain in the arse for me, as a midfielder who wanted the ball, so I didn't want to buy into it. I thought it was a load of bollocks. I couldn't wait to get away, and then I got stuck out on the left wing, so we had two fat wingers and Corky or Stewart Evans down the middle. Harry put me up there, and we did score lots of goals; I got and made a few, and my set-pieces were a different class. But it wasn't really until we started winning every week that everyone got on board.

We were getting close to promotion, and it was exciting and everyone was always at it. It seemed to improve as we went along, and in every division we adapted it. We couldn't have played exactly the same way in the First, Second and Third Division as we did in the Fourth. And in the final third we could and did play – it was just that we didn't hang about in getting it into that final third. That is where I came into my own, getting in the final third and creating or scoring goals. I think I got 18 goals in one Third Division season. It wasn't how I was brought up to play but it was so effective and it was helping me and my team win football matches, so it was a win-win situation.

Wally

When Harry changed the way we played, the three players who were most unsuited to the style were Glyn, me and Corky. Glyn and me because we considered ourselves midfield players who liked to contribute with the ball, and Corky because he wasn't physically equipped to run in behind defenders. As the system progressed, we adjusted our games and became adept at what we were doing: Corky was bright and aware enough to time his runs in behind, while Glyn and I delivered the crosses into the box that enabled us to pressure teams into making mistakes – that was if Corky or Stewart Evans hadn't already headed it in.

The bane of my life was remembering to get in on the back stick to get a tap in if all the strikers and defenders had missed it. You had to be brainwashed into getting there as, invariably, I'd be watching Hodge beating someone before swazzing one in and forget to get into the bastard POMO. Hodge was normally as dozy as fuck and nothing would please him or me more than coming in and grassing, or helpfully pointing out for the good of the team, that we'd put the ball across and no fucker was there! The amount of times we said it's a waste of time putting it in if no one's there. We were always rebuked by Harry with, 'You put it there and I'll find some cunt who will be there.'

It was hard to stifle a giggle when Hodge would lose his head and say, 'I ain't putting it in there no more,' only for Harry to go ballistic at him. The three of us loved dropping one another in the shit when we had done something right. Glyn and I sat together in the corner of the dressing room and Hodge used to read the programme at half-time, just to piss Harry off – it NEVER failed. We both took the set-plays as well. Corners and free-kicks are critical in football, and boy could we take them. I knew when Corky would make his run, and could always deliver it into the danger area. If he didn't score, Smithy, Potsie, Wilf or Evans would be tanking in as well. That won us untold games – all the POMO routines were well worth the time we spent on them.

Corky was such a great finisher with his head and the timing of his runs, but nothing gave him more pleasure than to scuff or trundle one in the corner – the amount of times we'd laugh at him celebrating a crap goal! A keeper would expect a ball in the corner and Corky would scuff it on purpose and throw him completely – which takes some ability, that does! (Well, he said he meant it!) Then, of course, there was the infamous occasion when Corky threw his boots into the corner of the dressing room at half-time and refused to go back on. When Harry asked what the problem was, Corky pointed at me and Hodge and said, 'It's them. They keep passing to my feet. They know I'm no good with my feet!'

There were a couple of seasons when myself and Hodge were the two most violent wingers in the game, both up before the FA for record disciplinary points totals. Midget had won that honour the first year, followed by me, and then Hodge blew it apart the next year. As neither of us were blessed with pace we had to use different means, and occasionally we got frustrated and tended to smash into defenders like they were supposed to smash into us. We found a way! Trying to be as technically gifted as Glyn (I never was) spurred me on – but, then again, in all my years of coaching I never came across a better left foot, ever. Fat bastard!

As for Harry, yes, he got the tactics that worked, but that didn't stop us calling him any variation on the best foreign manager at the time we could think of. 'Harry Basquillero' was a favourite, normally used when he tried a new coaching session that didn't work and we had to go running instead . . .

Harry

Along with the tactical principles I adopted, I also had – and still have – firm principles on the way you should manage. What are the most important characteristics a football manager should possess? Well, I reckon you need the following:

The Ability to Motivate

To be in charge of players effectively in winning games, to be able to inspire them. Orders alone are never enough – if their hearts aren't in it, they will simply 'consent and evade', as they say in the army. A manager who can enthuse a football team will generally do better than one who rules by fear or lethargy.

Domain Knowledge

As a manager you are in charge, so you must be endowed with sufficient technical understanding to obtain the respect of the team. You need to know the competitors and myriad details that provide insight and knowledge. This requires time and study, whether working in football or any other business.

The Ability to Listen

The boss should not dominate team talks and discussions. Encourage feedback and suggestions – by hearing what is said you gain invaluable knowledge. This provides a pathway for individuals to openly discuss matters. You manage by contact with everybody – from the boardroom to the laundry section – to hear what they have to say. You get amazing results.

Decisiveness

Ultimately football clubs and companies cannot function effectively as pure democracies. Someone has to make decisions. Procrastination or wishy-washy thinking are not the habits required by a leader. Groups of people working together need a sense of direction, or their energies are dispersed. That is why you are called a football manager.

A Sense of Humour

Sometimes this trait is vital but might seem out of place. Life is short and, as they say, 'a day without laughter is a day wasted'. This applies in my opinion as much in football as it should in a corporate culture. It is essential, while remaining deadly serious about winning football matches. I tried to make the majority of meetings enjoyable, so one looked forward to a day working together.

Reliability in Crisis

Every football club or business suffers problems – sometimes these can become full-blown disasters. Those who cope best are the organizations where those in charge don't panic but roll up their sleeves and get down to work in a professional and diligent manner, without histrionics.

Frugality

The most impressive principals with whom I've worked have adopted a thrifty approach to business and, indeed, life. Ron Noades and Sam Hammam were particularly strict in this respect. In my time, extravagant chief executives, chairmen and football managers have all set bad examples and typically lived beyond their means, which in many cases ends in trouble.

Delegation

You need to learn to identify, promote, trust and empower people with talent. Hiring and retaining superb staff is without doubt a vital ingredient.

Adaptability and Flexibility

Football, just like any other business, is extremely competitive, so you have to be at the top of your game to deal with a rapidly evolving situation. No football business model remains secure for long, therefore intelligent managers thrive on change and are constantly learning, and should not have a dogmatic mindset. There is a crucial difference between being firm and being unrealistically stubborn.

Courage

Leaders need bravery to make unpopular choices. That can often mean personal sacrifice or risking their position for a strongly held belief. I must say I am disappointed how many football and eminent public figures fail to speak out on controversial issues and prefer to abide by the consensus in order to not be seen as troublemakers. These are not real leaders, they are at best followers.

12
Scoring for Fun

Wally

THANKS FOR THAT, Harry. Can we get back to the fucking football now?

Our 22-match unbeaten run came to a shuddering halt as we set foot in the Third Division in August 1983, losing 2–0 at Bolton. However, with Corky back in the side after he had returned from a summer playing with Örebro in Sweden, and yours truly returning from suspension, we hammered Newport 6–0 at Plough Lane, although there were only just over 2,000 there to see it.

There was one new face in the Wimbledon line-up, and despite the fact that little was known about him at the time, he would prove to be one of the most important players in the club's history, despite the dodgiest of perms. In fact, Harry says that he wasn't his first choice for left-back because he was originally after Arsenal's Brian Sparrow, but they wanted £15,000 for him!

So, step forward, Nigel Winterburn, for his Crazy Gang memories.

Nigel Winterburn

I was at Birmingham with Jim Smith and then Jim got sacked and they brought in Ron Saunders. Ron released me so I rang up Jim, who had gone to Oxford, and asked if I could do pre-season there while I looked for a club. I was there maybe two weeks and they offered me a six-month contract, but then Wimbledon came in and took me for a month on trial. They didn't have a left-back for the start of that season. I met Harry and basically just stayed, I never went back.

To get that opportunity with Wimbledon meant everything – playing football was all I ever wanted to do. I knew nothing about Wimbledon. When you're desperate you take anything and try to prove yourself, so in that sense I owe Harry a lot, because I could have ended up playing non-league.

The sense I got was of camaraderie within the team. It was a fairly relaxed club, and felt like a small club, which suited me because I felt if I got in the team I would be given a chance, once I had proved myself. When I joined in '83 in the Third Division we were on such a fantastic run. From '83 to '87 it was unbelievable, because every year, no matter what division we were in, we were relegation favourites. That team just rolled through those four years I was there, and those big successes were down to Harry's team spirit. I wasn't that experienced, I hadn't been with many managers, but there aren't many managers you associate with having a fight in a car park, or throwing them out of a window into a swimming pool, without getting any come-uppance for it – but I do with Harry.

I was the new boy coming in, but early on one thing that stood out was there didn't seem to be any difference between the players. We didn't have superstars, everyone was the same. Some fellas were really loud, others like me and Gagey were quiet, but out on the pitch I felt equal to everyone. I never felt intimidated by anyone, and I think that is why we were successful.

Everyone prepares differently for games. You have loud people and quiet ones. We used to have the stereo on booming, and we were the first club to do that. But I remember at Arsenal, Wrighty was a nightmare getting ready, he was a nutcase. He was mad up until kick-off. Fash and Vinnie were a bit lively, but they didn't intimidate anyone, they left you alone to get on with preparing for the job we had to do.

We used to make teams kick it off – we used to pressure them so high up and so hard that they would rather kick it out than try to play it out. Sometimes their goalkeeper would kick it but we would always, always, win the header and knock it back into their half, and we would play from there.

I was very quiet and only a young kid. They left me

alone, they didn't know much about me, but they didn't try to intimidate me. Wally sums it up well when he says, 'I watched Nigel in his first ever game for us completely splatter someone and thought, "You'll do for me."' And with that I was part of the Wimbledon team.

We had a good team spirit at Arsenal when I first joined, we did a lot of socializing. If anyone asked me what Wimbledon was like, I would say a pub team – a very good pub team – and I don't mean that disrespectfully, rather just in the sense that we all stuck together and knew our jobs and our limitations, and I think we scared a lot of teams. We knew everyone was in it together and no player got above their station. It didn't seem like there was a pecking order, everyone felt equal, while at other clubs there was a pecking order. The tradition at Arsenal was completely different, but George Graham was more or less just doing what Harry was doing by bringing through lower-league players and being really organized.

I remember one Wimbledon match in particular when we played four midgets up front. We beat Sheffield United 5–0, we hammered them; Wisey even missed a penalty. They played four big centre-backs because they thought we would be all big and powerful, but instead Harry played the four smallest players at the club up front. Even our small players had strength and power, though. Everyone was saying all we did was smash it long to giants, and then we went the other way and caned them.

We weren't on a lot of money, but I don't think there were many chairmen who would race one of their own players for 50 quid. I think that was Sam's way of making it up to us and keeping the team spirit: you could beat him at any game for money, and he would let you. Apart from backgammon – he was shit-hot at backgammon.

Wally

The ball may have been in the air half the time, as Lurch pumped those monster punts upfield (except for one time that season when he tried to dribble the ball as far as the halfway line before Harry screamed at him to fucking hit it), but the goals continued to fly in, especially in the rarefied atmosphere of Plough Lane. Three against Bournemouth, six against Southend in the Milk Cup, four more against Port Vale, against whom there was no love lost. The pundits had a field day taking aim at our style. Harry didn't help by being quoted as saying that 'energy accomplishes more than genius'.

But proof the system was as effective as it could possibly be came when we were drawn against Nottingham Forest in the Second Round of the Milk Cup. Their side was packed with star names – Hans van Breukelen in goal, Viv Anderson, Kenny Swain, Colin Todd, Ian Bowyer, Frans Thijssen, Steve Hodge – and as was expected, they didn't like it fucking up 'em. We shut down their strikers – Garry Birtles and Peter Davenport hardly got a kick – and Evans and Corky gave Todd and Paul Hart a torrid time. Forest were completely outrun and outworked. Midget gave us the lead under the floodlights at Plough Lane – one of his rare strikes! – before Hodge (Glyn not Steve) curled in a pearler, and I've been told by many fans that was one of the best performances Wimbledon put in in that era. All of a sudden we were thinking, 'Jesus Christ, we can beat this lot.' And we could have beaten them by a lot more. Cloughie was made to stew on his side's shortcomings all the way back up the M1, but we were then full value too for a 1–1 draw at the City Ground, after which Cloughie came into our dressing room to offer his congratulations – and a crate of champagne. Proper gentleman.

Forest had had their own fairytale, of course, winning the league the season after coming up from the Second Division, then winning the European Cup the next year, and this was only three years since they'd won the European Cup for a second time, so the victory really put us on the map. They were the first really top side that we beat, so it gave us a profound sense of belief.

And, of course, we got absolutely hammered after the game. Fish's later recollection, in public at least, was rather modest. This was when we had Forest's number again the next season in the FA Cup: 'The last time we beat them,' he said, 'we stayed up in Nottingham and visited a few discos throughout the night. Two days later Scunthorpe beat us 5–1.' I think it was rather more than a few discos, Fish. And Harry had us in for training on the Sunday, even if it was all his fault. Here's his version of events.

Harry

We were on a high and I gave in to a request for a night in Nottingham. We ended up in a nightclub and simply got pissed. Some of the lads met a female Forest fan called Amazing Grace. She was a lady that was to later play a cameo in the life of Vinnie Jones. When Vinnie made his debut for the club at Forest in 1986, his job was to mark Neil Webb, a player he said he had never heard of. I told him he was likely to be the next England captain, the dog's bollocks, so just to stay close to him. Vinnie nodded and eventually returned to the room he shared with Wally.

He had escaped the usual initiation ceremony because Wally had told the players Vinnie had developed a bit of a wild man reputation at Wealdstone. But I knew that couldn't last with my mob. It didn't. Around 11.30 the night before the Forest game the phone rang in his room and Vinnie realized the worst when Wally slammed it down and shouted, 'Wankers!' It rang again and Wally said it was for Vinnie and handed the phone over. Several of the lads shouted down the line, wishing him good luck and saying things like, 'Shitting yourself yet, tosser?' and 'Lucky sod, First Division player, are we?' Vinnie was chuffed, but when it rang again and he saw Wally smiling he knew something was up. A few minutes later there was a knock on his bedroom door and Wally bounced up and opened it. In spilled four of the team and Amazing Grace. I could hear shouts of, 'Come on, Jonah, this is your initiation!'

He told them to piss off and he pulled the covers over his head just as Amazing started to strip off. Drinks arrived and tears of laughter were rolling down Wally's face. Vinnie was panicking. Eventually he cracked, his famous rage there for all to see as Amazing Grace started singing, 'If you're happy and you know it clap your hands.' At that point he snapped and leapt from his bed, grabbed all her clothes and tossed them out of the door – along with the players.

But, back in 1984, little did I know when I gave the nod to our night out in Nottingham that it was going to come back and haunt me. We got to Nottingham station the following morning after our boozy night out and one of the players remarked that, 'We look dirtier than the train.' It then got worse when a TV crew waiting for us in London interviewed our chairman, Stanley Reed, who went on air to describe how Forest were magnificent in defeat, and talked about their champagne gift and how 'the ladies of Nottingham were very friendly'. You can imagine how that went down with the wives and girlfriends.

Wally

Fish scored with his first touch to put Oldham out in the next round of the Milk Cup – their manager Joe Royle admitted that they 'were lucky not to be beaten by five or six' – so it was gutting to lose 1–0 at Rotherham of all places in the last 16, Hodge hitting the post late on. But neither that, nor a 3–2 loss at Brentford in the FA Cup shortly afterwards, could halt our charge in the league. I had a look at the match report from that Bees game: 50 fouls, 31 by us, 19 by them; Joe scored against us, of course, even if I did pull one back. Now that was a proper Cup tie.

In November we had temporarily knocked Oxford off the top of the table; they were the best team in the division, even if there was no way I should have been sent off in a defeat at the Manor Ground. A couple of months later I got hold of the ref's report: '. . . in the 53rd minute my linesman signalled to me and informed me that the Wimbledon number 10, Downes, had emerged from the fog and made contact with the Oxford number 3, McDonald, with head, chest and legs, rendering him unconscious. I had no option but to send him from the field of play.' My brother was at the game, watching from the far end, and didn't even know I'd gone! It was a bad fog. I lost my bearings! Harry went nuts and I got fined. I think I took his command to 'go out and make something happen' the wrong way. They were managed by Jim Smith, the 'Bald Eagle', who would take them all the way to the top flight before joining QPR, who then lost to Oxford in the League Cup final. But the other promotion places looked up for grabs, and after we lost our long unbeaten home record against Burnley, getting our revenge on Brentford at Griffin Park in another thriller, 4–3 to us this time, was sweet. We then beat Millwall 4–3, despite my contender for goal of the season, right over Lurch's head and into the back of our net!

We made it four wins from four over the holiday period by beating Sheffield United, with Corky in unstoppable form, two more headers making it 23 for the season already. In a 6–2 win at Orient in February he scored his 100th goal for the club, and he would end up with 33 for the campaign, a record 29 of them in the league. Didn't stop us from taking the piss out of him.

Later that month, we went top ourselves, albeit briefly, but you wouldn't have put us down for a goalless draw. We scored for fun – 97 league goals by the end of the season – as well as letting in some howlers, Lurch being responsible for a fair few of them too. Only four teams – Orient, Brentford and the relegated pair of Port Vale and Exeter – conceded more goals than our 76. I'm told that no other team has been promoted having conceded so many goals. And at a quick calculation, that tally of 173 goals in 46 games makes for an entertaining rate of nearly four a game.

So March brought the TV cameras to Plough Lane for the visit of Walsall, who had recently reached the semi-finals of the Milk Cup, losing to Liverpool. And if you

Google 'Wally Downes goal' you will find a link to YouTube, under the headline WALLY DOWNES SCORES A GOAL (more than 400 views, unbelievable!) and a clip of a Dean Thomas throw-in to me by the corner flag, from where I curl another contender for goal of the season, with the outside of my left foot, over the head of the Walsall keeper and into the back of the net. 'Thomas to Downes . . . That's his cross. It's awkward. *Oh, it's gone in! Well, would you believe it? Wally Downes!*' screams John Motson. 'Tony Godden deceived completely!' Less of it, Motty.

My season ended in the worst possible way, as it had a habit of doing, when I did my ankle against Hull after a clash with their keeper, in front of a big crowd of 4,495 too. They were head and shoulders above us that day, absolutely battered us. So my season ended on a stretcher, and it would be another long road back, personally. But, without me, the boys got vital wins in our next two home games, against Brentford and Plymouth, when Nige scored his first Dons goal. Then there was a massive 2–1 win at Sheffield United, which had us on the verge of promotion. We were 2–1 specialists at the time and that was a feisty old game at Bramall Lane. They fancied us as they were going for promotion too – basically, whoever won was going to get one of the top two spots. The atmosphere was unbelievable, in fact. It hardly helped that Evans headed us into the lead, as a Yorkshire lad, and one who had twice been released by the Blades boss Ian Porterfield. His goalscoring celebrations were cut short by a cut eye after one of their young fans threw a coin at him. Corky got the second, also a header you won't be surprised to hear, but the Dons fans were pelted with coins from the Bramall Lane end and called 'southern shits' all afternoon and were then stuck inside the ground for hours after the final whistle. This was during the miners' strike, and there was a bus strike in the city too. The streets of Sheffield were lined with protesters, and it turned into a full-scale riot, with police horses racing up and down the roads. When they did finally escape, the fans didn't have much of a better time of it, as their train was bricked and stoned while leaving the station. Fun times.

We needed three points from two games to win promotion, and over 6,000 fans packed into Plough Lane to see us take on Gillingham, who now had John Leslie up front. Gagey got the party started prematurely with a goal inside ten seconds, but the night took an agonizing turn after the break when both Steve Bruce and Tony Cascarino were on target, and the visitors eventually cruised into a two-goal lead. It looked like the dreams of those gathered inside Plough Lane had been wrecked, but news gradually filtered through that Sheffield United had lost to Bolton. Division Two would be the next stop on the amazing journey.

Despite being out with my broken ankle, I travelled everywhere with the team, so I was still part of all the celebrations. On the pitch the atmosphere was great. Ron Noades came back to help us celebrate, and the emotion was amazing. I remember later seeing Alan Cork kissing Les Briley in the boardroom! Les, who later admitted he regretted leaving, doesn't drink, but we made sure he bought us a few.

It was a marvellous moment. From going up and down twice then jumping into the Second Division – playing, working, laughing with what were your mates – that was a great, great day.

Someone once wrote that we are all 'part of one stupendous whole', so at this point I would like to mention some of the unsung heroes who helped Wimbledon become the club that became so well known. Few will remember Roy Davies and Ray Knowles, yet these players played their part in what is considered one of the greatest achievements in English football. Some made huge contributions to the Crazy Gang story: Dave Beasant, Alan Cork, Paul Fishenden, Kevin Gage, Steve Galliers, Glyn Hodges, Andy Sayer, Vaughan Ryan, Mark Morris and Andy Thorn. Others, like Dennis Wise, Lawrie Sanchez, John Fashanu and Vinnie Jones, iced the cake. But Mick Smith has his place in Wimbledon history, if only for the fact he was the first player to have a moustache and an accent we couldn't understand. He was from Newcastle, and had been Mick 'hard bastard' Harford's best pal at school. (Mick Harford was another player whose impact at the club won't be forgotten.) Mick Smith played in all four divisions for Wimbledon, but ended up being treated brutally. Signed from Lincoln, he was never happy when we played with a sweeper. He simply enjoyed being a typical son-of-the-soil centre-half who went in, won the ball and cleared it. Nothing fancy, just his way. Great guy, as strong as a fucking ox.

Mick just had too many injuries to make an impact when we got to the top flight. His final game for us was against Newcastle, his hometown club and the one he supported as a boy. They won through a single goal scored by a youngster. His name was Paul Gascoigne.

Mick played against the background of his wife's mum being ill, and knowing a new breed of player was just around the corner to take his place. Like me, he never fitted into the plans of Bobby Gould, who took over from Harry, and we both left soon after his arrival. Mick never earned more than £180 a week and was promised a testimonial by owner Sam Hammam after spending eight, in my opinion, great years at the club. He never got it. He wrote to Sam and didn't even get a reply. I thought that was sad.

Then there was Ray Knowles, a former gas worker, a centre-forward, who I drove mad. He used to pick me up near Hammersmith Bridge for a lift in, and I was invariably late every day after going to Covent Garden first to pick up our stuff for the stall. He was a proper bloke, a strong 25-year-old from non-league Southall, whereas we were just youngsters. Alan Devonshire, the former West Ham player, had been on our radar but we couldn't afford him and signed Ray instead. I played alongside him when I made my debut.

Ray used to say to me, 'Wally, I will fucking slug you

if you are continually late and mess me around.' He never did, but he flung me around a few times, mucking about. Then one day he was sitting on an upside-down traffic cone at the training ground and I kicked it from under him. Everyone rolled up. He gave me the beating of beatings, not a proper fight, but he man-handled me and threw me around like a rag doll for making him look silly. Dead arms, dead legs, the fucking lot. Worth it for the laughter of others, although I knew not to fuck around with him any more. Ray eventually joined Millwall. It's safe to say you could describe him as a bustling centre-forward. Everyone knew not to fuck with him.

Then there was Roy Davies, a really funny bloke. He was funny in a different way to me, but we got on well. Once, we were travelling home on a train, having a beer, returning from playing Halifax, and I asked him if he fancied a night out. He said he couldn't, he needed to go home to his wife. So we came up with an idea that he had been hit by a can thrown by a Halifax fan and was concussed. On the train we got the physio to bandage his head up. We got to London, we went into a pub and he kept the bandage on – then we went to a little club in Chiswick called the Burlington. Around 2 a.m. we got a cab back to his place and he'd had the bandage on now for hours and gone through his story numerous times, about how he was hit by a can, concussed, slept on the train, had a couple of beers, and that was why we were late home. There was *no way* we were going to deviate from this story.

We got back to his house and the first question his wife asked was, 'Where the fuck have you been?' and the whole story went out the window. He unravelled the bandage, he collapsed like a dime-store suitcase when confronted. As he was telling his missus he was continually unwrapping the bandage and it seemed never-ending. The wimp. I also got it in the neck from his missus, who blamed me for leading him astray.

Fun days. Happy days.

While Dario got in kids he had known from his days at Chelsea or QPR – kids who were young and who he knew he could work with – when Harry took over the signings became a bit more manly: like Ray Knowles and Francis Joseph, two strong bastards out of non-league, who were both ready to go straight in. They joined the Tom Cunninghams and Les Brileys, players who had come from bigger clubs, whose thinking was to join Wimbledon and then use the stage to get back up again to a higher level. It was a mixture of youth, throw-outs and those who believed they still had something to prove – a colourful cocktail. And it worked. Harry was into coaching as much as Dario, but he was happier to deal with older players, while Dario was more keen on the younger players.

Roy Davies was also unlucky in the fact he was the first player ever to go to a tribunal when he went from Slough to Torquay. The disputed fee was around £40,000, and in those days five per cent went to the league and five per cent went to the player, so he was due around

£8,000 out of the deal. The clubs, obviously, could not agree on the fee, but unfortunately the tribunal came up with the decision that it was a free transfer, so Roy went for nothing. Because he was the first to attend one of these meetings he didn't negotiate with agents, or have anything down in writing, so he became the first, and only, player to lose money on a transfer. Good player, though.

These were the players who were in my mind when we suddenly made the breakthrough into the Second Division.

And here's two more of them, who I was delighted to catch up with in another boozer in Chiswick as we put together this book. Mark 'Guppy' Morris and Mick Smith were inseparable on the pitch, so the pair of them can have the floor together now!

Mark Morris

I remember shitting myself at 16, 17, going up into the first team and thinking, 'What the fuck is this?' The club was in a transitional time, with Dario trying to make it more professional. When I first joined there was Roger Connell, Jeff Bryant, Dave Donaldson and Harry – can you imagine a 16-year-old coming straight out of school and getting slung in with them fucking nutters?

It was a tough school because of where the club had come from – non-league. I remember playing in the midweek league, the reserve league, and you would be all excited, but then you'd be going to Dagenham, where some 30-year-old hairy-arsed nutcase would be belting fuck out of you for an hour and half – longer given the chance. I remember breaking a rib in one game. I couldn't breathe, let alone shout or walk or run, and when I told Harry I needed to come off he told me to just hang about near the halfway line and 'make a nuisance of myself'.

There were the young established players who Dario had brought in, then the youth-team players who had come through – and then there was a two- or three-year gap before Geoff Taylor brought through all the rest, like John Gannon and Gage. I think that was half of the success: two full youth teams coming to fruition one after the other. Dario signed me, Paul Fishenden and Hodge, and I think the mix of established players and the local youth-team lads worked. I look at that and think that's what makes football clubs successful, when a club can bring through a generation of their own players. We got pushed through, and then when we were moving on, Geoff Taylor brought the next lot on, like Gayley, Andy Sayer, Vaughan Ryan and Andy Clement.

I remember going to Huddersfield needing to get a result to get in the top division, and being barely able to believe it. We were doing well and going up, but getting to that top league still seemed a dream. But then we realized that we would be playing Arsenal and Liverpool, and it just didn't seem right. I remember Sanch hitting the free-kick and wondering what the fuck he was doing, because on a good day he couldn't hit a cow's arse with a banjo – only the two centre-halves would be behind him in the pecking order for a free-kick on the edge of the box. And at that moment, personally and as a football club, I just felt like it was the exact sort of moment you play football for.

I didn't just look forward to training or enjoy going in, I wanted to get there early because the team spirit and the atmosphere was so good. You'd start at 10.30 but you were there at 9 a.m. because you didn't want to miss out on anything.

I watched the TV show and I saw from Fash exactly what I expected to see. He did exactly what he has always done. People were surprised or disappointed but he did what he has always done, so it didn't bother me.

Mick Smith

I first came to the club in 1979–80, when we finished bottom of the Third Division. They bought me from Lincoln City for a very small sum, because I wasn't doing much there. At the time there was Tommy Cunningham and Paul Bowgett in the centre-half positions, and it was a baptism of fire, even in training. My first day I got seven stitches in my head – I had no idea what was going on, it was such a different culture.

When Harry took over he enforced on everyone this

winning attitude. For me it was always about winning and not about how you won. We used to get bonuses then, so you could double your wages if you won. Harry asked me one week how much I was earning and then told me he had a way I could treble it. When I asked how, he told me there were two games that week, so I could earn my wages plus two win bonuses. He asked me if I knew what I had to do to get the wins and the money – and I did: I had to be tough, I had to work hard and I had to want it more than other teams.

We had a squad of around 15, so even if you were injured you usually had to be on the bench. We went to Rotherham and I was having these duels with their centre-forward, Ronnie Moore, now the Hartlepool United manager, and I smashed my face against the back of his head going up for a header. At half-time Harry said I looked a bit lethargic out there, and I told him I couldn't breathe, but he told me not to worry and to get back out there and liven up a bit. I managed to finish the game, despite being unable to breathe through my nose. When I got back home I told Lurch I had to go to the hospital – they swiftly told me I had a broken nose and a fractured cheekbone. Back then you didn't get six weeks off, or masks, you just played the next week and hoped you didn't get hit in the same spot again.

There were three players who came from the north-east and played for Wimbledon: me first, and then John Kay, who arrived from Arsenal. Because we were both from up north, Harry asked me to put him up, take him under my wing and look after him. He was a great lad, but he was a handful when he'd had a few.

When I first came down no one could understand a thing I was saying with my Geordie accent, so I used to try to talk cockney. The craic with the lads was unbelievable. There was a bit of intimidation, but you don't get to know a character like Wally without a bit of intimidation. He had a nickname for everyone, it was like *The Wally Show* in some aspects.

When Harry led us into the style of play that we later adopted, that's when we moved up a gear. When we changed our style of play after Dario left, it just suited every player down to the ground. We all knew exactly what we were doing. When me and Guppy played at the back together – he came through very quickly from the youth team because of his ability – we got so comfortable that we didn't even have to talk to give instructions or messages, it was all done with looks or little hand signals. We knew our full-backs were always in front of us, so we would catch teams offside all the time.

Harry was one of the first people to start using statistics. They used to go through how many times we got the ball in the box, how many times we got in the channels, how many clearances we won first-time. Everything was about getting balls into the box because that is where things happen. You can knock that and prefer the 'pure' style of football where everyone passes the ball about, which is considered aesthetically superior, great to watch.

But our games were all-action, and exciting to play in.

When Andy Thorn was coming through as the next centre-half, Harry came to me and told me to tell him absolutely everything I knew. I had to explain exactly how we played, what the signals were and why we did things that maybe other people didn't even see. He was more or less coming through to take my position, but we still had to teach the young kids – that doesn't happen these days. We would always try to teach a young kid a trick you had for yourself, and then have our own attributes. I personally could head the ball further than I could kick it. I could head the ball 40 or 50 yards – with one header we would be on the attack and in on the other team's goal. We had to pass our skills down, so the continuation was brought through and passed on happily.

There was a pattern of play that was set whether we went home or away, and everyone had it down. That is part of the way we were successful. Later on Harry would ask our opinion and ask us to come up with our own ideas for set-pieces or patterns of play. He would challenge you to come up for corners and make little blocks – when you see those on the TV now people think they are revolutionary.

I played against Fash when he was at Millwall and I played with him – and I would always rather play with him. I couldn't get near him when I played against him. But I thought the TV show they did was overblown. For me we were a team and we all won and lost together. We never just wanted to batter anyone.

13

Up for the Cup

Harry

BACK-TO-BACK promotions were more than I could have hoped for in the dark Fourth Division days of 1982. Personally speaking, of course, all this was great news for my profile, my growing stature as a manager. And my contract had just come to an end. So who got in touch? None other than Ron Noades, who was now at Crystal Palace.

Dario hadn't lasted long at Palace, leaving in November 1981 after a less than stellar start to their season. After being relegated, getting straight back into the First Division was the priority, and that didn't look like happening. Neither his successor, Steve Kember, nor Alan Mullery had had better luck, so Ron approached me and persuaded me that I should go to Selhurst Park for a new challenge, as I had probably done my time at Wimbledon. Plus he was willing to pay more than Wimbledon could or would.

I'd like to stress that I was perfectly happy at Wimbledon at the time (this was June 1984), but Ron could be a very persuasive man. I had known him since the age of 15, and had rented the office space from him to start my insurance business.

Back at Plough Lane there was the usual haggling over bonuses. Bonuses would come in the more wins we got, the more goals we scored – and if that didn't convince a load of skint blokes then nothing would. Hodges, however, was always putting in transfer requests – normally every time I dropped him – and asking for more money. I always told him to fuck off. One season he was angling for an extra fiver and I said I'd toss a coin for it. Before he could even agree I'd tossed it and he called heads and I said, 'You're right. You've got it. I hope you're happy, 'cos that's coming out of my own budget.' I always intended for him to have the extra but I wanted him to fight for it. I hadn't a clue whether it was heads or tails, I didn't even look at the coin.

Anyway, back to Palace and my decision to take the leap and join Wimbledon's rivals in the Second Division. Despite Wimbledon's natural antipathy to anything to do with Chelsea, their rivalry with Palace has stayed particularly vigorous, especially since the years of Premier League ground-sharing at Selhurst Park.

Back in the summer of 1984, I admit to having had my head turned, to being flattered at being wanted and having the chance to manage a bigger club with better facilities and better wages – for myself included. At

Wimbledon I even once had to put up a £25,000 guarantee on them. That was in 1981 when Sam Hammam told me he didn't have millions available to buy players because he had no assets in England (they were still abroad), but Sam was quite happy for me to take the risk. It wasn't until the following day that I realized what an unnecessary thing I had done. Wimbledon director Peter Cork, himself a banker, found out and explained to foolish old me how I had left myself wide open to having my house sold if I couldn't find the necessary money. Former chairman Joe McElligott, another great friend, simply told me, 'You are raving mad.' Those words were plain compared to what my wife Christine called me.

With Sam, I went to see his lawyer Peter Cooper, who was later also to become a director, and I found a sympathetic ear. But he also said the deed had been done and there was no way out unless Sam agreed to have my name removed from the guarantee. In the end, with Cooper's help, we agreed I would receive shares in the club in the event of the bank wanting their money. It at least eased my worries – although in reality the shares were worthless at the time – and Sam told everyone that the reason I had put my money where my mouth was was to show I cared for the club, was committed and had their best financial interests at heart. The loan remained for another year until the directors took it over. I was to do something similar when manager of Sheffield United.

As soon as I arrived at Palace – literally as soon as I

walked through the door – I realized what a bad mistake I had made. I knew instantly that the new challenge I wanted was actually at Plough Lane. We had just been promoted and it was completely the wrong time to leave the Dons. If Ron hadn't convinced me to leave in the first place the thought would never have even crossed my mind. So, as it turned out, I left Wimbledon on the Friday . . . but three days later, on the Monday morning, I went back again. On the Friday I had attended a dinner where I met Keith Fisher, the sports editor of the *Daily Mirror*. His first words to me were, 'You must be fucking mad!' I was already thinking that myself. Thankfully the door was still open for me at Plough Lane – but, as I later quipped, my stay at Palace must go down as one of the shortest reigns by any manager anywhere; Cloughie at Leeds was a marathon in comparison!

So I was back at Wimbledon, a wiser and happier man, but my relationship with Sam was never quite the same. He never forgave me. I think he saw it as an act of treachery, and he did not like the thought he had lost out to Ron. Sam doesn't do finishing second. Yet even he thought of leaving Wimbledon for Palace once, when Ron led his walk-out. I was totally honest with him, everything was up front, but the die was cast in our relationship. Sam did, however, put me back in charge and offer me a new three-year deal. I accepted and slipped into the shadows, hoping things would right themselves. All I wanted to do was prepare for our new life in Division Two. I was ready for it.

And we could not have made a better start to life in the Second Division. There was a bumper crowd of 8,365 to see us take on Manchester City on the opening Saturday, and we were 2–0 up within a quarter of an hour thanks to Evans and Hodge. We should have been four or five to the good to be fair. We didn't win the game, of course – this was Wimbledon and the opening game of the season we're talking about – and we were hanging on for a point at the end, in a game City manager Billy McNeill called a 'boxing match'. It's fair to say, though, that we took the step up in our stride – City had some top-quality players like Phil Power, Neil McNab and Kevin Bond, with Gordon Smith and Derek Parlane up front, and they would go on to win promotion at the end of the season – so the match report which described our play as 'alternating between the scintillating and the lamentable' was probably about right. But I think everyone at the club, including the fans, started to believe that we could actually compete in this division.

After that positive start, a fantastic Cup run would prove the highlight of another improved season, even if some of our defending would still send me apoplectic with rage on the touchline. We ended up conceding 75 goals in the league. Only the bottom two clubs, Cardiff and Wolves, were worse.

John Kay at right-back was the main new face in the team on the opening weekend, after signing from Arsenal for £25,000, with Paul O'Berg also starting against City – he had impressed me playing against us for Scunthorpe.

Phil Handford from Gillingham, Dave Martin, a £35,000 purchase from Millwall, and Andy Sayer, 18, one of our own and full of running, all made their debuts in the first couple of months of the season. Getting Kay in and dispensing with the services of our skipper, Gary Peters, ruffled a few feathers – all that effort getting up two divisions and he dropped back down into the Fourth to play for Aldershot – but he took it like a man.

I signed Kay on the advice of Don Howe. He was quick, tenacious and turned into a top lad – when Frenchie witnessed him fall into some bushes, pissed on a pre-season trip, he reported to me that, 'He's one of us.' The other players called him 'Tut Tut'. Fuck knows why. John was as quiet as a mouse when around his missus but a raging bull with the lads. I remember one night in Magaluf seeing dancers on a stage turning away – the next thing I heard were cheers as John joined them in just his underpants! Dave Martin just didn't fit in, though, and I realized my mistake within a few months and eventually sold him to Southend, taking a £15,000 loss on the move, money which a club like Wimbledon could not afford. You make mistakes.

There was a more significant makeover off the pitch, though: new or improved 'anti-interference' fences, turnstiles, floodlights and a PA system – all costing something like £60,000 in total. Every summer brought the same story: trying to get facilities up to a safe and acceptable standard for the authorities, against the wider footballing backdrop of violence and tragedy.

On the pitch, the boys struggled to put together a consistent run but a season of mid-table consolidation was fine: I imagine it came almost as a relief to the fans not to be involved in a relegation battle or a promotion race for a change. And let's face it, three promotions and one relegation in four years was pushing it. I'll hand over to Wally again to take up the tale.

Wally

For me, 1984–85 was another season of hurt and frustration, but as Harry says, we adapted well to life in the Second Division. We got the first win under our belts at Shrewsbury, then another at Middlesbrough just three days later. We had a settled line-up: Ketts, Corky and Stewart Evans were all finding the net, with Leo Sayer chipping in with a few too, and a first home win in this division came against Brighton, thanks to a goal-line clearance by Steve Hatter at the death. Mid-table we remained. We were particularly solid at Plough Lane, where a win over Steve Coppell's Palace put a big smile on Harry's face, and Midget's too. Three goals in the space of six second-half minutes sealed that one.

It was following a game against Grimsby at the end of November that Harry was the centre of attention again – for attending the press conference without an item of clothing in sight. The story goes that Harry was naked as the day he was born, but he assures me there was a pair of Y-fronts involved. Why he did it was anyone's guess, but then I'm hardly one to talk, am I?

There was arguably less excitement on the pitch, although away from home we were once again leaking bucketfuls of goals: three at Sheffield United, Fulham and Wolves, then five at Leeds in front of the TV cameras. Harry wasn't happy, accusing us of lacking professionalism, and neither were some of the players. John Kay and Steve Hatter asked for transfers; Corky was dropped for Micky Welch, signed from non-league Grays Athletic and soon on his way back there again despite two decent games. He was paired up front with Fish, who had been sent out to Sweden again to get games – there was always one or two out there, or in Finland or wherever. Harry said it helped the players' confidence, as well as broadening their horizons. Luckily for me, I mostly got to stay in London. Funny that.

Much more significant was the signing of Lawrie Sanchez. Wimbledon seemed to be a recurring factor in Sanch's career – as Harry said earlier, he had made his debut against us for Reading in October 1977 – one of many midfield battles he had had over the years at both Elm Park and Plough Lane – and after he left the Dons, his last start for Swindon was against Wimbledon. As it turned out, Liverpool were to be a recurring theme too, as he reminded me recently: there was a certain goal at Wembley, of course, but then as a manager he took Wycombe to the FA Cup semi-finals before losing to the Reds, and then kept Fulham in the Premier League with his first win as a manager over Liverpool in 2007. He's got a good memory, Sanch.

Sanch was now 25, with loads of games under his belt, and that experience would prove to be invaluable – five goals in 20 games was his tally for the second half of the season with us. That was good value for money – at just £29,000 that transfer turned out to be one of the all-time bargains. As did Carlton Fairweather, who cost just £7,500 from Tooting & Mitcham, and soon got his first goal, in a 1–0 win at Oldham on New Year's Day.

Carlton gave an interview in the spring of 2015 to the *Independent* – he now manages Sunderland Ladies who, at the time of putting this book together, were riding high at the top of the Women's Super League – about how he was 'the most level-headed' player at Wimbledon. Well, he didn't drink, so you could hardly have got a better designated driver. Carlton remembered that when he arrived at Wimbledon, the club 'was like a Sunday morning team but with a professional element. You had all the antics you would have with Sunday morning players, where they stitch each other up, and a lot of mickey-taking, but when it came down to playing the game the professionalism came out.'

And that was the key to it, really: have fun, then knuckle down. Carlton credits Harry with a lot that he learned about looking after players: 'A lot wasn't done through brute force, it was talking to players – an arm around you if you needed it, or if you needed a bollocking, he'd give you one.'

But it's true that, contrary to popular expectation, Harry was always one for asking players what they thought, what ideas they might have for improving things. He wasn't a tyrant dictating everything we had to do, even if he made you know, in no uncertain terms, that you either had to shape up or ship out. That's how you create a team, and a winning unit.

Our Second Division status ensured we started in the Third Round of the FA Cup for the first time, and when the balls in the bag produced Burnley, ten years since the famous victory at Turf Moor, we knew Harry wouldn't shut his trap. Luckily we saw them off 3–1 at Plough Lane, thanks to a howler from their keeper from a Gagey free-kick and two late goals from Fish, the first a thumping free-kick, the decider a penalty. It wasn't plain sailing, though, with Burnley the lower league club on this occasion, and Harry unhappy with our customary dodgy period after the interval.

By the time the Fourth Round came around, I was fit enough to be back on the bench, with a plum tie at the City Ground my reward for fighting back to fitness. Mindful of the previous season's League Cup loss to us, we learned that Cloughie, expecting 'one hell of a fight', had taken his Forest players off to Tenerife before the game. As if we needed added motivation. They certainly didn't lack for effort, and threw everything at us bar the kitchen sink, but Lurch had a blinder, helped by Gagey clearing a couple of shots off the line, and their strike-force of Gary Birtles and Peter Davenport once again drew a blank, although the latter should have scored a couple of times. Midget, having scored in the League Cup game, was really up for this one and, as he recalls it, Forest's Ian Bowyer gave him a right-hander on the left ear – he says it's still a bit cauliflowered now.

There were more than 10,000 at Plough Lane for the replay on the Wednesday, and Harry's hoodoo over Clough continued – six games against him as player and manager, no defeats. Forest's famed fluid style was once again stymied by our resolute approach, described by Jeff Powell in the *Daily Mail* as 'rudimentary football, so brazenly aggressive and forcefully organized that it is monstrously difficult to resist'. Fish was again the hero, his 13th-minute winner being deflected past one Hans Segers in the Forest goal by Kenny Swain, after an Evans cross-shot hadn't been cleared. We harassed them all over the park, not giving them time to get their passing game going. Despite Midget, always an avid disciplinary points collector, incurring Cloughie's wrath for a particularly ugly challenge on Steve Hodge – Old Big 'Ead stomped to his feet, only to be poked in the back by an old geezer with an umbrella or walking stick – we held on to the 1–0 lead. As the game fizzled out nicely we were in the Fifth Round for the first time.

As Midget recalls it, 'I just knew that I had to look after myself. How else was I supposed to react to that threat? You had to look after yourself. Clough said it was "common assault", and it was a bad tackle, but it was one of those things. Forest were a great footballing side, but we used to go man-for-man so they could not play their football and, to be honest, some of their players didn't fancy it when the tackles started flying about.'

'We didn't dominate like last time,' Harry said after the game, 'but we showed fantastic spirit.' That was after we had showered him with beer when he bounced, beaming, into the dressing room. 'It's elation and lager at the moment,' he went on, 'but it will be champagne all the way when we get to Magaluf on tour at the end of the season.'

It was another of the great Plough Lane nights. Cloughie, as I have mentioned, was always a gracious loser, and he was no less so in the aftermath of that FA Cup shock, even though it was the one trophy that would always elude him. He even went so far as to contribute a special piece at the season's end for our supporters' club handbook. Here it is:

> I swear to you I didn't have any special thoughts about us facing Wimbledon in last year's FA Cup just because they had knocked us out of the previous year's Milk Cup. But I had a few thoughts afterwards and, once the bitter disappointment of losing had subsided, they were quite pleasant thoughts too.
>
> Believe it or not, I was pleased for Wimbledon that they had managed to whack the same First Division side for the second successive year. They struck me as a remarkably honest bunch of players, who got on with the job of winning a match without any cribs or

complaints. I'm now getting quite used to hearing them singing in the bath after a match at our expense and, you never know, one of these days we might succeed in putting the record straight.

One thing I did put straight at Wimbledon's ground in the FA Cup replay was to flatten an issue that some members of the press had tried their best to build up. I went out of my way to meet the manager, Dave Bassett, and say, 'I am Brian Clough – this is an official introduction.'

Evidently a lot had been made about the fact that he had never had the opportunity of speaking to me during our meetings, but the truth of the matter is that every time I had tried to say 'hello' he was busy talking to the press.

Mind you, I suppose he did have something to talk about.

We had the run of the balls again in the Fifth Round draw – West Ham, and at home, and we fancied our chances at a truly packed Plough Lane, especially having just put five past both Crystal Palace and Sheffield United to ensure our morale was sky-high. And before that West Ham game, Tony Stenson coined the phrase that would become our nickname. 'Meet Dave Bassett's team of all-sorts,' Stenson wrote in the *Daily Mirror*. 'Rag-arse Rovers – soccer's Crazy Gang.'

It was a classic Cup tie: a fiery atmosphere, loud and intense, with Hammers fans seeming to have taken over the whole of Plough Lane for the day – on another shitty, snowy afternoon. I was freezing my bollocks off on the bench, so itching to get on and get stuck in. Alvin Martin proved a barrier to most of our attacks, but with the game still goalless, Hodge managed to hit the post. Midway through the second half, Tony Cottee grabbed a typical poacher's goal after Ray Stewart's shot had fallen in his path. With eight minutes to go, we equalized. I had come on for Hodges and found space on the right. I was fronted-up by Ray Stewart, who was a right-footed left-back and very fast, so my thoughts were, 'Don't come inside on to his strong foot and don't go down the line because he's way quicker than you.' All this left me with the option of a touch to the side, then dink the ball up to the back stick. Corky would always run across the centre-half to the front post; Stewart Evans would always pull to the back stick. That was our preparation and attention to detail. Stewart Evans duly headed home. Pandemonium.

The replay at Upton Park came just two days later, and despite Fish scoring again with a first-half equalizer – going through with me and putting a bobbling ball past Phil Parkes – we were outclassed by Alan Devonshire in midfield, and by Cottee and Paul Goddard up front. It didn't help that me and Fish had over-elaborated our celebration in front of the West Ham fans, who wanted to kill us for the next 70 minutes. Still, 5–1 was a fucking shocker of a result, and one we didn't deserve. Harry laid in to us afterwards with more than a few choice words.

His official line to the press was that, 'We lost our discipline. We didn't lose with dignity.'

The Cup run may have come to an end, but it had resulted in not just increased prestige for the players, and the confidence that instilled, but also the intangible joy and satisfaction the fans feel when you really give it a go in a one-off game against a bigger club. Then there was the not inconsiderable sum of a reported £50,000 in the club coffers.

That said, we looked knackered and played worse in the aftermath of the Hammers defeat, losing at Portsmouth, Oxford, and then 6–1 at Carlisle, before steadying the ship by thumping Shrewsbury, with me at sweeper behind a central defence of Micky Smith and Brian Gayle, making his debut.

And then I broke my fucking ankle again.

All the injuries and suspensions did at least give Harry the chance, or rather forced him, to blood new players from our increasingly fruitful youth development scheme, which had already seen me, Fish, Hodges, Morris and Sayer make the grade. Gayle, who had been sent out on loan to New Zealand of all places, played all of the final 12 games of the season; Andy Thorn took over at sweeper once I had got crocked – he played the last 10 games – and both took to the Second Division like ducks to water. In fact, we were a fair bit tighter at the back in those end-of-season games, which doesn't reflect altogether well on yours truly!

The first-team players always took a deal of interest in

youngsters coming through. We'd had a great bunch, but now the game changed in the form of those two centre-halves, Brian Gayle and Andy Thorn. What a partnership they were, and both of them born a stone's throw from the ground. Gayley was conscientious, physically daunting, lightning quick, great in the air and a born leader; Thorny at the time was tall, but physically not so developed (boy, has he developed!), but technically excellent, very bright and strong in the tackle. These two complemented each other so well. I had played centre-half with a few players – from Tommy Cunningham and Paul Bowgett through to Smithy and Stevie Hatter then, for a while, with Mark Morris – but this was the first time I looked about and thought, 'You can forget any long-term position here.' These two had been indoctrinated into everything that we did at the club, and when they came in everything remained like clockwork. Geoff Taylor had been telling everyone they were ready, and they were.

We'd all come through the lower leagues and learned our trade, but these two had to come in as kids in what is today's Championship, and they went on to form the backbone of the team that went into what is now the Premiership just 18 months later – then all the way to the Cup final. Gayley wasn't selected, or on the bench, for that game, and it shows his character as a man that he was with the lads on the day, having been part of it all his life up to that point. Thorny made his most important contribution at Wembley by making a rare error of judgement with a tackle, and Peter Beardsley scored, but the ref stopped the game and gave a free-kick. The outcome might have been different if that hadn't happened!

Thorny and Gayle were a fantastic pair at Wimbledon, but also went on to have long Premiership careers elsewhere. I had the pleasure of coaching them separately later on and witnessed them becoming not just top-class centre-halves but also the stand-out men in very strong dressing rooms. They were great players.

I'd taken Thorny as my apprentice when he came in, purely because of a story told by Geoff Taylor. Geoff had been training behind the main stand at Plough Lane one Thursday night with the under-14s when Thorny had rung in sick. During a short break, Geoff happened to look up above the wall and fencing surrounding the training area, only to see a perfectly healthy-looking Thorny reading the *Racing Post* on the top deck of the bus, whose destination was Wimbledon dog track, where the first race went off at 7.30! This boy needed guidance and I felt I was the man to do it. He was my apprentice for the year, to basically look after my gear, wash the motor, get my laundry and so on. Kids got sod-all wages, about 20 quid a week back then, so getting a tenner or score every week was always handy. The amount was always results-driven.

One day Gayley and I were recovering from minor injuries and had completed our treatment and rehabilitation under the watchful eye of the cab driver from Watford (aka Frenchie). Harry used to like to get his pound of flesh by sending the injured back to the main ground to the weights gym with our strength and conditioning guy, Mike Winch, who was number two Great Britain shot putter behind Geoff Capes. Harry did this to discourage players from thinking little injuries were an easy way to skive off a day's training.

Anyhow, Gayley was feeling slightly lethargic, both hungry and thirsty, and with me being weak-minded and open to suggestion, one thing led to another and we dodged the weights session for lunch in the pub to discuss team tactics. After much discussion, we agreed that the mixed grill in the Sportsman was tactically the way forward! Gayley loved a pint of Guinness and, purely from a team point of view, it was decided that the food should be accompanied by just the one Guinness, which is renowned for its iron content and nutrients, and in moderation can, in some instances, speed up the healing process!

I had up until this point never drunk Guinness, as I'd had a mouthful as a kid and hated it. Anyway, Gayley railroaded me into drinking it, and apparently I was helped into a cab ten pints later. I couldn't train the next day, got fined a week's wages, before winning man of the match on the Saturday. I haven't touched a drop since. Cheers, Gayley!

As well as Gayle and Thorn there were also first appearances that spring for Doug McClure, a teenager who came in on a free transfer from QPR, and, finally, the 18-year-old Dennis Wise, on as a sub on the final day of the season. I had known Wisey for a while – his family came from round the corner in Shepherd's Bush – and had recommended to Harry that we take him on when he left Southampton following a falling-out with Lawrie McMenemy.

A falling-out? Who? Dennis Wise? Even then he could start a fight in an empty house. It was the way of the West – west London, that is.

Dennis was to play a huge role at Wimbledon, and I'm proud of my part in his arrival. Pat Deller, one of our scouts, also suggested him to Harry, but Geoff Taylor was not so sure because he was keen to keep bringing Wimbledon's kids through, and felt this might be a problem. Harry decided it was worth giving him a trial and asked me what I felt. I replied, 'He's good, Harry. Trials are hit and miss. Give him £100 a week until the end of the season – you'll see it's a good move. He'll fit right in, and you'll love him.' He did just that and Dennis was signed. It was the first time, really, Harry had asked my opinion and trusted my judgement. It was to be the first of many.

The youth team had a great season too, finishing runners-up to Luton in the South East Counties League, above the likes of Palace, Spurs and West Ham – and after Gayle and Thorn's promotion, hopes were high for more new boys on the production line: John Gannon, Simon Tracey, Andy Clement, Gary Fiore, Vaughan Ryan and Ian Hazel were all getting write-ups.

In the league we finished in 12th place. Job done. There was the usual carping about Wimbledon's crude style but, as the fans said, even when we lost we gave value for money. And ask Brian Clough what he thought about our tactics or ability. Nigel Winterburn, as usual, was the unanimous choice as player of the season, and one of the other highlights was the emergence of Paul Fishenden. Without his 14 goals in 25 games, especially the Cup goals, it would have been a different season altogether. I still have fond memories of his hat-trick in a 5–0 thumping of Crystal Palace at Selhurst Park that season. Here's Fish for you.

Paul Fishenden

Dario was my way in because I had come from Chelsea. It was me, Hodges and Gary Waterman, and Dario sold the club to us by promising we would get a better chance, or at least a quicker chance, at Plough Lane than anywhere else.

All that talk about a non-professional, Mickey Mouse outfit . . . that was everyone else. It was never from anyone within the club. That wasn't Wimbledon. With Bassett, work was work and play was play. We knew never to step over the mark; training was serious, it was hard work but he treated you like adults. You were given a bit of rope and you knew how much to take.

Harry's hands must have been tied when he

actually put us in the side because he put four or five of us in at once. I must have only been 17 when I made my debut. We were struggling down the bottom, we had injuries, but we all got a chance. Initially, it might have been intimidating but it made you grow up, because you had to deal with it. It was playful abuse. Today it's called banter. It was never vindictive, you grew with it. I saw that show with Fash. The in-built foundations for Wimbledon and the successes they had happened long before he arrived. That show came across like he started it.

In my second ever start we got knocked out of the Cup by Enfield 4–1 and Harry hammered us. Their team was full of ex-pros and ex-amateur England internationals. They were a top non-league side and we were near the bottom of the league, and Harry had to play all the kids.

A few years ago I might have been more critical of Harry and the way he did certain things, but I've mellowed. I'm older and wiser, and it's great to look back. I wish I had known then what I know now. Harry was like your dad, he treated you like one of his own kids, but I had loads of fall-outs with him because I would be in and out of the team, and in and out of his office every other week. Most times I would come out of the office and go back in the reserves for a week, but laughing as well. He was so up front and honest with you that you couldn't help but like him. You knew where you stood, you knew when to have a laugh and not to cross the line. You hear about Fergie and the hairdryer, but Harry would scream sometimes, actually scream.

I actually played with Harry when he was coming towards the end of his career, and he just would not let it go. He was getting stuck in, plenty. I remember Guppy, a young centre-half, getting beat up, and Harry done a bloke with his ring and then fined himself a fiver. Harry would mostly get the hump, go berserk, when he thought we were getting bullied or pushed about and not standing our ground; he would have a right go at us. I remember Jimmy Case wiping me out in a reserve game at Brighton once – he had won European Cups and he tried to break me in half – and Harry bollocked me instead of Jimmy or the ref! He told me I had to man-up, and you had to take it on board. We weren't thugs, but if we were hitting good, accurate long-balls and the front four weren't up there, challenging, pinning their man, then you were for it. He would shout from the touchline. He wasn't asking us to smash them, he was demanding that we make challenges.

I remember the goals towards the end of our promotion, particularly one against Halifax. We were already up but Harry had the hump over our set-pieces. He said our free-kicks had been shit and if we could score from one he would buy the drinks. I managed to score a flick-on, so he had to get them in.

14
The Case for the Defence

Harry

THE MOOD OF positivity going into our second season in the Second Division was tangible. Many people were tipping us for relegation, but I knew differently. We had done well the previous season, had a good Cup run and were on a big learning curve, with the likes of Nigel Winterburn – who arrived as an Oxford reject, remember – Dave Beasant, Kevin Gage, Mark Morris and Andy Thorn. I also believed Alan Cork was one of the most underrated strikers in the game, and his partnership with Stewart Evans had flourished. I also knew Glyn Hodges had the ability and could handle the next level, and that Sanchez would cope and get stronger. There was also the juicy thought of a next generation emerging, players like John Gannon, Simon Tracey, Vaughan Ryan and Andy Sayer, while behind them came Neil Sullivan, Chris Perry and Stewart Castledine.

Consolidation in the league had vindicated my

decision to stay at Plough Lane. In fact, it gave me even greater satisfaction to see the league table from the previous season, with Palace three places below us in 15th – plus we had smashed them twice, with our best performance coming at Selhurst Park! The general feeling of everything being all right with the world even made me come over all poetic in my annual address to the Dons fans in the club handbook. Here are 'the manager's thoughts' at that time:

> The crowd had gone, just a few people lingered in the bars. The late evening sun was giving another reminder summer was on the way.
>
> We had just drawn 2–2 with Leeds and my mind was still racing through the match, going over moves and players, when a bulky figure walked on to our pitch. He was overweight and softened by obvious good living, but I recognized him immediately. Don Revie, one of the most controversial managers ever seen in England.
>
> As he chatted away with the Leeds Manager, Eddie Gray, it immediately released a flood of memories. My thoughts swiftly danced back to those FA Cup days a few years earlier. Revie had just left Leeds for England but the side he fashioned was the one that we met as a non-league team.
>
> Now here we were meeting again in our first ever season in Division Two. It gave me a great deal of satisfaction standing there. And if forced to

give an end of term report I would say, 'With pride.'

I think we gave a lot of people red faces by doing so well. I know a lot of 'experts' had tipped us to go straight down again.

Charlton Manager, Lennie Lawrence, told me what we achieved was what he actually set out to do. And if someone had said at the start of last season we would beat Nottingham Forest again and have little trouble establishing ourselves in the Second Division, I would have settled for that straight away.

Last but not least: a special word of praise to my assistant manager, Alan Gillett, plus youth team manager, Geoff Taylor, and hard-working, hard-moaning physio, Derek French. All work extremely long hours, mostly unrewarded, for the club. To them I say, 'Without thee, without me.' They are deserving legends in their own right.

So maybe this is a good time to hand over to my assistant, Gillett, who joined from the start of this story, in 1977, and hear his side of the story.

Alan Gillett

I had just returned from coaching in the Yemen and was looking for a job. Football in Yemen had been a shambles, as it was in many Middle Eastern countries those days, and I wanted club football again. Thankfully, Dario Gradi got in touch and invited me to be Wimbledon's youth team coach. He suggested I meet Dave Bassett and discuss a few things. I mentioned to my wife, Kate, that Dave was a horrible, absolutely shitty person, who would kick or punch you when you played against him, as I had when playing for Sutton United in the Southern League. We went out to dinner and afterwards my wife said, 'What a charming man . . . nothing like you described.'

Wimbledon only had two apprentices at that time, Wally Downes and Nigel Blazey. Dario made it tough for me, every day, demanding the kit be picked up, boots be cleaned, and when I mentioned we only had two apprentices, he said I should also clean boots, and demanded I develop more players. I would train in the morning, go to matches in the afternoon, and then return for evening training. It was a full-on job, but also the best learning curve I could have had. Dario had worked with Dave Sexton at Chelsea and Colin Murphy at Derby, and had loads of experience. So I listened.

In those days most of the local clubs would be feeders for either Chelsea, QPR or Fulham, and it was tough trying to find the kind of youngsters we wanted who were not tied to the bigger clubs. I worked with Peter Prentice, and the only promise we could give them was that if they were good enough they would get their chance.

Some youngsters, like John Gannon, came to us and mentioned the likes of Arsenal also wanted them. Dario would say, 'Let them go. They'll be back.' He was confident that once they got to other clubs they would discover they became faceless, a number, while Wimbledon offered much more. We offered hope of a breakthrough and, being much smaller, a close-knit group, it usually worked.

Dario kept a lid on his feelings – unlike Harry who, still being a player, was closer to others. He would let senior pros have their say. Dario was more comfortable working with youngsters, and when they grew hair round their chins he would invariably lose them. His joy was developing players. He was married to football, and still is.

When Harry took over, he lifted spirits and the atmosphere. We were struggling in Division Four, and the lowest point came when we lost to non-league Enfield in the FA Cup. After the game we could hear their manager Eddie McCluskey being interviewed by John Motson, saying how wonderfully they had played. Harry refused to batter anyone. He knew we had been hit by injuries and were short of players, being forced to use kids. In fact, we had to play our best striker, John Leslie, at right-back. Harry simply said, 'Right, let's get out of here.' He knew how to treat people and assess the atmosphere. He could also be ruthless and must have released over one hundred players during his career – but when he chopped their legs off, he did it in a way that no one held a grudge against him, never said a bad word.

His wage negotiations were a masterclass. He knew what to offer players, mainly because he didn't have money to spend. He also knew what players would ask for. He always wanted me with him, and it was my job to work out how many games the likes of Downes or Corky had played. So in would come the players. Harry gave them a figure, they demanded more, then Harry would turn to me and ask for the facts. I would spell it out, and in the end the players would look at me, accept the deal and walk out. It was the bad cop–good cop routine, and I was always the hated one.

Despite all that, Wimbledon was a wonderful place to be. There were no big-time Charlies – several players from the Southern League days were still around – so there'd always be lighter moments.

When Harry was Dario's assistant, he would take the first team and order me to take the youngsters for a run. Off we'd go, but then Harry and the boys would disappear into the trees and waylay us on our way home. We all ended up covered in mud and bruises, and Dario would ask what had happened. I invariably told him we fell over. He must have thought we were a clumsy lot, because it happened virtually every day.

We had fun, but training was serious. No one messed around, no one missed training. There were no overnight hotels in those days, trips long and short were all done in one day. There was also a lot of drinking, and you could tell those who had been on it the night before in training, but they never slackened. I recall Mick Smith asking one day for a bin-bag to be cut into the shape of a body-top so he could sweat out the remains of the night. Mick was a good pro and took his responsibilities seriously. No phoning in and saying he didn't feel well. He just got on with the job.

The happenings of those early days blur into each other. We didn't have much depth but we had a determination. Harry was always planning ahead. If we were in the Fourth Division, he'd be planning for Division Three, and so on. He was driven to succeed. He turned youngsters like Glyn Hodges into men. We were criticized for our style, but it was a style of substance. We had much more than that and we all knew it. When I met people from the FA and told them I worked for Wimbledon they would invariably say, 'Aren't you that long-ball side?' I wanted to punch them. We were more than that. I recall talking to Tony Pulis when he managed Stoke, and they received similar criticism. He told me to let people think what they like: 'We know better and we can also play.'

Today's footballers have it on a plate. Good luck to them. But I also think they have it easy. They no longer have to clean boots, collect the kit, sweep dressing rooms. To me that was character-building, part of the growing-up in football. It forged a togetherness. The kind of bond that made Wimbledon into a football story that we will never witness again.

Harry

Back on the field, we achieved the unthinkable to kick off the 1985–86 season by actually winning our first league game of the campaign – for the first time in my Wimbledon history. The last time the Dons had started with a win had been in 1970! Middlesbrough were the victims of our new-found autumn energy, trailing back home with their tails between their legs after a 3–0 kicking – and, aside from a 4–0 hammering at Bramall Lane when the Sheffield United players got Stewart Evans sent off, clean sheets were the order of the day: six of them in our first seven league games. Finally, the players had taken on board what we had been trying to get into their heads, and they did it with aplomb. The transformation from a side haemorrhaging goals to miserly masters of defence was astonishing – and vital to our continued progress up the leagues. Concentration was a major part of it. They say you can't teach an old dog new tricks, but young ones you can.

That super start to the season took us up to second in the table in fact, and to celebrate I put pen to paper on a new two-year contract.

The system was as sound as it could be – we were lean and mean – and the squad was settled. There was Bez in goal, ever-present as usual; Kay and Nige at full-back, with Gagey an option; Thorn, Gayle and Morris or Smithy the big centre-halves; Fishenden, Hodges or Ian Holloway (a £35,000 signing from Bristol Rovers) and Sanch in midfield; Cork, Evans and Sayer up front. Whoever came in did a job, and I, with Wally as my special envoy, made sure they all knew their jobs.

When we were hit with injuries, we coped. Both

Gayle and Thorn had cartilage operations during the season, and we had to recall Guppy, who had been on loan at Aldershot, but it was as if he'd never been away. Nige apart, Guppy was my player of the season.

Being defensively sound made us as unpopular as our so-called rough-house tactics – we were booed off the field after a 0–0 Friday night stalemate at Stoke – but this was (and is) a results business, and we stayed up at the business end of the table. When we needed to, we could let loose. After the Stoke game, we were 1–0 down at home against Carlisle at half-time and I was screaming blue murder at the players, giving them a right fucking bollocking. Luckily for their futures and their families, they turned it around, Mick Smith and Corky both scoring twice.

Around then, I brought Hodge back into the starting line-up; Carlton Fairweather was also starting to make a big impact, initially from the bench. Carlton had made a few appearances the previous season but was now really showing his worth and would prove to be a great asset to the team, scoring seven goals that season and setting up countless more. Most importantly, despite the usual red cards – Corky at Sunderland, Smithy at Boro – we remained hard to beat. Then, over the Christmas period, we slaughtered Sheffield United 5–0 – they did have two men sent off, but it was nice that it was them and not us for a change – blew away Palace 3–1 at Selhurst Park, in front of the watching Millwall manager George Graham, who called us 'absolutely brilliant', and then had Wally to thank, now that he was fit, for a perfectly executed free-kick at Barnsley which Sanch converted.

The critics had to sit up and take notice. In Nigel Winterburn we had clearly the best player in the league. His work-rate, his energy, his sorties down the left flank, were second to none. We were on a roll. Could little old Wimbledon make it to the First Division? Too bloody right we could. And people who knew their football were paying us the credit we deserved. I began to believe we were finally being accepted when I took a phone call from Danny Blanchflower, captain of Tottenham's Double-winning side, a former Chelsea manager and at that time a writer for the *Sunday Express*. Danny was one of my heroes. A Northern Irishman who played with a twinkle in his feet and eye. He was an artist on the pitch and eloquent off it. 'Can I come and see you?' he asked, saying that he wanted to weigh up our chances of promotion. Of course he bloody well could.

'When I first talked football with Dave Bassett in his Wimbledon office eighteen months ago,' Danny opened his article, which we later got permission to reprint in the *Supporters' Club Handbook*, 'he was honest and passionate about the game and his club. His eyes sparkled and his face shone as he considered the tasks ahead. He was not over the moon, where everything looked bright. But he was ready to challenge the difficulties without the fear that will get you nowhere. Perhaps it was some disappointment in his youthful days that urged him into a positive approach.'

Danny went on to describe a training session at Richardson Evans: 'I put on my old tracksuit and joined them in some of the action. If you want to judge a team properly, the nearer you can get to them the better. Bassett ran a two-hour show with a variety of small games that suited particular aspects of the big match. It was good, practical practice, devised by Bassett and his assistants. One challenging game followed another, allowing the players little time for boredom. And Dave was having arguments with a few of them who complained he was not adding up the scores properly!

'Bassett, assistant Alan Gillett and youth team coach Geoff Taylor,' Danny concluded, 'can be proud of their work at Wimbledon. The players and officials should feel the same. Wimbledon have done wonders with their limited resources. But would it not be a miracle if they did make it up to the big-time?'

Danny obviously knew and could smell things were about to happen. And so as 1985 turned into 1986, our sights were firmly fixed on the prize.

15
Bish, Bash, Bosh

Wally

THE START OF 1986 was, to put it lightly, shit. On New Year's Day there was a massive Plough Lane crowd of 9,025 to see us lose 3–1 to Portsmouth, with Mick Channon, at the age of 37 no less, scoring twice. Those were a precious three points dropped. Then in the Cup at Millwall, without the injured Andy Thorn and suspended Sanch, we lost by the same scoreline. The fans felt let down – completely deflated, in fact – and they were openly questioning whether our early-season form had been a flash in the pan. Too many of us were off the pace that day, seemingly lacking application and co-ordination. It was fucking unacceptable.

The Millwall game was significant in one other respect, though. John Fashanu, himself having just completed a five-match suspension, absolutely tore us to shreds. He bashed us about all over the park, and both Wimbledon players and fans absolutely hated the very sight of him for the whole ninety minutes at the Den, never the nicest of places to play in the first place. At one stage it got a bit hairy between Fash and Hodge, with Fash grabbing the Welsh winger by the throat.

Then, at Oldham of all places, despite Harry having read us the riot act, we were shit again, losing 2–1, which would have been worse had Lurch not saved another pen. Pathetic. If it could not have got worse, after that it could not have got better. What followed was a 16-match unbeaten run that took us to the promised land of top-flight football.

Norwich, the league leaders in March, couldn't cope with our four up front. Pompey took over at the top, by which time Fash was in a Wimbledon shirt, having signed just before the transfer deadline, and we were up against Pompey at Fratton Park on Easter Saturday. That was such an important game. Titanic. Millwall's Cup run hadn't done much for their crippled financial situation, so following that game Harry spoke to George Graham and asked them how much they needed to survive. When he said £150,000 he ran it past Sam for confirmation, as they didn't really want to go above £125,000.

We had first come across Fash when he was starting out with Lincoln, in the 1983–84 promotion season from the Third Division, so we had known for a while what he could potentially bring to the team. Harry had said just after Christmas that we needed a bit of impetus and another centre-forward. Fash was identified as the prime target and was followed for about half a dozen games. We also knew he was wanted by several other clubs, including Aston Villa. Fash had played for Millwall against Portsmouth just four days before we played them at Fratton Park, and even though he started on the bench – Harry said he wasn't fit – he would prove to have an instant impact. Lurch saved a penalty from Kevin O'Callaghan after Sanch had brought Vince Hilaire down, blocking the ball with his knees only, early in the second half, for Noel Blake to give Pompey the lead from Hilaire's corner. Fash immediately came on for Fish, Gagey swung over a cross which Evans headed against the bar, and Mick Smith popped the ball in the back of Alan Knight's net. Share of the spoils. A good result. Beers all round.

Fash was involved in an incident in the tunnel after that game, and their players went mental as the ref tried to calm things down. The Pompey fans hadn't forgotten Fash's antics for Millwall a few days previously and had been on his back the whole game, whether he was off the pitch or on it. It was bound to go off. Along with Blake, they had Mick Tait, who was the hardest of the hard men, and Kevin Dillon, Mick Kennedy and Billy Gilbert too. They could give as good as they got.

Pompey manager Alan Ball, who was always on our case, completely lost his rag, saying that Fash's physical approach had turned the game. 'Fashanu did three players with his elbow,' he ranted to the press, 'and butted Billy Gilbert in the tunnel coming off.'

Fash gave an eloquent response: 'It seems as if somebody's trying to blacken my name – if that's possible. I don't need to resort to that sort of thing. Alan Ball has to be very, very careful. We are all professionals, and to accuse somebody of elbowing and butting is a little bit below the waist.

'I was certainly enjoying myself,' Fash continued. 'But if I left a trail of destruction, I am sorry. If you compete in this game, you tend to get a reputation. But you don't kick and tell – I certainly don't. I would be very surprised if any of the players said that I was doing what Alan Ball claimed.'

Well said.

Fash concluded his case for the defence by saying that 'compared to Millwall's match here last Tuesday, this was not a rough game, it was just kindergarten stuff' and received the backing of his new gaffer.

'I think Alan Ball lives in a fantasy world,' Harry said when it was his turn to face the media. 'It's tragic when people have to say things like that. It's just ridiculous. If you are upset with the way your team has performed you don't say your opponents have done things they haven't. People get hysterical when they're in for promotion, and obviously Ball is worried about his job. But let's face it, he doesn't like the way we play, as we are difficult to combat, and he uses every chance he can to criticize us.'

Fash then started the next game against Palace and headed his first goal for the club. Whatever you may say about him – he was a right poseur, capable of hearing a camera click from about five miles away – you can't deny that his arrival gave us a shot in the arm that spring. Pain in the arse, yes. Handy player, yes. You wanted him on your side. And he earned the dressing-room respect, even if he was a man apart. We felt invincible when we were playing properly, and Fash led the line fantastically well.

Fash had told Harry before signing he wanted nothing to do with our famed Crazy Gang antics, and Harry had no problem with that. But that didn't stop me from filling his tea with salt and nicking his favourite silk socks. We had a confrontation, but it was nothing serious. He took me in an empty dressing room, and I thought, 'Oh shit, here we go.' And it seemed an eternity till Kempy came in and put a stop to my impending doom. Dodged a hiding there . . . and I can now say, after all these years, that it was VJ who nicked his orange juice that day.

I had been in and out of the team with injuries, as usual, but was back on the bench for our final home game of the season. We had to beat Stoke, in the pissing rain, and nerves, tension and tiredness got the better of us for long periods. Corky's header, from Gagey's free-kick, gave us all three points, and the crowd flooded on to the pitch at the final whistle. Harry addressed the throng: 'We still need one more win, so let's keep it calm for now,' before continuing, 'Here, stop all that pushing down the front. We don't have any hooligans at this club, apart from the players, of course.'

At the post-match interviews, he was more honest

– and used a few well-worked football clichés: 'As far as I'm concerned, we can't get it over quickly enough. We have three more games in which we need to get the three points we need – three Cup finals, in effect, and we only need to win one of them. But I'm praying it will all be done and dusted at Huddersfield on Saturday. Then we can all relax and get drunk.'

Corky's goal ended a seven-match drought – during which time Carlton had been playing out of his skin, Fash had scored a few, and Hodge got a hat-trick against Sunderland when Harry brought him back in after months out of favour – and he paid tribute to the gaffer after the game: 'Our success is all down to Harry. There's something about him that keeps us plugging on. He's not like a boss, he's like a mate. When I first came to Wimbledon eight years ago he was still playing. He hasn't changed a bit, and it's because of him that players have stayed with the club.

'Quite honestly,' Corky continued, 'the money we get here is terrible. But I've just signed a new two-year contract and I was happy to do so. I suppose we've never had real ambitions before. We all thought it was a miracle we got into Division Two. But Harry has given us the belief that we can go on and reach the top.'

Being so close to promotion now really made people sit up and take notice. There was a write-up in *The Times*, with the usual lame tennis headline (WIMBLEDON'S GAME SET OF MATCHWINNERS), which paid tribute to what the club represented while, of course, taking the piss out of our backgrounds. The club, they said, 'still *feels* non-league – home-made, rough and ready, with ordinary blokes instead of stars, and a crowd that is more like a clique. Wimbledon are almost poseurishly unpretentious.'

A backhanded compliment that was spot on.

Plough Lane was, they said, a 'rootsy little ground' and with the big-time beckoning, 'the club [was] rootsier than ever'. To my obvious amusement, though, the writer, Simon Barnes, then turned his attention to Harry: 'Bassett was a classic non-league player with limited skills; now he is directing Wimbledon at a level of football he never dreamt of playing. He is 40, but looks as if he were about to audition for a part in *Grange Hill*. Bassett does the perky little cockney act to perfection. It is a sound method of deflecting the routine criticism that is levelled at his team's unpretentious style of football.'

Right you are. Unpretentious. Poseurishly so. Years of this shit. Even on the radio, apparently – the BBC broadcasted the Stoke game live from Plough Lane – they were ranting on about Stoke 'continuing to play football under an incessant bombardment' and us being 'chronically short of refinement' when Stoke were completely outplayed and only had one half-chance in the whole ninety minutes.

The Broadwater Farm riots in London earlier in the season had caused a number of games in the capital to be postponed, so we ended up with two games in hand on most clubs at the end of the campaign – but our final three matches were all away from home. It was going to be hard, but the only way to silence the critics was to do our talking on the field. And, fortunately, we did it at the first time of asking, at Huddersfield's Leeds Road, on Saturday, 3 May 1986, in what many would say was the most momentous game in Wimbledon's history.

As usual, it was absolutely pissing it down up north, complete with thunder and lightning to make it all appropriately dramatic. As many as 300 Dons fans made the trip, and they were to witness what Joe Lovejoy in his match report described as 'a match littered with fouls ranging from petty to downright spiteful', reflecting 'little credit on either side. Dave Bassett and his bargain-basement team had their big moment soured by an explosion of violence which saw Huddersfield reduced to nine men with the dismissal of Terry Curran and Paul Raynor by World Cup referee George Courtney.'

Ah, those were the days. Curran got his marching orders for hacking down Fash, who was himself booked, needless to say – and a few minutes later we scored the goal that took us up. To much consternation, Gagey touched a free-kick to Sanch who rifled the ball home, before starting a demented dance with Gagey and two others. They looked like something out of *The Wizard of Oz*.

'I struck it so sweetly, it was always going in,' Sanch told Lovejoy, who reflected that it was the most important goal Sanchez was 'ever likely to score'. Well, he could hardly have predicted Wembley in two years' time . . .

When Raynor got his early bath for taking out Midget, the fans started to do the conga all round the ground, and the party would continue all the way down the M1 and into the early hours at the Sportsman. The major incident that people remember from the aftermath of that Huddersfield game took place in the dressing room, however. The players were singing, 'Where were you when we were in Division Four?' Most were naked, following their showers, when in came actress and Wimbledon FC life president June Whitfield, followed by comedian Cardew 'the Cad' Robinson. June wanted to shake the hands of the players and congratulate them. Being footballers though, a few accidentally forgot to wrap a towel around their bare bodies. June needed all her acting skills to keep control and only looked into the players' eyes as she went round shaking hands. Then she got to Dave Beasant, all 6 foot 4 inches of him, who was standing on a bench, albeit with a towel around his waist. June, slightly flustered by this giant of a man looking down on her, decided to glance away as she held out her hand. With that, off came the towel and June was shaking something that certainly wasn't a hand! Collapse dressing room. And, if you'll excuse the expression, she took it well. She calmly let go of the object in her hand and carried on with her duties. It was an Oscar-winning performance.

We had two more away trips to round off the campaign, the first of them at Charlton, which turned into a bit of an anti-climax, with both teams having already been promoted. The players had been boozing non-stop since Huddersfield in any case, so our limbs were not exactly in perfect working order. Still, Lennie Lawrence and Harry cracked open another bottle of champagne after the game and toasted our success. After the 0–0 at the Valley, we needed to win at Bradford to clinch the runners-up spot behind Norwich, and ahead of Charlton, but that wasn't to be. Third it was, which meant missing out on something in the region of £7,500 in prize money. But the stat that was most pleasing at the end of the day was in the goals-conceded column: we had only let in 37 goals all season, less than half the 75 of the previous year, and that was testament to a fantastic team effort.

The other huge factor in the promotion was the unity of the players – call it what you will, but I think we can safely call it 'the Crazy Gang'. Of the 12 players who played at Huddersfield (I was injured), eight had been part of the first-team squad that had gained promotion from the Third Division two years previously. And look at where the players had come from: Lurch – peanuts from Edgware; Midget and Carlton – non-league too; Nige – rejected by so-called bigger clubs; Gagey, Guppy, Thorn, Hodge and Fish – home-grown the lot of them; Corky – practically the same since he'd come down from Derby at 18. Only Fash and Sanch had cost any money. That is one hell of a fucking team-building exercise.

We were also now becoming famous – well, to a degree. So as Wimbledon's longest-serving player, I had a bit of fun with Steven Howard of the *Sun* ahead of a game against Sunderland in April 1986. As he mentioned in his foreword to this book, he was doing a piece profiling this bunch of upstarts who were heading, against all odds, towards the First Division, and Lurch and Stewart Evans lent me a helping hand as part of a forum providing Steven with some snippets of information for the nation's delectation and delight, under the headline THE CRAZY GANG CLEAN UP!

Dave Beasant (goalkeeper, 27). Ever-present for over four seasons. Penalty expert – saves more than 50 per cent. Allegedly weak at both near and far posts. Known as Lurch for obvious reasons, and gave up riding to work on a moped when the players kept filling his crash helmet with talcum powder.

Nigel Winterburn (left-back, 22). Dons' first England international. Picked up an under-21 cap against Italy this week. Loves a tour – and a tackle. Known to lose the ball on purpose so he can get in another challenge, all the time waving to the crowd. Rated at £250,000 and interests Spurs.

Mick Smith (central defender, 27). Sunderland-born and in his seventh season. Known as 'Rock Nuts'. Recently headed the ball from the halfway line into the penalty area. Complained of nose bleed later.

Mark Morris (central defender, 23). Watches *Rambo* and *Rocky* videos the night before a big game. Known as 'Wear 'em out Wilf' because he never stops in training. He loved heavyweight Frank Bruno's 'I could have taken care of six baboons tonight' after beating Gerrie Coetzee. Before the recent Millwall game, he was heard to say, 'If I can get up to the nine baboons factor, we'll handle 'em.'

Kevin Gage (right-back, 22). Made his debut five years ago at 17 – the Dons' youngest ever. Quick, likes to attack and known as the SW19 answer to Italy's [Antonio] Cabrini. Bleached-blond – usually shocking ginger. Caught in the showers on TV recently when the truth was revealed.

Lawrie Sanchez (midfield, 26). Rumoured to be an Ecuador international. Played more than 400 games for Reading before becoming a bank-breaking Wimbledon buy at £35,000. Ex-skipper and now nominated as the worst player in the side. Supposedly Dons' most intelligent man as he studied accountancy and has letters after his name.

Steve Galliers (midfield, 28). Just 5 foot 4 inches and known as 'Midget'. Quick with tackles that look worse than they are. Once picked up a record 49 disciplinary points. Only held the title for a year before teammate Glyn Hodges clocked up 51 . . . allegedly by Christmas.

Wally Downes (midfield, 24). Joined Wimbledon in 1977. Barrow boy, and the forgotten man after bad ankle injuries. Waiting for manager Harry Bassett to move on so he can take over. Plays anywhere and is rude to everyone. His forward line would be Stan Bowles, Rodney Marsh and Alan Cork. Started eight games this season and Wimbledon lost the lot.

Glyn Hodges (winger, 23). Good player, injury-plagued and volcanic. Has been known to be booked for 'visual dissent'. Has an excellent left foot and has played twice for Wales. Rumour has it that after his first appearance they had to sew two caps together as one wouldn't fit.

Alan Cork (striker, 27). Known as 'Beagle' – short form of Bald Eagle since QPR boss Jim Smith claims the original. Incredible scoring ratio – 120 goals in 250 appearances. Suffered financial collapse and beer gut after failure of pub venture. Unpopular, but wealthy, fines-system treasurer.

Stewart Evans (striker, 25). While Cork is 'Grab', 6 foot 4 inches Evans is 'Smash'. Favourite manager is Ian Porterfield, who off-loaded him at both Rotherham and Sheffield United. Often mistaken for Dave Beasant, who he doesn't like: 'I'm up at the other end, the ball is coming down with snow on it, the centre-half is belting me round the ear . . . and Beasant keeps raining 80-yard punts down on me.'

John Fashanu (striker, 23). The managing director paid £100,000 of the recent transfer fee to Millwall out of his own pocket. Likes the vigorous Wimbledon style of play but hasn't really beaten anyone up apart from Portsmouth. Had car keys nicked by Wally Downes on first day at the club to make him feel at home. Doesn't like fines system and no one has been brave enough to take money off him yet. Doesn't drink.

Paul Fishenden (striker, 22). Shares flat with full-back Kevin Gage and known as one of the Wham! boys. Best striker of the ball in the club. Curious relationship with manager Bassett. Scored twice against Exeter in the Third Division and was promptly dropped. Going grey.

Carlton Fairweather (striker, 24). Once fined £5 for being so well behaved he received no fines during the season and contributed nothing to the players' pool for the end-of-season tour. Very pleased Fashanu has joined the club.

Harry Bassett (manager). No comment.

16

Aim for the Stars

Harry

THE JOURNEY BACK from Huddersfield was riotous and carried on into the early hours, when we got back to London and eventually found a club that would take us. As the taxi finally dropped me home, I didn't want the night to end. I opened the front door to my house, crept in so as not to wake my wife, Christine, and my two girls. But sleep was impossible, so I poured myself a generous measure of scotch, slipped in the ice and plonked myself down in an armchair. I was a bit inebriated anyway but wanted to saviour that moment. I was drained, I was euphoric and I raised my glass to all of those, past and present, that had helped us achieve the impossible: 'Cheers. Here's to Division One.' The rag-bag army had tilted the windmill and there was no way I was bailing out and going to bed. I reflected on what had been achieved, and on those who along the way had been employed by the club, from our kit man Sid

Neale to Alan Gillett, Derek French, Geoff Taylor, Vince Craven and Neil Lanham and the players who had been with me every step of the way and bought into my ideas and vision.

I also felt for the Wimbledon fans who had been with us on our journey, watching away on cold terraces, which were often half-empty, and for years squeezing into our run-down Plough Lane. I don't believe there would have been one who could honestly ever say they thought their team would play in the top division. Some still couldn't believe we had actually made the Second Division, but to believe the likes of Manchester United, Arsenal, Liverpool and Chelsea would one day come to our ground only happened in fairytales. Even our gates that year had been piss poor, and the away fans had also stayed away.

The following day the press were all over us, and I glowed with pride at what had been achieved. It made me feeling fucking glad I returned from Palace so quickly. I'd believed Wimbledon were on the verge of something and that I might be missing out. I knew in my heart I was leaving a team of character: players who had grown and matured into men and had spirit, perseverance, ambition and determination. I thought they had those things, then they actually proved it in those two years in Division Two. They were winners.

When I was going through some old papers for this book, I came across some notes I had jotted down after we achieved promotion to Division One for inclusion in the forthcoming 1986–87 season's *Supporters' Club Handbook*. They are as relevant now as they were then. Memories might fade; words don't. So here is what I wrote in the aftermath of THAT match on 3 May 1986, a few weeks after the reality of what we had achieved kicked in, under the headline MY THOUGHTS . . .

> Huddersfield Town dressing room. The crowds had gone, leaving just the corks, empty champagne bottles and the echoes of laughter. I should have felt jubilation, satisfaction from a long, arduous journey. Yet nothing. I stood in the shower and let the water pour over me. I wanted to shout yet something still held me back. The greatest moment in my managerial life and I couldn't get with it. It was only later I fully realized what had been achieved and what efforts had been put in by so many to achieve it.
>
> That epic day in Huddersfield will never leave me for many reasons. I recalled the yo-yo days of relegation and promotion, the drive through the divisions and even my few 'away' days at Crystal Palace. It was a dream I set out to achieve when I first became manager of Wimbledon just five years ago, and yet when I arrived I was numb. I've spoken to many sporting people and journalists since and they've all understood the moment. Someone said that perhaps we always appreciate the journey more than arriving. I'm still not sure if that's right but I certainly had some fun getting to the First Division.

I don't mean these notes to sound far out, deep or sombre. I'm just recalling those madcap moments when this club could suddenly look Liverpool and Manchester United in the eye. Now the grass has grown, we've come back from a marvellous trip to Spain and begun planning again, and I can only just appreciate what we've accomplished. A lot of people have asked how it's been gained, and I've said, 'Hard work, dedication and a feeling for others.' If pushed further I would say it all began during the early days of last season. And that was when Mark 'Guppy' Morris left us for a loan period with Aldershot. A marvellous, whole-hearted defender, who I honestly believed was extra to my needs. Aldershot wanted to buy and I was ready to listen. It was that kind of situation. Then suddenly I lost three central defenders and Mark was recalled.

So he stepped out of the Fourth Division and immediately plunged power, lungs and enthusiasm into trying to lift Wimbledon and himself into the First. There was no anger, no, 'I'll show you.' Just a good professional going about his work. And as the impossible journey continued no one gave more for this club than 'Guppy'. He was an inspiration to us all. And if I had to separate the marvellous effort produced by the team there would only be one winner of my player of the year. Mark would never figure in Bobby Robson's plans, or join the million pound lira train to Italy. But to me and the others on my staff, he was, and still is, a hero.

We all enjoyed the night beating Stoke (our last home game of the season), and many of you danced and shouted with us on the grey day in Huddersfield when promotion was achieved. We set out with hope and I hope no one here loses that feeling, fan or player. Reaching the First Division would delight even the most humble, but to me we have to capitalize on our situation. I just wish I could erase 20 years and be there to start in the First Division; if any player doesn't give their all here and enjoy playing against Liverpool rather than Scunthorpe, then we might as well give up.

But what a season:
No one did the double over us.
We were the only team to do the double over champions Norwich.
We recovered from having four central defenders out with cartilage trouble.
We never lost a London derby.
Our reserve team reached the final of the Capital Midweek League Cup (the final held over to this season).
Wimbledon's youth team finished second in their league.

A lot of people have said to me this summer that we've reached the pinnacle. I believe it's just the first foothold, I want . . . no, I expect . . . more. Every player here should be thinking of being the best, of being ambitious and successful. Next season will no doubt be exciting for all, in our tenth season. We must push on and not become complacent, as the majority of people throughout the country will be expecting us to fail.

On the back of promotion Alan Gillett and I were given Nissan cars to drive around in. The trimmings of success! The club also had cablegrams, letters and cards of congratulations from many of the clubs that we had fought against over the years: from George Graham (Millwall), David Pleat (Luton), Jim Smith (QPR), Terry Cooper (Bristol City), Brian Horton (Hull), John Hollins (Chelsea), Ray Graydon (Oxford), Sam Ellis (Blackpool), George Kerr (Lincoln), John Lyall (West Ham), Denis Smith (York), John Rudge (Port Vale) and, of course, Dario Gradi (Crewe), the man who helped me on my journey. Ted Croker of the FA and Gordon Taylor of the PFA even sent their best wishes. There were also good wishes from Sir Matt Busby C.B.E. of Manchester United. That was when I knew we had arrived.

Being promoted into the top division with Wimbledon was obviously going to make more than a few football faces and Fleet Street hacks eat their words. Luckily there were always a few of them on our side, including Tony Stenson, the man who coined the Crazy Gang moniker. When we decided to put this book together, he was the obvious choice to get involved. Tony had his column in the *Mirror* – under the name of 'Sten Gun' ('Tony Stenson, the Man Who Shoots from the Hip') – and I've kept the cutting from the week we went up, in an old scrapbook that takes me down memory lane. Here it is.

> Dave Bassett lives in a house called Bees Nees. He must feel that way after leading Wimbledon into the First Division. He took the club built on promises on an impossible journey. They were the no-hopers . . . footballers who played for pennies and washed their own kit. But they have defied all logic and made it to the big time after just nine seasons in the Football League. Halifax, Torquay and even the Upper Balls Pond Road Working Men's Club should take hope from that. There is a place for romantics among the fools who think only of Super Leagues.
>
> Bassett is 41, rich and could live without soccer. But he stays because he loves soccer. Passion for the game burns through his every conversation. Ask him, and he'll probably name every player in the league.
>
> Southampton wanted him. Coventry do, and a cluster of Middle East clubs are knocking at his door. But his chances of winning the manager of the year award aren't very high. That honour will probably go to Kenny Dalglish after leading Liverpool to the title in his first season. Bassett wouldn't be my choice as manager of the year. It should be manager of the decade. I think even Dalglish would agree with that.

I have to say Tony's probably employed a little bit of journalistic licence there. Middle East? I don't fucking think so. But I can live with the flattery. Ask me and I can talk about non-league to First Division in nine seasons any day of the week. And there were plenty of others talking about how I should have been manager of the year. Here's one just for a flavour of what we had to put up with, and I'm sure you're all getting used to the language now: 'Bassett's all-sorts are a rag-bag assortment of misfits, cast-offs and former Southern League players who have cost – by today's standards – peanuts to bring together. To take that team into the First Division is little short of a miracle – and it's the bouncy Bassett who should take the credit.'

Elsewhere, though, there were the usual moans from the establishment. FA secretary Ted Croker, who could say a lot of shit most of the time, and despite his letter of congratulations, openly questioned our right to be in the top flight, citing our 'limited facilities'. Wimbledon, he said, and this is his actual quote, were 'totally incapable of staging First Division football. To bring top clubs like Manchester United and Tottenham to a ground like that is ridiculous.'

Utter drivel.

Although we were, of course, paupers in the company we would be about to keep. Despite Sam's investment in Fash, the top wage back then was still only £310 a week and, as I admitted in an interview with Joe Lovejoy in the *Mail on Sunday* in May 1986, 'It's difficult trying to sign a married player from the north. He's horrified to find what sort of house his money buys down here.'

But even though we were seen as a novelty ('We're not a variety act, we're a football team,' I'd respond to that), the jibes kept on coming: 'Wimbledon have got the best pitch in the Football League . . . because the ball never touches the grass'; 'Wimbledon have given up selling tickets in favour of boarding cards'; 'Next season the floodlights will be replaced by searchlights'; 'They have more high-balls than a New York cocktail bar'; 'Spectators are not given seat numbers but flight numbers.' These were just some of the lame comments fired in our direction. Someone even said that we were 'a pygmy club that played like apes'.

Bring it on. Of course we had a plan, and it worked. Against Blackburn in March, the week before that pivotal clash with Pompey, we forced 15 corners in the second half to the opposition's one. David Lacey in the *Guardian* wrote after the game that our style was 'original Watford with a touch of Sheffield Wednesday' – but he was wrong, it was Wimbledon. He was correct, though, in identifying the importance we placed on getting corners and free-kicks, and that we needed a natural finisher to get on the end of Corky and Stewart Evans' flicks and angled lay-offs – Fash would join days later.

Bobby Saxton, the Blackburn manager, also revealed what it was like to play against us. 'Nobody can condemn Wimbledon's tactics,' he said. 'They go for the direct style of play, put you under pressure and make it very difficult for a defence. They don't mess about, they get the ball into the danger area as quickly as possible and everybody piles in after it. It's very hard to combat. They don't play fancy tip-tap stuff, it's pure and direct and it's successful.'

If only Bobby knew what was going on in our dressing room. We'd had a blazing row about not converting all those chances – I called the players sloppy and slovenly, as if they were waiting for things to happen rather than making them happen.

So our tactics were, as usual, described as crude, but I had plenty of ammunition for anyone who wanted to discover more about our football philosophy. The lazy 'long-ball' generalization was pinned to Wimbledon because we were an unglamorous club. You have to build your tactics around the players at your disposal, but even with the likes of Glyn Hodges and Nigel Winterburn, who could have graced any team, the media ignored this and always focused on flair players in other teams.

In an interview with the *Independent* in September 1986, when we were top of the league, I pointed out that teams are entitled to play whichever way they want as long as they stay within the laws of the game. 'You can play with a sweeper, without a sweeper, with wingers, without wingers. It's up to the manager.

'Everton and Liverpool play a long-ball game and nobody says anything about it,' I went on, warming to my theme, and my voice no doubt getting louder with every sentence. 'Or maybe they don't notice. Make no mistake, they don't play the short-passing game all the time. I'm not saying they play our style, but the long ball comes into it more than some people seem to think. At Wimbledon, we try to play to our players' strengths by using a system that suits them.'

And a lot of it was just downright inconsistent. 'Why is it,' I asked another reporter, 'that when Arsenal play high balls to a 6 foot 3 inch Irishman, Niall Quinn, it is quality football, and when Wimbledon play high balls to a 6 foot 4 inch coloured striker, it's football that's ruining the game?'

The system had evolved over the years, as all systems have to do. Players change, the opposition changes, the laws change – look at an old game today and how odd does it seem to see a keeper picking up a back-pass before launching it up the field? The game changes.

Under Allen in Wimbledon's Southern League championship-winning years, I told the reporter, 'we played a kind of long-ball game. In 1981 when we were promoted from the Fourth Division, we played with a sweeper. Later we had another think about it and moved back to the long-ball because it suited us better. Seven of the players who started in the Fourth Division are still with us, so it wasn't just a matter of changing the system to suit new players.'

Going into the First Division was always going to be a challenge, but we weren't there just to make up the numbers. 'We set out to win the league and the Cup,' I continued. 'That may sound boastful, but it's true. That was our objective. We didn't set out to be 16th in the league. Aim for the stars, and you might get somewhere on the way.'

One of those stars, in more ways than one, would turn out to be John Fashanu. Here's Fash.

John Fashanu

I spend a lot of time in Nigeria now, but the scrapbooks of my sporting life are always by my side. The biggest, funniest, most memorable of all were my days at Wimbledon under Dave Bassett, and playing alongside the likes of Wally Downes. You could not find two bigger characters.

You had to be mad to manage Wimbledon, and Dave was the craziest. Wally was similar, but both in the nicest ways. We had our moments, fall-outs, but we were always a family, and in families there are bound to be one or two arguments. But I loved every one of those guys. Still do. Will always do.

When I arrived, I thought I had joined a local village side, one full of hooligans, lager louts, touts and Arthur Daleys, where they'd sell your shoes if you left them off long enough. Wally was behind most of the pranks, and many times I thought I would sort him out – but when it came to the moment, I would simply burst out laughing. He had that way about him. When I left I think I was more Wally than myself.

Dave Bassett was one of the greatest managers I have

known, also a wonderful man and wonderful person. He had a way about him that made you listen. He was also completely mad, of course, but you had to be to manage a squad with so many complexities. You simply couldn't manage me the same way as Vinnie Jones, Alan Cork, Wally, Dennis Wise or Lawrie Sanchez. We were all off the wall, with different intellects, beliefs and characteristics. Harry managed the impossible, bringing us all together, getting us playing to a well-honed system. Most days it must have felt like he was herding cats, but it worked, and he worked hard to do it.

What I also found was that you had to fight to be a Wimbledon player, and woe betide anyone who didn't. We had rows, but if any outsider took liberties and tried to take us on we were all in it together, scrapping side-by-side – and that included our 77-year-old chairman Stanley Reed. It was impossible to split us. We were family first and foremost. I had my spat with Lawrie Sanchez, but if I saw him today I would go and kiss the guy. As I said, inside families you are always going to have rows, but we could never be divided.

Other managers took over after Harry left but hardly changed anything. They stuck to his well-thought-out blueprint, adding newcomers along the way to ensure the success continued. We were blessed having a man like Harry, and infectious people like Wally and Corky. They were exciting, certainly crazy days.

I knew I had joined something special when I made my debut at Portsmouth, just a few days after playing against them for my previous club Millwall. It was war. But I knew from that moment I would never be alone. They were by my shoulder every minute, and afterwards I knew . . . I knew I had joined a special band of brothers.

I was told I was crazy to join them. I ended up being as crazy as the rest, and I am proud of it.

17

Unsung Heroes

Wally

HERE'S SOME MORE unsung Wimbledon heroes who deserve their recognition. If you want to know what life was like as a young player back then, have a good read of what John Gannon, Kevin Gage, Andy Sayer and Andy Thorn have to say.

John Gannon

Wimbledon was my local club: I lived just round the corner from Plough Lane – sadly now a block of flats. I see AFC Wimbledon as the same club. I remember when I was working for Notts County and they played MK Dons and I was asked to do a programme piece, I refused – I could not recognize them as a football team. I come from Wimbledon.

Fulham and several other clubs wanted me in to train

with them as a youngster, but Wimbledon were more active in getting kids in. I always felt you were much more involved at Wimbledon – they would get you in throughout the school holidays, and the people there were fantastic. Fulham were the bigger club, but you felt a warmth at Wimbledon – it was a nice place to be; everyone would say it was a great place to be. You always felt like you wanted to get to training – almost everyone would be getting in there early, there were people and characters who attracted you. Facilities and everything were poor, but it didn't seem to matter. The café was there but the food was limited – everything was limited, in fact. I had bad knees from the age of 16 because we were training on concrete from the age of nine, behind a stand at Plough Lane. There was a sandpit for the goal-keeper to dive in. We just didn't have the facilities. But it was the place you wanted to be and wanted to go back to.

I was Wally Downes' apprentice one year. You weren't asked, you were told. It wasn't good if you were down the betting shop on a Saturday at two o'clock and you got his bets wrong – there was hell to pay. He had a tongue that could cut you to pieces, but he was also a very thoughtful human. If Wally was in a difficult mood then it could be an awkward morning, and that is how it was – other days he would be delightful. His moods would swing and change just like Harry. Wally was never far off being a mini-Harry; there are a lot of similarities.

I made my debut on the last day of the 1985–86

season, at Bradford, after we had got promotion from Division Two. I scored in that game, which helped in terms of trying to establish myself for the next season in very difficult circumstances. When I was a schoolboy we were in the old Fourth Division, but by the time I was a first- or second-year pro we were in what is now the Premier League. That ride was incredible. My first wage was £18 as an apprentice. Harry was learning all the time and the team were learning.

Our preparations were years ahead of their time. Harry was a master at mind games, tactics and organization. We were also the first team to introduce a dancing celebration – the 'Magaluf Shuffle' was way ahead of its time. Thirty years on players pre-plan their moves or have a trademark celebration, but Wimbledon were doing that 30 years ago.

Us apprentices were all best mates as well – we spent all of our time together socially. Vaughan Ryan arrived just after his dad had died, and his mum got involved with the club and started helping out with the kit and the kitchen – the club tried to look after them. There were a lot of difficult characters there but I think Harry liked that, he liked that spirited type of boy, one who would fight back and had a bit of edge. Personally, I wasn't really one of those but there were certain players, like Dennis Wise and Vinnie Jones, who, at the right time and in the right doses, gave the team that bit of energy and edge. When Vinnie arrived he was wild. Dennis was unbeatable as a runner. He could not be beaten around Richmond Park, he had phenomenal stamina and desire. He had heart. He was a tough boy and aggressive, he would drop his shoulder and go. He had a tough background and he was a tough man.

Fash had a very hard upbringing too – like quite a few of the players – and maybe that was the element that made him a good fit for Wimbledon. In his first top-flight season he was fantastic, because he did what he was good at, and he was wearing orange boots and trying to market himself long before anyone else. He was very different and probably a bit ahead of the curve in that sense. He loved being the pantomime villain, he loved it.

Harry loved to get us out on loan, to places like Sweden. He felt it was character-building. I did a nine-month loan in Sweden that was fantastic. I still have friends over there now, and my brother married a Swedish woman. It was probably one of the best periods of my life, for growing up. I went with another lad who ended up living out there. It used to get us off the wage bill.

But it didn't work out for everybody, of course. Andy Thorn did fantastic. As a centre-half he was massive – not particularly quick but he was the sharpest mentally. He would step up for offsides and his positional play and organization were second to none. But Ian Holloway never settled, and he was a fantastic player. He was young when he arrived and he used to stay at my auntie's house – we used to lodge players with us. Ian found it particularly difficult, but he had glandular fever while he was with us.

Alan Gillett was the perfect assistant manager for Harry, and a very good coach too. He got a fair bit of stick from us players, but everyone did. They were a good combination because Bassett was the screamer and shouter and Gillett was more of a school teacher, but he would put on some very good sessions. I think people learned there, and we had some sharp individuals.

One thing that I think is desperately lacking in football now is a sense of 'I'll show you'. Even when Harry was fucking negative towards you, we all had a determination to prove him wrong. I don't think that attitude is there with players any more, players don't react like that today – they walk away when you dig them out. I couldn't do it at Wimbledon, but when I got to Sheffield I wanted to show Harry that I was fucking ready and I could do it. That attitude and determination isn't there now.

Geoff Taylor was fantastic with the youth team, but also a sergeant major. You were told the bus was leaving at 7.30 a.m., and if anyone was running late it wouldn't be a surprise to see the bus start up and leave without you at 7.20 a.m.

I remember a time when I had just turned full-time and the training was extreme. Geoff asked me what was wrong – he could see that I was physically struggling – and I told him I was fucked. We didn't eat, we had fuck all money, so we either bought a bottle of Coke to quench our thirst and starved ourselves, or we bought food and dehydrated. We had no energy, but then Geoff sorted it out so we got two free rolls every day. Geoff would always fight every inch for the young players like us.

Derek French, the physio, was great as a middle-ground between us and Harry. As soon as you got to the training ground he would let you know if Harry had the hump. He would say, 'He's got the hump. Chris [his missus] has had a go at him.' So we would know then to tread carefully – things like that were so helpful. Frenchie was great to have around because he knew Harry so well – he was usually the first in and he could help set the tone and calm things down when the more volatile people around him were going off.

After Wimbledon I never ever walked into a changing room and felt intimidated. Because it was extreme and I was young but I had to deal with it, everything else was a walk in the park. Later on in my career, whenever I went to a different club as a player or as a member of staff, whenever youngsters came and asked about my playing career, the minute you said Wimbledon their interest in anything else faded. They still want to know about the Crazy Gang, even now. Gagey will tell you that too.

Kevin Gage

All the apprentices would go to the launderette on a Friday in a minibus. Geoff Taylor would drop us off with a week's worth of training kit, and we would have to wash it. We would be in there for three hours, over the bridge in South Wimbledon – that's when APs were APs. We would go back afterwards and sweep the terraces and the changing rooms. I was a year older than Gannon and Sayer and there were only two APs my age, but we didn't have to clean boots.

Wally Downes was the instigator of a lot of the shenanigans that went on. He was unofficially in charge most of the time. If something was going on you could bet Wally was behind it, or involved, or had wound someone else up to do it. He was very cute and clever and devious. He was very funny when it was directed at others, but in a nice way, and you just had to get on with it. There was no bullying, absolutely not.

Wimbledon were getting more professional as the years went on; Wally was the first apprentice, then it was Hodges and Guppy and Fish. They were still learning how to be a professional football club and how apprenticeships worked. Even the pros had only been pros for a year or two, so everyone was learning, and I think we got away with an awful lot – off the pitch – because Harry didn't have any experience as a professional football manager, he had come from non-league. Harry let a lot go, and that created the team spirit, the camaraderie and the Crazy Gang ethos.

Your debut is so personal, so we all remember our debuts. Mine was against Bury, in May 1981, the promotion party from Division Four. It was only a week after my 17th birthday. The game I remember best, though, is the one when we got promoted to Division One – Huddersfield away. We won 1–0, and it was never in doubt. God knows what I was doing taking free-kicks, but I took one quickly and touched it to Sanchez – and he spanked it in. Maybe this is where we were quite cute, because Harry made us think like that. We realized they didn't have a charger in the wall, so I told Sanch this, and before they were organized he larruped it in.

I remember being on the coach going home and we were all at the back getting pissed, and it suddenly hit me what we had achieved. We would be playing Manchester United, Liverpool, Arsenal – how the fuck did that happen? In the lower leagues, I remember going to Hereford, and we had to get a connecting train. We had nowhere to sit on the last leg of the journey because of all the skips of kit, and on the way back we were sitting and drinking with all the fans and talking about the game.

We always got the impression that Harry thought he was a good coach because he used to put on the odd session. But he was never a brilliant coach, not just at Wimbledon but going on to Sheffield too. Harry was about organization, leadership, set-plays and getting the best out of players. There was a lot of fear as well – fear of letting him and your teammates down; we were all in it together.

When you first joined it was like being at school with your mates. It was great fun and everyone just happened to be great footballers. It turned into an extended family, and that must have been where a lot of the success and motivation came from because, as has been well documented, we were not on a lot of money. I never dreamed of leaving – you signed any contract that was put in front of you because you wanted to be at this club that was going somewhere, and doing something, getting these promotions. You just did not want to leave.

Vinnie used to sit in the back of either my car or Dave Beasant's, because Lurch lived in north London and I was in Hatfield. We used to pick Vinnie up on the way through because he had no car and not a pot to piss in. He was loud and full of himself. I do remember him saying one thing that was quite funny: after about a month, when it looked like he was about to get a contract, he was sat in the back of our car jabbering on about how much he should ask for, and he came out with a ridiculous sum for the time, like £200 a week. I looked at Lurch and didn't say anything, but thought, 'You've got no chance.' My next thought was, 'I've been here seven years, so if you get that I'm steaming in to get it as well.'

I went on loan to Sweden at the start of my career, but unlike a lot of the lads I hated it. I think I only lasted four weeks, and I had another English lad from Lincoln to keep me company. I was in the middle of nowhere doing absolutely nothing all day. My tennis improved but not a lot else. It was not about football but about growing up. It gave us responsibility.

Hodge was the best player I ever played with. He

probably should have done more, but to be a really top player you have to have pace, and he didn't. He had everything technically. Wisey did supremely well career-wise because he wasn't particularly great when he arrived – he had set-pieces and an engine. I never saw anyone so durable in my life.

None of this would ever be talked about if we were not successful on the pitch. Loads of teams got up to silly stuff and were idiots, but you don't become successful unless you have good football players. We were fortunate in those five, six, seven years, with those who came through that youth side and could cope with the level of football.

But in a team like that, full of big characters, you cannot have everyone chiming in all the time. You have these personalities. Me and Nigel Winterburn used to sit there watching Vinnie and Fash getting up to their antics, and we would just look at each other as if to say, 'What the fuck is going on?' We just wanted to play the game and get on with it; they were from a different planet sometimes.

We appreciated Fash's presence on the pitch, so we let the stuff off it slide. We were always so pleased he was on our side, because when we played against him he was a nightmare – he was like a lunatic and I remember someone in the dressing room saying, 'We have to sign him.' Soon as we signed Fash we knew he was perfect for getting us promoted. He got us over the line, so we ignored the other stuff.

There was a period when the media didn't seem to like us, but that came later when we started getting successful, after we had beaten Clough's Nottingham Forest. When we were younger and coming up through the divisions I always felt people were very kind to us. When we got in the top flight people started to dislike us because by then we were fitter, stronger and better players.

I first broke my nose playing at Southend, away in the reserves when I was 15. I was out cold and then woke up in the dressing room half an hour later and was taken to hospital. The first time you break it, it really hurts, but after that every time you get a knock you just have to crack it back into place.

We were all, more or less, playing reserves football at 15 – not because we were that good but because we didn't have anyone else. It toughens you up. The first time I ever saw Bassett I was playing in an FA Youth Cup match at Plough Lane. We played Tottenham and I had only just joined, from the suburbs of Addlestone. It was my first big match for them, and we lost 2–0, but I thought we had played OK, and I had done pretty well personally. Gillett was giving a pretty basic post-match team talk, going through the players and being positive in places, but then the door burst open. This bloke stormed in, looking official, and the room went silent. I had no idea it was Bassett. He had a go at every single player, starting from the goalkeeper, right through, and not just about football stuff. I was number 8 and when

Top: Putting pen to paper on a new contract. No one earned a fortune.

Above: A day at the races with Stanley Reed.

Right: No fancy dress here. Army training camps got the boys in shape.

Top: You do it like this…

Right: You go over there…

Below: Oh, for fuck's sake!

Above left: Fash was a huge factor in our success, as was Nigel Winterburn (**above right**), Player of the Year all four seasons he played for us.

Below: The luxury training facilities just off the A3. I can't remember Harry's question but I'm not sure the answer is up there!

Above: We were only top of the league after four games of the 1986/87 season!

Below: Vinnie and me after his goal against Man Utd. I suppose you could say it looks like we are 'having ourselves a bit' here.

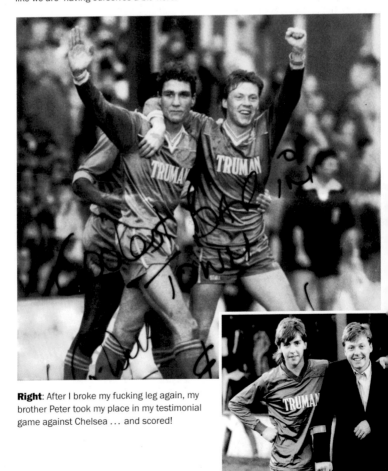

Right: After I broke my fucking leg again, my brother Peter took my place in my testimonial game against Chelsea . . . and scored!

We had two epic FA Cup ties at Plough Lane that season. **Above**, Brian Gayle chases down Everton's Paul Wilkinson, while Dennis Wise and Sanch get to grips with Glenn Hoddle (**below**).

Wimbledon

First D

Back Row: Lawrie Sanchez, Brian Gayle, Stewart Evans, David Beasant, John
Fashanu, Colin Gordon, Mark Morris.

Middle Row: Derek French (*Physiotherapist*), Mick Smith, Alan Cork,
Nigel Winterburn, Simon Tracey, Andrew Thorn, Carlton Fairweather,
Glyn Hodges, Alan Gillett (*Assistant Manager*), Geoff Taylor (*Youth Team Manag*

ootball Club

1986/7

Front Row: John Gannon, David Martin, Steve Galliers, John Kay, David Bassett (*Manager*), Kevin Gage, Wally Downes, Paul Fishenden, Dennis Wise.

Founded 1889

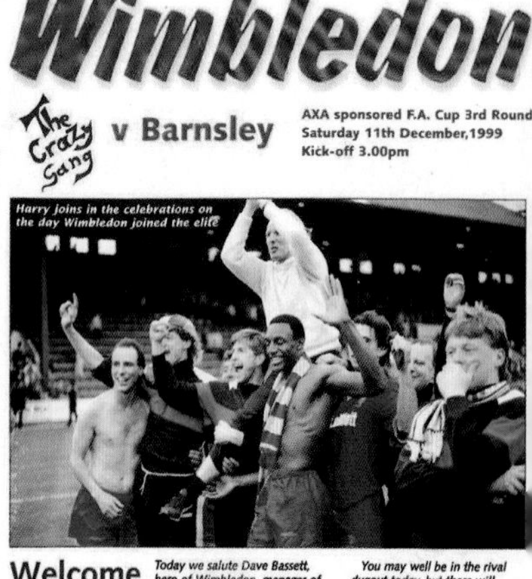

Price £2.00

Wimbledon

The Crazy Gang v Barnsley

AXA sponsored F.A. Cup 3rd Round
Saturday 11th December, 1999
Kick-off 3.00pm

Harry joins in the celebrations on the day Wimbledon joined the elite

Welcome Back Harry

Today we salute Dave Bassett, hero of Wimbledon, manager of the Millennium.
What you did by taking us from the Fourth to the First Division will never be equalled.
Other wonderful managers continued the miracle, but it was you who made it possible.

You may well be in the rival dugout today, but there will always be part of us in you and you in us.
This will always be your spiritual home. It is an honour to welcome you back.
Sam

Club Sponsor tiny
Match Sponsors Kingswood Print & Display Ltd
Programme Sponsor ALAN BAILY

Top: I'm proud to call Alex Ferguson my friend, but we did the double over Man Utd that season!

Above: Leaving Wimbledon to join Elton John's Watford was a mistake.

Right: Sam Hammam's tribute on my return in 1999, with a photo from Huddersfield. What's Wally doing?!

he got to 6, I thought, 'Fucking hell, what's he going to say to me?' He did number 7, and then got to me – but he said I did all right. He probably never gave me more encouragement in the rest of my career than in that moment. He was more stick than carrot. He went through the rest of the team, and even had a go at the sub who didn't get on. He said, 'How shit must you be if you can't even get in this team?!'

In the early days it was Harry's way or the highway, but later on he started to develop more and bounced off the players he knew and trusted. But who were we to really tell him after all he had done? The football was rough and ready but personally I felt I developed very much as a man.

I left Wimbledon in '87, just after Bassett had left, and went to Aston Villa, who were a big club – but, on the first day, I was treated like a god because I had played for Wimbledon. Everyone at Villa wanted to know how we had done what we did, what Bassett was like, were the rumours true? They had heard about us, and we had beaten them twice. They wanted to know how we had achieved all that with gates of only 3,000. I was held up in such high regard because of what I had done with Wimbledon. Graham Taylor would single me out as an example to the other players of the standard that was expected, and that was all down to Wimbledon and what can be achieved with a bit of graft and determination.

I remember playing one game for Villa at Crewe in the FA Cup Third Round in 1989, and we were 2–0 down in the first half and getting hammered. We were playing 3–5–2, or something like that, and Graham Taylor walked in and had a go at us and said, 'You got yourselves into this mess, you can get yourselves out of it.' Then he stopped and looked at me and said, 'We need some of that old Wimbledon spirit that your old team showed: get us back in the game.' We then went 4–2–4 and steamrollered them; we won 3–2 with David Platt scoring the winner. So that was Villa, the 1982 European Cup winners, using Wimbledon as the template – not just in how to win a game but in how to win a game from 2–0 down. It shouldn't have happened. We were held up as something to aspire to when the chips were down.

In the early days of the 1983–84 season, I was basically going off the rails a bit. Sharing a flat with Paul Fishenden was a recipe to party, it was an open house. Players from all over London would end up coming round, knocking on the door at any time. We got away with an awful lot that perhaps other players at other, maybe more professional, clubs would not have been able to get away with. But it worked and the roller coaster kept going. In my first full season we were relegated and I was not always in the side, but after that season it was more or less constant success with promotions or stability.

When I was about 19 and going off the rails a bit, Bassett summoned both my parents into the club for a meeting. I was never going to be an alcoholic but I was going out too much and it was affecting me. They went into Plough Lane, and he said, 'Gagey is doing all right but he's going out too much and not doing as well as he could.' Well, I got the bollocking of my life once I got home. That showed what sort of family element we had at the club. But the players' lounge doubled up as a night-club, so drinking was inevitable.

I would not swap my Wimbledon time for anything in the world, not league titles or cups. Aston Villa was a huge club, but when you told people you had played for Wimbledon that sparked their interest and they gave you respect. When I walked into that Villa dressing room with Gary Shaw, Andy Gray and Nigel Spink they all wanted to talk about Wimbledon. I probably only really realize now how good it was. At the time it was the norm; there was nothing to compare it with. But when you look back it's amazing.

For a comparison to show how much of a family and close-knit club Wimbledon was, I remember on my first day at Villa speaking with Graham Taylor when a smart, older-looking man came over. I was introduced to Doug Ellis. I said, 'Hi, Doug,' and we exchanged a few pleasantries. Finally he said, 'Best of luck, and, remember, it's "Mr Chairman" to you.' We didn't have any of those airs and graces at Wimbledon, far from it.

Andy Sayer

We didn't have to clean boots unless the pros wanted you to do it and wanted to pay you. Wally would pick his own apprentice every year. I don't know what his criteria was, maybe he did it on looks! You had to suffer it for a year – it was not a good gig. Wally was great with his time and help, and if he had a win he was very generous. My first pro wage was £50 a week, and that was a 'take it or leave it' offer.

I remember my first trip to Magaluf. I was 16 and quite naïve, I hadn't really lived. We used to play in the West London Cup. We played Fulham, who were a much better side – two divisions above us at the time – and the next day the first team were going to Magaluf, but someone dropped out so I was told the day before that I was the stand-in and would be going. Harry said, 'Get your bag, we're going tomorrow.' Going away with Wally and everyone was amazing, it was an eye-opener. Wally nicked my passport, and because we both had blond hair we went through on each other's passport. Then in Magaluf – I think it was after we had got promoted from the Fourth Division to the Third – Everton were out there too, and they wanted to hang around with us!

When we were schoolboys, every week – whether it was a Tuesday or a Thursday – Dario would come and take a training session. This was the first-team manager. He would come over and take the session for the under-12s or 13s. That was fantastic for us. You couldn't begin to imagine that now at any level, the first-team manager doing that, not just once, but every week.

When it came to contracts and money it was daunting

going to see Harry, because there was never any money and we couldn't afford anything. But one of the great things I remember was the minute he left Wimbledon and went to Watford, he was on the phone telling us all how much we were worth and what we should go in and ask for. He wanted to look after the club, and he maintained that sense of wanting to help the players after he had gone. But if we had asked Harry for it while he was still at Wimbledon he would have said, 'Fuck off and get out!'

I can hold my hands up and say I should have done more, but I wasn't mentally tough enough. I have to admit that. I underachieved. I was quiet, but there were other quiet players.

I played at Oxford away. I think we went 3–0 down and Harry said to everyone, 'Right, you've embarrassed me, now I'll fucking embarrass you!' He did the half-time team-talk on the pitch. Oxford fans were taking the piss, Geoff Taylor was doing the team-talk, and they battered us. But I remember when we used to get the train back from games up north, the players would hold on to Harry and not let him off at his stop at Watford. Micky Smith would pin him down so he had to come all the way into London.

I remember at 14 you had to sign schoolboy forms. At the time I was training with Chelsea too, so I had to decide, and it was a massive decision. But what swung it for me was Dario, the first-team manager, coming round my house to speak to my mum. Chelsea were a much bigger club and wanted me to sign, but Dario told me I would be in the first team and spoke to me personally.

Geoff Taylor had a huge influence on me as well. He was the one who was constantly in Harry's ear trying to tell him about us coming through, pushing to get us in the first team. He had a massive role in the careers of so many of us. He has to take credit for that. He would go to war with Harry; they would have incredible rows. They were almost complete opposites, but their mutual respect is huge. Geoff had a soft side too. I remember one year we had to go in on Christmas Day, and I reckon Harry had told Geoff to run us, but Geoff said, 'You have ten runs, but for every one of my ten presents you can guess I will knock one off.'

If Wally or anyone else ever went too far with one of the young lads Geoff would always get involved and put a stop to anything that might have been over the top.

Frenchie was great as well. I remember breaking my toe once. But when I told Frenchie he told me to fuck off. At the Richardson Evans training ground there was a private hospital nearby, and he made me walk there for an X-ray on my foot. I had to go back and tell him that it was broken. He didn't seem too bothered. Liverpool used to have 30 back-room staff, and Manchester City take a hundred people on a tour, but he had four people.

In those days there was one sub, so only 13 would travel. When away trips to places like Carlisle, or anywhere far afield, came up you knew it was going to take up your whole weekend, travelling up and back and never knowing if you were playing or not until the morning of the match. You would go down to breakfast, and the players who more or less knew they were starting would have beans on toast, a light breakfast. The way Harry would tell whoever wasn't involved was by saying, 'Have what you like, son – a fry-up.' Then you knew you were missing out and your weekend was fucked. His catchphrase was, 'I'm going on my gut feeling – eat what you like.'

My favourite match was probably the one in which I got a hat-trick against Newcastle, which made me the first Wimbledon player to hit a treble in the top flight. I would love to see those goals again, but I don't think it was filmed. They were all in and around the six-yard box, not great goals, just tap-ins, really. I have still got the signed ball – it might be at my mum's, in the loft.

18
Survival Instinct

Harry

BEING THE FITTEST team in the league was going to be a vital part of being able to push above our weight. So it was an easy decision to take the players on a nice little holiday to Germany to get ready for our assault on the First Division. Krefeld, the place was called, a lovely little resort which was home to the 28th Signals Regiment. The army had even flown over an extra specialist, Jim Wood, a former Olympian and biathlete, to get the boys in shape.

'To be honest,' Jim told me when he first assessed where we were at, 'they aren't as fit as I thought they would be.'

'That's why we're here,' I said. 'I don't believe footballers are as fit as they could be. We kid ourselves in our game. I know it's all about different sets of muscles, but when you see the young army boys go through the same exercises, it makes you realize we have a way to go.'

A week of early morning runs and the camp assault course – Wimbledon became notorious for this later, of course, when pictures of our training were aired on *Football Focus* – did the trick, though. Jim put his finger on what we had as a club when a journalist caught up with him: 'They have come on really well, and the main reason for that is their wonderful morale. You can see why they have gone so far in football.'

It was obvious, really: you need a fighting unit, you need them fighting fit, and so you go to the army. A barracks is like a football club – you're in it for each other, and you need a structure, with leaders on and off the pitch, or the battleground, or whatever.

Of course, it wouldn't have been Wimbledon without a bit of fun too, as Wally recalls. I imagine he was once again responsible for Corky finding himself on the wrong end of the stick.

One morning, the sirens went off to get the players out of bed; we were told it was an emergency, and that we had three minutes to get into chemical suits – a giant radioactive cloud was on its way from Chernobyl. For some inexplicable reason, Corky's suit was a few sizes too small, and he could barely fit in it, the trousers were halfway up his legs. He was jumping around like a fucking madman, pointing at his bare feet and ankles: 'I can't have these dropping off! I'm a fucking footballer!'

Corky had, of course, seen every one of the four divisions, so I'll let him take over the story, from an interview back in the day: 'We work hard and to a purpose down here, but it is also one big laugh. If you look back on the banter and the things that go on in the dressing room you'd think that you were in a kindergarten with five-year-olds rather than with grown men. Sometimes I think the whole club is geared for getting the biggest possible giggle out of any given situation.'

Corky was responsible for coining the phrase 'a giggle factory' in relation to Wimbledon. He went on to compare me to Ivor Powell, the former Cardiff City manager who was infamous for saying things like, 'We must have more harmonium in the dressing room.' 'Our 'Arry sometimes gets things mixed up,' Corky confessed. 'It's a question of his mouth and his brain working at different speeds. He's been saying "well done" recently and that's the first time in ten years I can remember it. Usually when we have done well he has insulted us – in a pleasant way.'

Cheeky bugger.

'Mind you,' he continued, 'there is no way anybody down here will ever get the chance to be complacent, because there are too many people looking for the chance to put Vaseline on your car windscreen, let your tyres down or put treacle inside your shoes.'

That pretty much sums it up.

I remember there was another article that ran in the *People* newspaper midway through our first season in the First Division, when our training methods raised a few eyebrows. It was headlined DIRTY HARRY! The reporter, Brian Madley, had come down to Richardson

Evans to witness a 14-body pile-up in the middle of the training pitch. He wrote that 'Wimbledon's players don't exactly practise a punch-up routine. It just looks that way.' I told him it was 'a nice little warm-up exercise' – the culmination of a seven-a-side American Football routine I used to run, and I told Brian I had no worries about anyone getting injured. 'A player can twist an ankle jogging round the pitch. The harder you try to avoid injury the more likely you are to get one.'

Training was fun, but strict as well. Anyone caught daydreaming was given an instant punishment of ten press-ups. Anyone skiving would have to stay behind for extra training. Work-rate not wizardry was paramount to our performances. 'Just because we beat Manchester United doesn't mean you're a bloody superstar,' I yelled at a player in front of the man from the *People*.

Brian Madley then recounted a dinner for football coaches in London that I had attended the previous week as a guest speaker. I started my speech by producing a screwdriver, a hacksaw and a hammer. 'That's what I hand to my players before every match,' I said. Of course, this was all to wind people up – and to make people fear us. 'So we're a tough team and no one likes playing us. Good. The day they all want to play us I'll know I'm a failure. But I will defend the team to the death when people start calling us cheats.'

Camaraderie was the key. If you've got disharmony and discord, success is impossible, especially if, as I once quipped, you've got 'a bunch of Third Division footballers playing in the First Division at a Fourth Division ground'.

And we also needed a physio who was up to the task of looking after the players. Medical expertise, as we have heard, possibly came second here to sheer bloody-mindedness and a hardened survival instinct. Frenchie, over to you.

Derek French

The transition from being a bad cab driver to a bad physio, for me, was easy because I was bad at everything. Being bad was part of my nature – but I wasn't that bad. I had always wanted to work in football. I was probably one of the finest amateur footballers known to mankind – I had several trials for Watford, none of them successful. The start for me was at Barnet with Barry Fry, who I thought was mental. And then I ended up at another club where everyone, from top to bottom, was mental, so again it was another easy transition.

I got a call from a friend called John Cornell, who knew Harry, and he told me there was a job going at Wimbledon. At the time I wasn't very experienced, but he told me not to worry as they didn't want anyone experienced and the money would be shit. Harry never even bothered to phone. Alan Gillett called me and told me there were several people in the running for the job but that he had heard good things about me, so he would let me know over the course of a few days. I politely asked if there was any information on what the finances might be and he said, 'NO.' I waited two days and then Alan called again and told me Harry thought I was the ideal man for the club and to get over there ASAP. Alan informed me that I was not chosen because I was good but because I was cheap – which is a stretch when we had never even discussed salaries – so I knew from the start that the job was never going to be about money.

That was in the summer, so I went to Lilleshall to complete the Treatment of Injury course. I was still shit by the end of the course but they still gave me the job. I had been at Barnet for two years and done my first year of the Treatment of Injury course but I would never have dreamed of calling myself a physio – I was a bucket and sponge man. That said, the bucket was too heavy, so I just used to run on with a sponge in a small bag.

Wimbledon was a funny set-up: they were a great bunch of lads who were always out to get you one way or another, and they usually did. I came in after the relegation; in 1983 we then won the Fourth Division. There wasn't much difference between the set-up at Barnet and Wimbledon – although I didn't see much of the lads at Barnet because they were part-time. There wasn't a lot of money at either club. Barry used to pay the players on a Thursday night after the disco. Everyone had to wait until about 10 p.m. – by which point the club disco had had a few people through the door – to get their dosh. I used to get paid out of the one-armed bandit, but only if Barry won.

At Wimbledon I was always watching my back – there was always stuff flying around, you could smell it. Harry tucked me up on the first tour to Finland, which was a steep learning curve. We had just come out of the sauna and there was a beautiful lake near where we were staying. When I commented on how peaceful it looked Harry told me to have a dip and enjoy myself. The moment I took a serene stroke out from the bank the entire squad dived in and tried to drown me – and I am not a good swimmer. That was more or less day one.

It felt like I was a good fit straight away. They were all just good honest lads who wanted to play football and have a good time – and we managed to do it. There were training sessions when there were not enough players to practise set-pieces and free-kicks so me, the kit man and the tea woman were always called up and I was always, ALWAYS the charger, every time, getting smashed to fuck. There were loads of things happening like that.

A lot of managers are suspicious of the physio room because they think players might be skiving in there, but I liked to keep it lively and happy. I was the first person to ever have music in the dressing room – I was playing a lot of real R&B and jazz and blues, and then the players brought their own in. Harry didn't mind or think players were taking the piss because in those days players just didn't. There was no malingering or work-dodging. He wouldn't have stood for it. And the other players wouldn't have tolerated it – they policed themselves.

There was a huge togetherness; no outsiders were allowed in. If anyone was bought in or loaned in and they couldn't adapt to what was going on, then they didn't last five minutes. We used to have so many coming through, loans and triallists. Ian Holloway had to work very hard to be part of the system. Dave Martin had a pet duck, he was mental.

But that was the criteria for the people Harry wanted to come in. He wanted characters; we wanted people who were going to work tremendously hard and then have a right laugh. Working and playing for Harry was a test all of the time. Even later on, on pre-season tours, you were always allowed to be men and go out and have a drink, but if you could not train and do your job and keep up with your teammates the next day then you were in shit. It was always a test to see if you were up to the job. We had a few who struggled over time. Some players would come in like these *Big Brother* characters and say things like, 'I am nuts – you're going to love me – I am fucking mental.' And I'd be sat there thinking, 'Oh great. You're gonna need to be, son.'

It was a tough school. I remember up in Sheffield when Harry got a sports psychologist in, and one of the tasks was to physically form a circle with their bodies, all the players linked together and holding firm. Then a few people on the outside had to get inside the circle – by any means – so there were players trying to climb over, punch a hole in the circle, bribe their way in. It was to make the players in the circle work together and stay together. Then the players saw that the ones who got in really wanted to be there, and the ones that didn't want to know probably weren't going to make it. It's possibly the most perfect physical example of the ethos and ethic that Wimbledon had.

It was such a thrill to be involved in the football club, with the chance to get promoted with people that you genuinely liked and wanted to see succeed. I used to get a rush running on when a player went down. I had a rapport with the home fans, and would have a laugh with the away fans when I would run on with a little pink hat on my head, maybe do a little effeminate walk, all sorts of funny little things. And then if you knew a player went down, you knew he was injured too. It wasn't a time for namby-pambys, you had to be rough and tough. I remember Mick Smith took a blow to his face and played on, but then he blew his nose and his entire face puffed out.

The relationship between Harry and Wally was always like father and son. I think Harry would have liked to have been as naughty as Wally, but he always had to be a bit more reserved. They are both very intelligent people but, together, a dangerous combination. Wally, like most of the people Harry worked with, had almost a sixth sense in how he knew exactly what Harry wanted. Harry worked 24/7 and he expected everyone else to do the same – over all the years I have known him that has never changed.

I would never breach the confidence of the players to Harry. I always told them that what they said to me was private. If anyone ever came in to me and said they didn't feel right, then I would know there was something going on and they weren't right to train – it usually wasn't the reason they had given me, but I knew something was up – so I would let Harry know, or we would make something up. Well, that was until Fash came, and then it was a different story.

Fash used to walk up and say, 'Frenchie, I am expecting a very important phone call at 11 a.m., so you will see me limping at about 10.45 a.m., but don't say anything to Harry, will you?' And I would put on my James Bond secret service voice and whisper, 'Of course not, your secret is safe with me, John.' But I think Harry knew what was going on, the way Fash played back then you could forgive him plenty in training. I never got into any dispute with Fash about his fitness because he was always very much his own man, set apart from the rest a bit, and I knew he was one for Harry to deal with rather than me.

Because Harry is such a personality he can be your absolute best friend one minute and your worst enemy the next. But he will always end up back being your best friend again. He has that ability, he's a very strong character. When you think about all the flak he took during one time or another – accusations he was ruining football and all the rest of it – it never phased him, and he got people in who could help and support him. He needed that circle around him too because we had some tough times. He knew what he wanted from a player, but it's hard to know their character, so they would be given a tough time to see how they could cope.

Stevie Hatter always made me laugh – he was an East Ender, but I wouldn't say he was the toughest kid in the world. He would come in and gasp, 'Frenchie, my ankle! I have never seen an ankle like this in my life, the swelling is unbelievable.' As a centre-half that wasn't ideal, whereas someone like Mick Smith was virtually nuts.

Harry wasn't really interested in the medical side of things; he cared about players' well-being, but not particularly how it was achieved. He helped improve all the facilities we had, but it took a long time. We started off in the little room at Plough Lane where they kept the tills. The physio room was a tiny room at the end of the tunnel, 6 foot by 4.

Harry tested me throughout. One pre-season we were travelling over to Sweden at night when the players decided to hang me over the edge of the ferry. It was terrifying at the time, but if you went to Harry to complain he would tell you to fuck off. That went through the whole team, you had to be part of it. When you were ignored and not targeted that's when you knew you were not part of it.

Vinnie was made for it. When I told Harry about him he was at Bedmond, our local side – me and Vinnie had played together. I was always on at Harry about Vinnie because he was ideal for what we wanted to achieve.

Vinnie always wanted to make something of himself, he was driven. He travelled in with me for a year and he never offered me a penny for petrol money – tight bastard. But the beauty of it was I never had a company car: I just used my cab, and then an old banger, and then the club got me a VW Jetta which used to break down every fucking morning on the A3. Jonah had to get out and push it, and we would say that was his training programme.

I remember Corky breaking his leg. Although Corky was quiet he was a very strong man, and character, and he worked ever so hard to come back from his break. He returned as good as ever. We didn't have that many bad injuries back then. Wally had terrible luck with injuries, and I can imagine it was very hard for him. He was so lively and the instigator of so much that was happening. For him to have been out for as much as he was . . . how he coped with it, I don't know.

The problem for physios in those days was you were a one-man band. You had to look after maybe 30 pros, and even when we sent them to Lilleshall you never got a chance to speak to them. Wally was such a strong character, and people had a lot of respect for him. He is like a brother to me: we lived together and he has been such a big part of my life. He can be a nuisance and a pest but he is such a character, and he made characters of others. You didn't have to be in Wally's gang but it helped almost every one.

There was almost nothing that could have been done

with John Gannon's knees, certainly not back then, and it's testament to him that he had the career he did, because lesser men would not have got close to what he achieved. He had osteoarthritic knees as a kid, but he was such a battler. In 1983 I don't remember words like 'cruciate ligament' or 'metatarsal' even existing. I don't know if it's the change in footwear, or that players weren't as fit or didn't test their limits as much in those days, but I can't remember problems like that.

Games never really stuck with me, but I'll never forget Huddersfield. Gagey touching the free-kick to Sanch, and everyone thinking, 'Fucking hell, what's he knocking it to him for?' And the next second we were all giving it the big 'yeehah!' because he'd smashed it straight in. Harry went over set-pieces over and over again, and everything was done to death and by the book, so when that went in – a free-kick they had never ever worked on! – it was great. Going into the First Division then was nirvana, it was just so exciting to visit big clubs, to see the boot room at Liverpool. First Division sides would come to Plough Lane and be stunned by our facilities – or lack of – but we used that to our advantage. That corridor at Plough Lane, between the two dressing rooms, must have been, for a time, the most dangerous strip of land in England. There were some amazing fights down there, with opposition players sometimes getting dragged into the Wimbledon dressing room for a good whipping. It certainly wasn't the tunnel of love.

I saw the TV show and from a personal point of view

I thought Fash made it out to be far worse than it was – they tried to make it out to be like *Pulp Fiction*. I'm not saying no one got kicked or slapped, because they did, it happened, but it happened at most places back then. If people had a bit of mouth they would usually have to take a bit on the chin; other people gave us plenty as well. Alan Shearer always used to try to take the piss out of us. One time he was going on about how we were poor and our gear was crap, trying to look big in front of his mates. He didn't realize Jonah was behind him – Vinnie grabbed him by the ears and moved him politely out of the way.

Fash was made for Wimbledon: he was rough and tough and no one was ever going to take the piss out of him, and on his day he was unplayable. He frightened the life out of everyone; when he was shouting 'put it in the mixer' it would terrify defenders. It doesn't matter who you are – the fear factor always works. If you can frighten two or three out of 11 you've got an advantage; it was sledging but there were no TV cameras like there are now.

My whole life was fun – we had to have fun at work; we had to have fun after. I went on an acupuncture course once, to help improve vitality and vigour among players before games. I did it for three weeks then Harry came in with the hump over something else completely but decided to lay into me: 'What is this bollocks? There's been no change, I haven't seen any improvement.' In the end I said, 'Neither have I, Harry, but at least four of them have stopped smoking.'

Wally

Here's something the Frenchman didn't tell you. On this first trip to Finland we had a team meeting where Harry introduced him as a new addition to his staff, and asked him to say a few words by way of introduction. All was going well and everything was quite plausible till he had to finish off with a slight mistake. I think it was along the lines of, 'All I DEMAND is respect.' Oh dear. A few of us started to shift about in our chairs, one or two exchanged glances, and the blood drained from Harry's face. That evening we were playing a local team. It was always a big deal for them, the whole town would turn out. They were just warm-up games for us, and we'd always win comfortably before playing more difficult sides as the tour gained momentum. In this game we were 2 or 3 up at half-time and all was going well when I said to Hodge, 'Go down on the far side as though you're injured.' He did, and Frenchie was called on by the officials for his first professional appearance with the bucket and sponge. It was a very hot night, and while he was diagnosing a non-existent injury I emptied the bucket of water over his head. He went nuts and jumped up, fuming and soaked. We all pissed ourselves, including Hodge, who had made a full recovery by now. Frenchie couldn't control himself and started coming towards me. I was 5 foot 11 inches and 12 stone of muscle at the time. Frenchie was 5 foot 3 inches, 8 stone and soaking wet but I still decided to turn and run, and he began chasing me. It was like *Benny Hill*. Even the ref was laughing! Frenchie stopped when he knew he couldn't catch me, and stormed off.

He'd calmed down after the game, and we were over it – although at first he flatly refused to go out that night. Eventually he saw the funny side and had come round by the time we were on the coach, going to the night-club that was laying on the hospitality for the two teams. When we got there it seemed the whole town was queuing up to get in and meet us. Unfortunately for Derek, once inside, they were showing the incident with the bucket virtually on a loop all night, and people were rolling up about it . . . and then laughing even more when they spotted him. It didn't take him long to turn this to his advantage, and he became a Swedish TV star overnight. He became such a big part of everything we did from then on, and played a great part in getting me back through injuries over the years. I must have been a right bollock-ache for him, with three breaks in four years, but his help and friendship made it easy to come in to work every day. That physio room was such a funny place to be, and he's a great physio – if slightly unhinged. I love him.

Frenchie also told me that: 'I want it on record that Harry never won anything without me being at the club . . .'

Harry

I'll have you for that, Frenchie.

One other honour bestowed upon the club after our promotion was the first ever Bernard Joy Memorial Award, named after the *Evening Standard*'s former football correspondent. Joy was an ex-Arsenal and England amateur player whose guiding principles were commitment, resilience and integrity, so obviously it was a proud moment to be associated with the same qualities. I'm not sure the wider football fraternity would have agreed, though!

As the *Standard* article published to coincide with the award revealed, with average salaries at around £240 a week, money was hardly the major motivating factor for the players, especially when you took into consideration how much they'd then lose in fines. Our poor disciplinary record continued to haunt us: we were hauled before the FA for the third consecutive year and hit with a whopping £2,000 fine that summer after massing a total of 289 penalty points. Of course we had a physical approach, and sometimes it was just a touch of over-enthusiasm on behalf of the players but, obviously, we didn't want it weighing round our necks. 'It's something we've not been proud of,' I boldly assured the *Standard* reporter, 'and we've taken steps to improve it. I've tried to impress on the players the need to cut out retaliation. In the past when one of the lads has taken a wallop he's invariably felt the need to retaliate, but gradually we are getting that out of the system. We have our own internal punishment for dismissals and cautions and, for each offence, the penalty increases. We still get the odd stupid incident but we're improving and will continue to do so.'

Of course, even I came under this increased scrutiny, being known for the odd loud word or ill-advised action. Then I would have to fine myself, and I did. I remember when Fash turned up the morning of his debut, at Portsmouth on Easter Saturday 1986, the players fined him £30 for wearing jeans and a casual shirt. They loved it. This was all part of fostering the team spirit, the fact that we were all in it together. Sam, by the way, got a £30 fine too for the same offence.

Hodges was a particular serial offender. Here's how he remembers it: 'One year I broke the record for the most disciplinary points totted up, with 52. I had to go up to the FA quite a few times. At one stage they wanted to send a representative to check out my background and meet my parents. I was getting in so much trouble that they thought I was from a seriously troubled background, or some sort of nutcase. They wanted to unearth what the problem with me was. It was always dissent. I once got booked for 'visual dissent'. Work that one out – I didn't say or do anything physical and got done for 'visual dissent', and Harry fucking fined me. There were no gestures or anything; I just looked at him and got booked. With Bassett you could fight, punch and kick and hold your ground and not get fined, but dissent was the worst of the worst and was always fineable, so I was always in trouble.'

When you're the poorest team in the league, you're also closer to the fans; all the players contributed money – £60 each for the year in our promotion season into the First Division – to the club lottery. That sort of thing meant that we had more of a perspective than those fancy-pants clubs up north or wherever. 'Football's not life and death, is it?' was my response to one reporter in 1986. 'There's more of a problem in Soweto.'

As the First Division season drew near, everyone at the club paused for breath and took stock of what had been achieved. Reaching the top rung of the English football ladder within nine years of being elected to the Football League was simply a unique achievement, a part of football history that would never be written again. Wimbledon, a small, unfashionable club, had proved that anyone could be successful, without million-pound players, palatial stands and bags of money. It bugs me to this day, though, that Sam Hammam never treated all the players and staff to a memento for the remarkable achievement. A Rolex each would have been peanuts for him.

Sam and I had decided, as a treat after reaching the First Division, that we'd go to watch the 1986 FA Cup final between Liverpool and Everton. Perhaps it wasn't such a good idea. I remember Sam saying to me afterwards, 'My God! How are we going to cope with the likes of them?' 'Them' being Everton's Peter Reid, Kevin Sheedy, Kevin Ratcliffe, Trevor Steven and Graeme Sharp; then from the red side of town, Bruce Grobbelaar, Mark Lawrenson, Alan Hansen, Craig Johnston, Steve Nicol and Ronnie Whelan (although we did sigh when we got to Ian Rush. He was off to Juventus.).

I replied that on paper we had no chance, but I thought we would do all right. We had a team that had achieved the virtually impossible and secured their own piece of utopia. These were players who a few years ago were grubbing around the Fourth Division, earning peanuts – they still did in 1986 – but had a unique spirit. They had been told they weren't good enough for the Fourth Division and won promotion. They were told the same about the other divisions and were now in a land of fairytales. I knew they wouldn't buckle in the heat – bigger names would only give them a bigger challenge.

Then we had another ace up our sleeves in Dennis Wise. I believed he was soon ready to jump from youth- and reserve-team football into the first team. The same went for Andy Sayer who, as he said, went on to become the first player to score a top-flight hat-trick for Wimbledon. I wasn't frightened and I told Sam the team weren't either. For sure, I said, we would come unstuck on the odd occasion and get a hammering, but we also had the self-belief to succeed. Hellfire – of course it was daunting, but I knew there were a lot of strong characters in our dressing room that wouldn't back down.

But at the time the likes of Brian Talbot slaughtered

us in the press, telling the world, 'They will get killed with their style of football.' There were also a lot of other naïve people who didn't know what went into achieving our success. They spoke because they didn't know how to handle a side hell-bent on winning, a side who were well-organized and from the hard school of knocks.

There was an art to it. Some see a Turner picture and think it's fuzzy and uninviting; others see it as a masterpiece. My choice of art is more portraits and landscapes – like Italy's Lake Como in all its glory. It is a personal thing, but I wouldn't criticize those who like abstracts or Turner. Get on with life.

I told Sam I needed another striker and eventually we offered £90,000 for Colin Gordon from Swindon. Duff move on my part. My staff, usually excellent at spotting talent, said he would suit us, but I wasn't so sure. We concluded the deal and shook hands, and I immediately thought, 'Have I dropped a bollock here?' If I had been more ruthless I would have ended the deal and pulled out there and then. My gut feeling proved right. Colin made only two league starts for us.

My only other signing almost gave Sam a heart-attack. I said I wanted to buy Vinnie Jones from non-league Wealdstone for £10,000. Sam thought I was fucking mad. He asked, 'How do you expect a non-league player to go up against the likes of those we've seen in the Cup final? The step up would be too much for him!'

Allen Batsford, who was now the manager at Wealdstone, had marked my card about Jones. 'You might like this player,' he told me – and I went along to a few of his matches. I liked his determination, desire, belief, and had seen him do some good things. He could score goals and was strong as a lion. Sam still thought I was a loony. I mentioned to Sam that we were only going to pay him £120 a week and if it didn't work out he could always be used to help cut the grass or paint the stands. Sam liked the idea of not losing much money and agreed the deal.

During talks with Vinnie I told him he'd be on £150 a week, plus £50 a goal and £50 per appearance in the first team. Then I told him, 'That's it. See you tomorrow.' Vinnie loitered, so I asked, 'What's up?' He replied something like, 'Any chance of a signing-on fee?' I told him, 'No. Now fuck off. I've given you your chance.' (I later gave him £150 to buy his first suit!) Vinnie came to my house for those talks, and I remember Christine saying, 'He's nice, handsome, but not the brightest spark.' I replied, 'Don't worry, he's a footballer. They're all like that.'

I decided to send Vinnie to Sweden during the coming weeks, after telling the club Holmsund he was a Wimbledon player. Which actually he wasn't, at that point. I warned him that if he just once stepped out of line, blotted his and Wimbledon's copy-book, then the deal was off. He accepted the terms, secured himself his first passport, and left. He was a success there. The club and fans loved him and, although he was playing in a league lower than Wealdstone, was named their player of the season. But he still wasn't ready for us. There was a lot more learning yet. It eventually came against Brian Clough's Nottingham Forest in the November of 1986. He was crap, and even gave away a penalty. More on that shortly.

In our build-up to Division One we travelled to Finland for our pre-season, and it went reasonably well, even though we lodged in rather cheap dwellings. We had been invited to play Finland's under-21 side. So we took a coach to Helsinki and turned into the forecourt of a five-star hotel. I could see the eyes of the team lighting up like Christmas trees as we drew closer to the front steps. 'Now it's the big time and payback,' they thought, as the coach drove up the tree-lined driveway . . . only for it to keep going until we reached some youth hostel in the forest next to the hotel.

Each room had paper cups and paper towels. Fash's face was a picture: one minute he was contemplating five-star luxury, now he was confronted by bunk beds with no sheets. To their credit, the players simply got on with it, again proving to me this was a team of characters, not Charlie Big Potatoes.

19
Reaching the Top

Wally

I HAD A PRETTY good view of us gatecrashing the First Division party as I'd broken my fucking leg . . . AGAIN! I made a point of travelling to all the games that I could but, believe it or not, the finances were still such that it wasn't always doable for overnight stops. What I saw were the makings – and the breaking – of a very good side; the side that had got us so far, but had now lost some players who had served their time superbly and were being replaced by younger players with more potential.

Harry had allowed me to sit with him during games. His insight into how the game was going and how a manager could affect things would hold me in good stead later on when I embarked on my own coaching career – although how on earth he ever had the bare-faced effrontery to sub me, I'll never know: it defied logic!

Fash was the only real addition to the promotion push. Although it was late in the season, it was a great buy by Harry as Fash's impetus and presence, aligned to the fact that the club had paid a record sum for him, showed the opposition, our fans and, more importantly, the players themselves that we meant business and were not going to fall away as the winning line came into view.

I'm sure the glory of Sanch's goal at Huddersfield will be better described elsewhere (probably by him!) but in the stand nobody was screaming louder than me. It was a goal deserving of all the efforts that everyone – from the people at the café to Sid Neale, Joe Dillon and Judy Ryan in the laundry, up to all the chairmen – had put in over the years.

Then he goes and does it again at fucking Wembley! All the industry and work that Sanch did for the team went largely unheralded, but he was a strong fucker, who allowed you to play when you played with him, and here he was, finally getting the glory – bastard! Thank God I'd left before the Wembley goal.

Sanch raised his game, as we all had to when we went up, and although not as daft as a few of the lads, he was quirky and funny enough to become one of the Wimbledon greats. His single-mindedness and idiosyncrasies made him as crazy as any of the Crazy Gang, and it came as no surprise to me that he remained through all the difficulties that the club later went through – and went on to great success as a manager and coach.

None of us were overawed by the fact that we had made it to the top flight; we had always shown a certain degree of irreverence to all the challenges put before us, and this new challenge was no different. We always prepared meticulously and trained very professionally all week. To be able to test ourselves against the best on a regular basis was something we were all prepared to take on.

If we had been in any way unsure of our right to be in the First Division, opponents would have sensed this, and defeats would have come thick and fast. As usual, though, we took up the challenge and had a great start – to the extent we shook up the football world by being top after four games. This, while still having the smallest transfer budget, lowest wage bill and smallest crowds in the league. But by now all that was no big deal for us – it had been the situation in every division we had ever been in, the only difference this time around was that it was increased probably by a factor of ten.

The reason we had come to this point in our journey so unfazed by it all was that we had an unshakeable belief and trust in each other as a team – respect for all our individual talents and abilities whatever they were. We were the epitome of a symbiotic team, which came from the way we were managed and coached by Harry and Alan. As has been noted, they were very different characters, and also had very different coaching methods, but both were able to get across any relevant point to the entire group as quickly for the fastest learner as for the person who didn't quite grasp the detail of that particular session. Contrary to popular belief, footballers are far from thick – on any given day it may have taken a bit of time for the penny to drop for the brightest of the group, while the most cognitively challenged may have got it immediately. There was no way of telling, but Alan or Harry would get the message across. That's not to say that whoever was being a bit dozy didn't get ripped to shreds by the rest of us in this supremely gifted and intelligent group!

A lot of our work was based around repetition on the training pitch, but it was also backed up by statistical and video analysis – and while our critics were quick to point out how aesthetically repugnant they found our game, Harry would find video clips of the best teams, past and present, who played a high-intensity pressurizing game. AC Milan could adopt a more direct approach, believe it or not, and Liverpool, Everton and Arsenal played more balls back to front than any others. And so it would go on – examples every week of effective football, how to eliminate errors in your own half while in possession (God forbid anybody who played a square ball that got cut out!), the most effective way to score from wide areas, the importance of winning the ball back quickly in the opposition's half, which is now called 'pressing high', as practised by Barcelona, no less!

We were shown how important all these things were; if you got good players believing you and putting it into practice, you were halfway there. But now we were beyond halfway there. We were . . . THERE! All we had to do was stay there. It wasn't easy to play that way either. You constantly had to play the ball into the right areas, and everyone had to be on their game. Everyone knew exactly where they were supposed to be. We worked on it every day. It was complex and draining, especially the shadow sessions – without even a ball to kick around.

There were excellent players coming through our youth set-up: Geoff Taylor was always championing his players to Harry whenever his input was called for – or, more to the point, when it wasn't called for. Geoff was the perfect man for teaching kids how to play football – he had a sound football philosophy, a constant hunger to adopt and adapt new ideas, while maintaining the core beliefs of hard work and endeavour. As much as he loved all his kids, they all knew who was boss. Sean Priddle, Johnny Gannon, Brian Gayle, Andy Thorn, Andy Sayer, Andy Clement, Simon Tracey – all of them were brought through by Geoff, and all of them made valuable contributions and, as we went up to the First Division, all were, unfortunately, about to put pressure on some of us who were in the team. And that was credit to Geoff Taylor. Geoff kicked every ball of every game with the youth team – I even once saw him travel down the touchline at Richardson Evans at the same speed as the move the team were executing, culminating with his diving header on the touchline, much to the surprise of the linesman right behind him.

Johnny Gannon was a youngster who got a lot of stick

off the lads, as first Dario and then Geoff championed him to the first team. Dario even once told us he had an 11-year-old who was better than all of us! We couldn't wait to find him and scurf him about, but it proved not to be a million miles from the truth.

Geoff used to fancy himself at pool but would only play for 50p, so he got the nickname 'Bullseye', or just 'Taylor', from the first team. We were playing pool one day and I said, 'Come on, me and you, Taylor.' 'You're on,' he replied and racked them up, took my 50p and was rejoicing in his victory when Gannon, an apprentice at the time, said, 'I'm next, Taylor.' Geoff flew across the table, picked Gannon up with one hand, and said to him, menacingly, '"Mr Taylor" to you, boy!' The whole place erupted, and none of Geoff's 'young spunkers' (as he called them) ever called him 'Taylor' again until they were in the first team. Geoff was and still is a great coach, and our debt to him should never be underestimated.

We trained really hard and were meticulous in our preparation; we had signals for all of our corners and free-kicks, even down to how and when we'd come out to catch people offside. It was a different game then, and that was a legitimate way to catch teams that weren't too bothered about working on movement and losing markers at set-plays. We were self-regulating, all aware of our roles and responsibilities – but if you got it wrong you could be sure you would be told in no uncertain terms. There could be flare-ups over the tiniest thing that someone had forgotten but, as in all great teams, anything that was said was said for the good of the group and quickly forgotten. Nothing ever lingered and no grudges were ever held.

This applied to Harry and Gillett as well – they could roast you at half-time (if we hadn't already done it ourselves!) but by Monday it was gone and we were moving on. Everything was done for the good of the group, from the youngest apprentice upwards – there was no hierarchy, nobody was better than anyone else, and if anyone came for any of us they'd have the rest of us to deal with as well.

The reason we weren't liked when we made it to Division One was that we had come up the hardest way possible, from the Fourth to the First, and you don't do that with shrinking violets. But, in truth, we had become good players as well. So if teams wanted to try to outrun, outplay or outpass us, we could accommodate them; and if they wanted to come at it physically, then our upbringing as kids playing hard bastards up north in the Fourth Division stood us in very good stead too.

Everywhere you looked there was someone coming through – Vaughan Ryan, say – and they were often fast-tracked. Vaughan had been at the club since he was a kid and was, as usual, championed by Geoff; when he was a youngster he'd been allowed on a first-team trip and had had breakfast and the pre-match meal with us. I think he was even allowed in the team meeting; that may not sound much of a big deal, but when your aspiration in life is to be a footballer, it's the sort of experience that inspires you. We all took an instant liking to Vaughan as he was a lively kid, a bit trappy and generally full of himself – so he fitted right in.

I'm not saying it doesn't happen everywhere, but we were very inclusive at the Dons, and it was terrible news that Vaughan had lost his dad. Nobody can know how that affects a family, but it wasn't long before Judy, Vaughan's mum, had a job at the club's training ground – and what a great signing she was! She ruled the laundry in no uncertain terms, wouldn't stand any of our bollocks, and always had a cup of tea ready for you if required. There was a lot of love at the club, and I don't remember one real fight in my 11 years there – although we were like young lion cubs skirmishing every day. But you knew you couldn't ever fuck about with Smithy and the Midget . . . he was too strong and couldn't play!

When Vinnie arrived, he showed massive enthusiasm and was keen to join in with everything that went on. Harry asked me to look after him, saying he had something but that he might rub a few up the wrong way! To be honest, though, Jonah was coming through like a fucking asteroid heading for the Dons bar. He had great big ears, big eyes and was willing to listen and willing to learn. Vinnie travelled in with the country boys. Even if we were all in it together, like anywhere, there were different factions at the club. The country boys started with Peter Brown, Paul Bowgett, Paul Haverson, Phil Driver and Frenchie – then, for some reason, Gagey too. They would come into Richardson Evans in a convoy of shocking Vauxhall Vivas, Volkswagen Jetties and anything else.

I'm biased, of course, but they were never going to take over from the west London influence at the club. That started with me and Steve Parsons when we were kids – Harry's team hadn't seen anything like us two – then Lurch (or Dave as he's started calling himself), then Knowlesy, Joe and Wisey to top the lot off. We had so much belief in ourselves as a group that we could influence the shrinking violets to come with us anywhere we went.

Another faction were the boys away from home in digs: Corky, Midget, Paul Denny, Gary Armstrong – and the fella who we gave probably the hardest time to . . . Adolf Hitler! At least that's what we called Dean Thomas, a left-back with a long throw and a great shot – a great lad we signed from Nuneaton Borough, who came with a dodgy Midlands moustache and a ferocious side parting, hence the nickname. He just couldn't see the resemblance, though.

The 'spine' has become a buzz word for teams today – get the spine right and you'll be all right. Well, ours for all seasons and all eventualities had been Lurch, Smithy, Ketts and the Midget, with Corky up front. The rest of us sort of flitted around, but we could 100 per cent rely on those five. During the coming season, though, it would be all change, and my time had just about come.

We knew we had really arrived when we were invited to the Harry Secombe golf tournament at Kingswood golf club in Surrey – and to be honest, it was clear I was going to be spending a lot more time on the golf course. I probably played only about 30 games from the age of 24 till I packed up at 28, and that season I would manage only 18 games in the First Division before breaking my leg again against Coventry.

It was all my fault – we were getting the run around at home, and I said to Vin, 'We gotta do something here to disrupt their flow.' Which was our speak for putting a bit of physical about. So I went in very enthusiastically, shall we say, only to cop their player's studs right through my ankle. I tried to get up and get back but it was a mess, and that was the end of the Suburban League to the First Division journey for me.

After that Vinnie's personality and influence began to grow amongst the group. I watched and thought, 'This is a natural progression.' He got louder and louder, but he was good with it – and he was great in the dressing room. The one thing you can say about Vinnie is that throughout his career, whatever he has done, he has grabbed everything with both hands and made a success of it. He has done fantastic.

I've stayed in contact with Vinnie more than any of the other lads over the years, and all I'll say is, if one of your mates winds up being a Hollywood movie star, you'd want them to do it the way he has! He is still the same, and his door is always open – that is, on Mulholland Drive, in the Hollywood Hills, Los Angeles, California, next to fucking Quentin Tarantino!

When Vin got his debut, nobody was more surprised than him. He'd been doing well in the reserves and was training with the first team, learning all the time about what was required in midfield. When Harry handed out the bibs for the Forest away game, he threw the green bib at me and then slung the next one at Vin. Fancy making your league debut in the top flight! It wasn't the best debut anyone's ever had – he gave a pen away – but then he went and stuck one in against Man Utd on his home debut a week later, when we did them 1–0.

Vin got a bit ahead of himself later on in that game: Remi Moses got subbed after about an hour and Vin gave him a bit of stick as he went off, something along the lines of, 'You ain't had a kick anyway.' He looked over to me, winked and said, 'That's the hard work done now anyway.' I looked over Vin's shoulder to see Captain Marvel, Bryan Robson, just about the best midfield player in the world, entering the fray. I nodded to Jonah to have a look. He did, and when he turned back to me you could see it was an 'oh FFS' moment, but we both rolled up laughing as Robbo ran on. 'What the fuck are you two laughing about?' was all he said. Well, he was England captain! But he hated playing us.

Vin was my roommate and, contrary to popular belief, we always prepared professionally. In fact we were like a couple of old poofs, making tea, watching a film and going to sleep with quiz questions. His chosen subject was the living world, which is fairly expansive, while mine was *Caddyshack*.

I'll leave it to Harry now to tell the story of that amazing season when we went on to finish 6th in the league, our highest ever position, and get to the quarter-finals of the FA Cup for the first time. What a ride it had been for me: three broken legs, a broken knee cap, packed up at 28, then missed out on the Sky money when that came in! But I wouldn't swap it for one minute.

20

Wombles from the Lane

Harry

MY 42ND BIRTHDAY will always be one of my best memories because we were only top of the fucking league.

Our first game in the top flight was at Maine Road. Our chief executive, Colin Hutchinson, had been waxing lyrical before the match, saying that 'football is all about fairytale and romance', and when we took the lead against Man City, with an Andy Thorn free-kick drifting into the corner of their net, that really did seem on the cards. The game changed, though, when Paul Simpson came on as a sub for Ian Brightwell. He ran John Kay ragged and created three goals in quick succession, two for Graham Baker and one for Trevor Christie. City didn't win again for another 12 league games.

I thought we didn't deserve to get beat, but that match was also notable for David Beasant setting the record for most uninterrupted league appearances – 226 dating back to May 1981 – as Liverpool's Bruce Grobbelaar was injured. It was a fantastic run of consistency.

Our opening First Division game at Plough Lane was against Aston Villa, three days later, and a look at the match stats tells me there were 6,366 there to witness five goals, a red card and a penalty. You want entertainment? I dropped Kay for Gagey, and he scored the late penalty that gave us the three points, with Villa already down to ten men, Gary Williams having laid into Hodges. Up and running. Glyn had opened the scoring in that game, thus becoming the first Wimbledon player to score in all four divisions.

We then beat Leicester in midweek – Dennis Wise taking star billing, turning out to be the player I thought he was, and Corky on target to ensure he too had scored in all four divisions. Mark Bright was Leicester's dunce, missing a couple of sitters. 'We have had a hard and hectic week and have been surrounded by a helluva hullaballoo. We are completely drained,' I complained to the papers, but we were nicely set up for a trip to Selhurst Park to play Charlton the following Saturday. The eleven picked themselves really: Beasant, Gage, Morris, Smith, Winterburn; Galliers, Sanchez, Hodges and Wise; Cork, Fashanu. Charlton had just won at Old Trafford, but we kept it tight and they barely got a sniff. Then, with three minutes to go, Sanch drove the ball into the goalmouth, Fash's shot was blocked and Dennis looped the ball over their keeper. We were top of the league. I only realized when I was told the other results at the post-match press conference, but it was another milestone in the amazing story of the Crazy Gang, made even sweeter by the fact that a certain Ted Croker had been at the game (although he had left his seat in the directors' box before Wisey's late goal). Lennie Lawrence was, as usual, generous in his praise: 'What upset me most was that we weren't out-classed, but outfought. We were always second best.' He said that all the people who had knocked Wimbledon and written us off should think again. 'Their total commitment is fantastic.'

As for me, the papers were now falling over themselves asking for interviews. 'All I can say is, "Blow me!"' I said. 'It's not so much two fingers up to Ted Croker. We've made our point already. And he probably regrets saying that now because football needs clubs like Wimbledon. It's an example for all others to follow. It should give heart to clubs like Rochdale and Scunthorpe, who can believe they will do the same one day. The small clubs count. We've proved that the Wimbledons of this world should be part of the Football League and Division One. I think we've made our point. If you make the First Division a closed shop it will be boring.

'At least if we are relegated,' I then joked, 'we can say we have been top of the league. My mum will want the season to end tomorrow.'

Stanley Reed even got a poster of the league table framed. 'I don't normally make a thing about my birthdays,' I told the *Express*, but this time I think I can afford to have a little toast with the family.'

All the attention allowed us a chance to put our side of the story, to respond to the tired accusation from our many critics that we had no place at the top of the table. 'Where they're absolutely wrong,' I said, warming to the theme, 'is to say we're not good for football. I watched Barcelona in the final of the European Cup [that dreadful 0–0 draw against Steaua Bucharest] and thought it was one of the biggest yawns I'd ever seen. At Wimbledon we guarantee you goalmouth action . . . particularly at our end.

'Of course, it's all a bit of a joke,' I continued, 'but a lot of people would like to be a king, if only for a day. We're enjoying it.'

As it turned out, we were kings for a little more than a day. The players were full of confidence, and two days after my birthday we got a third 1–0 win on the spin, at Watford, scoring even later than at Charlton, thanks to Hodges poking the ball through their keeper's legs in the last minute. So much for action at our end – Lurch hardly had a save to make, apart from a brilliant one-handed stop to deny Luther Blissett in the first half, and although John Barnes looked dangerous, he didn't have a shot on target.

I tried to ensure the players kept their feet on the floor. 'We're trying to make sure we haven't got too many big-heads in the team,' I told the press, while Watford manager Graham Taylor paid us tribute: 'It shows how crafty they are because the longer people think they just play up-and-under football, the better chance they've got. I think they'll finish in the top half. Wimbledon are a very well-drilled side – they are good, honest lads and have every right to be top. It would be foolish for any other First Division team to underestimate them.'

Another Bell's Whisky manager of the month award was on my sideboard, but it couldn't last. Our eleven days as leaders of Division One came to an end with a 2–1 defeat against Everton, in front of an attendance of 11,708 at Plough Lane. I have to confess that I think Howard Kendall was more than a match for me that day. Knowing what to expect, they played five men at the back, including a sweeper, to handle our attacks. 'It was a mark of respect,' I said after the game. 'I take that as a compliment because I haven't seen them play like that before. It is up to us to overcome that sort of tactic.'

We didn't help ourselves by conceding an early goal, Trevor Steven taking advantage of a slip by Guppy to cross for Kevin Sheedy, who drove home. 'A bit of a Fred Karno goal,' I called it. Corky got the equalizer before Graeme Sharp was given a free header. 'That is the difference at this level. When you make a mistake, top players accept the opportunities, while others are not quite up to it.' I was referring to Wisey, who had the best chance late on. 'He couldn't hit a cow's arse with a banjo,' I remarked. 'And some of our crosses were rubbish. When you play against the sweeper system you have got to centre accurately. Today the pie man behind the goal was in more danger than Bobby Mimms.'

But 12 points out of 18 was hardly a bad start to the season, and Everton's England international centre-half Dave Watson paid us credit after the game too. 'There is just no let-up,' he said. 'The pressure is constant and you know that when you go for the ball there will be an opponent right at you. I finished on the losing side twice against them when I was at Norwich last season, and there are a lot of teams who are going to find it hard work down here this season.'

That Everton defeat, however, kicked off a run of eight games without a win, including a pathetic exit in the League Cup at the hands of Cambridge United. We steadied the ship by beating Norwich, and then there was an infamous game against Spurs at White Hart Lane.

Sanch was an idiot in that match, getting sent off along with Graham Roberts. He retaliated and he deserved to go, but even though Fash scored our winner from a set-piece routine, he was the centre of attention for being too physical, with a challenge on Gary Stevens resulting in the Spurs player being stretchered off with a broken collarbone.

Then at Stamford Bridge the following month, we gave Chelsea a 4–0 mullering but all the talk was about Doug Rougvie's red card, for headbutting Fash, an incident which sparked a mass brawl. He was a nutter that day, Rougvie – 'a one-man demolition squad' the papers called him – and he had already been booked for an off-the-ball incident with Carlton Fairweather. Yet it was us who got the blame for causing the fights, who got slaughtered for our bad image.

I was sick of the way we were being portrayed and didn't hold back in my comments to the press, talking about how soft players had become. 'They tackle like a lot of pansy potters,' I said. 'There's no comparison between now and a few years back. To say our players act like Desperate Dan is ridiculous. I reckon they are more like Lettuce Leaf. I think it's cleaner than ever now. It's just unfortunate the official organs have put more pressure on the referees and players than there has ever been. I'm not whingeing. This is a man's game, and my only regret is that it's gone a bit soft. There are too many wimps around in the First Division for my liking. There's too much moaning about everything. About referees, about decisions, and about players on other teams. Some of the bigger established teams think they should be given decisions just because of who they are.'

That Chelsea game came, however, after the Wimbledon debut of one Vince Jones, as he was called at the time, which was only going to add fuel to the fire in the debate about our approach to the game. I hardly need to relate the Vinnie story – he's become that famous, and we'll let him tell it in his inimitable way in a minute – but Vinnie had bundles of enthusiasm and, even though he may have lacked some of the basics, it was clear that he was desperate to make it as a professional footballer. That was enough for me. You always need someone like that in your team.

To be fair, though, Vinnie was so shit in his first game, against Nottingham Forest at the City Ground, that it's a surprise he ever turned out for us again. At half-time he asked Sid, our kit man, how he thought he'd played. 'If that's the best you can do, why don't you keep your shirt, because if it was left to me you'd never get another one,' Sid told him. Punching Franz Carr's cross away for a penalty was definitely not the brightest thing Jonah ever did. Nigel Clough converted it, and his dad got one over me for the first time, Johnny Metgod making it 3–2 to them in the end with a scorcher of a free-kick. Needless to say, I wasn't happy.

So, by all rights, Vinnie should not have started the next game, but with Midget injured and Sanch out too, I decided to give him another chance. We were at home to Manchester United, who had not been enjoying the best of seasons. After they went out of the League Cup in a replay at Southampton, clobbered 4–1, their manager, Big Ron Atkinson, had been given the elbow. In his place came Alex Ferguson, who'd been doing well at Aberdeen, but was new to the English game. It was 6 November 1986 he was appointed – a date with destiny written all over it. Two days later, Alex took charge of his first Man Utd match, and suffered a 2–0 defeat at Oxford. A 0–0 draw at Norwich hardly lessened the pressure on him – and he had to overcome a culture of drinking within the club – but when they came to Plough Lane, his team were on the back of a 1–0 win against QPR at Old Trafford.

To be fair to Alex, who I'm proud to say has been a good friend ever since, his team were well beaten that day, with only Bryan Robson, who came on as a second-half substitute, coming close to scoring for them. And letting Jonah get free from a Hodges corner to head home the only goal of the game just before half-time must have resulted in his players receiving the old hair-dryer treatment.

Vinnie was, of course, ecstatic, running over like a mad man to celebrate his goal with his dad Peter, mum Linda and 30 mates in the stands who had travelled down to Plough Lane from Hertfordshire. 'I didn't even expect to be playing,' Vinnie said after the game. 'Last week I made my debut at Nottingham Forest and it was my family's biggest day in years. Now this – it's a fairytale.'

I have always liked Fergie. He was one of the few managers who never, ever criticized us in public, either while I was there or after I left. He always invited me into his room for a drink and was forthcoming. But I think that defeat changed his whole perception of the club. He looked at us and witnessed a team of no stars but players who were willing to fight for their club. His team was littered with big names, but we actually did the double over United that season. Still, Sir Alex went on to do all right, didn't he?

Vinnie, the former hod carrier, then only went and scored in the next game – that 4–0 win at Stamford Bridge which was our biggest victory in the First Division to date (and our biggest brawl too) – and in the next game too, when we put Howard Wilkinson's Sheffield Wednesday to the sword, 3–0 at Plough Lane. To say that he was becoming a fans' favourite was an understatement. And before too long, his long throws were causing havoc in opposition boxes. As far as I can recall, the first time that led to a Wimbledon goal was when we took on Watford just after New Year, when Carlton flicked his throw on and Andy Sayer scored with a diving header. Vinnie scored in that game too! What a signing he was proving to be. A talisman. The cards certainly tumbled right for him and Vinnie was never to look back.

It was then FA Cup time, and what a run we would enjoy in that famous old competition. We started against Sunderland, then in the Second Division under the management of Lawrie McMenemy, and we were heading for an early exit before Sanch converted from Hodge's corner – set-pieces proving our salvation again – before Hodge got the last-minute winner himself. Portsmouth were easily disposed of in the Fourth Round, 4–0, with Fash again getting up their noses, and that of their manager Alan Ball, with a couple of goals. That brought Everton to Plough Lane for a Fifth Round clash on Sunday, 22 February 1986.

Everton had only been denied the FA Cup by Liverpool in the first all-Merseyside FA Cup final the previous year, and the two clubs, truth be told, dominated not just English but European football at the time – at least before the Heysel ban, which Howard Kendall's team was still seething about, as it had prevented them from having a tilt at the European Cup (they'd already lifted the Cup Winners' Cup in 1985). They were a seriously good team – probably better than Liverpool at the time – with Neville Southall in goal; defenders like Kevin Ratcliffe, Dave Watson and Pat Van Den Hauwe, who could match our physicality; skilful midfielders in abundance – Paul Bracewell, Trevor Steven, Peter Reid, Kevin Sheedy; and goalscorers up front in Graeme Sharp and Adrian Heath. They would go on to win the league at a canter that season, nine points clear of Liverpool, and in addition to knocking us off the top of the table in September, had given us the runaround at Goodison before Christmas, winning 3–0. Plus, for me at least, there was the memory of that 8–0 hammering they'd given us back in 1978.

So the scene was set for an epic Cup clash. Sunday lunchtime, live on the BBC, a party atmosphere, and I'm told many of our fans had come straight from parties that had gone on all Saturday night, clutching leftover cans of lager or lukewarm bottles of Blue Nun in their hands. Plough Lane was rocking. Luckily for us too, Sharp was missing – even our big lads at the back found him a handful with his aerial prowess – but his replacement, Paul Wilkinson, gave Everton a flying start, heading home from Heath's cross after he had rounded Bez, our defence having been split by a clever Steven pass to put the striker clear.

Just before half-time – always a good time to score, as everyone knows – we got the equalizer. Sanch won the ball in midfield to put Fash through, and he held off Gary Stevens for pace before going tumbling in the box. Did he dive? Who knows? Who cares? Gagey was our penalty-taker, and he had never missed from the spot, getting one against Charlton the previous weekend. But this time, in front of a sea of hostile Everton fans, Southall saved brilliantly down low to his right. Hodges was right on the rebound – as was Fash – to poke the ball home. Sniffing – just what the players are meant to do when a pen is saved. Good work, boys.

Fifteen minutes into the second half, it was Fash on target. Leo had got on the end of another huge punt from Bez, and when his shot was saved, there was our number nine to sweep the ball into the net again. And he returned the favour to set up Sayer for the clincher fifteen minutes from time. Same tactic, same result. It was one of the best results in the club's history, summed up by Martin Tyler's words on the commentary, which you can find on YouTube: 'There's yet another chapter in the glorious history of Wimbledon Football Club.'

Plough Lane shook to the rafters with the fans singing at the top of their voices.

We are Wombles
We are Wombles
We are Wombles from the Lane
We drink champagne
We snort cocaine
We are Wombles from the Lane

We were in the quarter-finals of the FA Cup for the first time.

Three weeks later, Tottenham were the visitors to Plough Lane. Another team with bad Cup memories for the Dons. Maybe that was an omen? Another Sunday, live on the telly again (this time ITV), the ground heaving, the atmosphere making the hairs stand up on your neck.

Leo had got a hat-trick in our last home game, against Newcastle, but neither he nor Fash, or Carlton or Corky when they came on, could find a way past Richard Gough and Gary Mabbutt in the Spurs defence. The game looked as though it was heading for a replay, but we had our opportunities, and when Fash was brought down on the edge of the box, I thought we had our chance to win it, but the ref gave nothing. Spurs went straight down the other end of the pitch, Chris Waddle turned Nige inside out and then, with his right foot and from an acute angle, beat Bez on his near post. It was heartbreak – right in front of the home fans too. Salt was poured on our wounds by Glenn Hoddle after Andy Thorn had brought Waddle down thirty yards from goal. It was, admittedly, a scorcher of a free-kick.

Spurs would famously go on to lose to Coventry and Keith Houchen's diving header in the final. Wimbledon would have their day in the sun just one year later, and I believe the Cup run of 1986–87 was one of the factors behind it. It gave the players the confidence to know that they could beat the biggest teams in the land. And it fired the players up with the desire to put things right after going so close the year before.

Just two weeks after the Cup quarter-final defeat, we again showed that winning mentality by beating Liverpool at Anfield. Sadly, that was without Wally, who had suffered that heartbreak with another broken ankle, against Coventry. This time, his recovery would be even longer and more painful, and ultimately unsuccessful.

Liverpool were top of the table, but we got our tactics spot on, with our three big defenders, Gayley, Thorn and Guppy, wrapping up Ian Rush, and then John Aldridge when he came on. Kenny Dalglish equalized after Nige had given us the lead, but a Corky header from a corner, after he had come on as a sub for Andy Sayer, gave us a famous victory. Throughout the match a fan had kept calling Corky 'spamhead'. He just laughed it off and went to shake the fan's hand after scoring the winner.

The journey home from Merseyside was a blast. Beating Liverpool at Anfield doesn't happen every day. Corky asked Stanley Reed if we could stop the coach at the next off-licence. Stanley, who loved good times and a sing-song, quickly agreed. Stanley, Corky, Andy Thorn and Tony Stenson, travelling with the team as usual, leapt off the coach and bought a bottle of scotch, a bottle of vodka and countless beers for the journey. We were wrecked by the time we got to Plough Lane, but thankfully the Sportsman was still open.

That was followed by five games without a win as the wheels came off our season again. On Luton's crap plastic pitch – they and QPR should never have been allowed to play on it – we were booed off after a dire 0–0 draw. At Oxford, as you have heard, I kept the players out on the pitch at half-time, calling them a bunch of poseurs and explaining afterwards that 'they thought they were on holiday, so I sent them out to continue sunbathing'.

There was also another descending of the red mist – and they were fucking stupid red cards too. Sanch, Fash and Thorn had already received their marching orders that season, but against Arsenal at Plough Lane I could have strangled Vinnie for reacting to a kick by elbowing Graham Rix in the back of the head. At least he says it was Rix, and that was what the match report said, but I still consider it a case of mistaken identity as Jonah was really looking out for Steve Williams, who a few days earlier had bad-mouthed us as a club for our style of play. Still, I was furious: 'Vinnie is a silly boy,' I fumed to the press. 'He has risen quickly and he must learn just as quickly. He is sick about it, and if I find out he did elbow the Arsenal player he will be fined. He'll now miss the game at Manchester United and that will disappoint him and should help him to learn.'

Then, in the next home game, against Spurs, it was Gayley's turn to go, but that was a scandalous decision. Brian had been booked for a tackle on Nico Claesen, and the Belgian then went down like a ton of bricks when the ball was thrown at him. The ref missed that incident, but sent Gayle off, for spitting he said, although he was miles from the Spurs player and categorically denied doing anything of the sort. Dennis Wise even went over to the linesman, saying it was him who was involved, and their player Richard Gough tried to intervene on our behalf, but to no avail. It was shocking. The ref also then missed an incident when Hodges should have been sent off, for elbowing Glenn Hoddle in the face. It was petulant, unprovoked and unnecessary; even Glyn didn't know why he did it. He was a Spurs fan, and I think he died a thousand deaths that day.

I fined the lot of them but shouted my mouth off as usual about Claesen after the game, saying something along the lines of Germany running through Belgium during the last war. Along with the FA, I got a right rollicking from my wife Christine when she saw the morning papers. 'You should keep your mouth shut,' she said. 'You're in trouble this time and you probably deserve it.'

I went public to defend ourselves against all the accusations of being a dirty team: 'Contrary to popular opinion,' I said, 'I don't tell my players to kick the opposition in the nuts. But I'm not running a Sunday morning outfit. It's not all beer and orange juice in the bag, a good fight and an even better drink afterwards. Sure, it sounds as though I'm defending the indefensible, but I don't think we're out of order. If we are, I let the players know.

'There have been times this season when people thought I was out of order with my comments. I made an observation about Peter Shilton early on that he was weak on crosses and got protection from referees. I was surprised at the attention it got. People probably thought I was a flash git, but I don't mind. It was just an opinion. I'm not going to get the hump.' I explained that it was the fact we were so high in the table that was really getting on people's tits: 'Many of the big clubs don't want us. They need Wimbledon and our gates of 6,000 like a hole in the head. They also don't expect to get beaten by us. Some clubs, to be fair, think it's nice and romantic to have Wimbledon around, but even they certainly don't expect to lose to us.'

'We were a fairytale, but the fairytale was supposed to end with us going back down,' was how I explained it to *FourFourTwo* magazine ahead of AFC Wimbledon's FA Cup game against Liverpool in January 2015. 'That didn't happen and nobody liked the fact that little Wimbledon came up and managed to stay up. By the end of that first season in the top flight, we were like a wasp in the room to the division's other teams.' (And what a night it was at Kingsmeadow, by the way. Just like the old days. Neal Ardley had his players fired up to believe they could win the fight. I was proud of them.)

To end the 1986–87 season, we beat four of those so-called big clubs in a row to put the seal on a fantastic first campaign. First it was Forest, who couldn't cope with Fash, thus restoring my dominance over Cloughie. Next we won with ten men at Old Trafford thanks to Wisey's late winner, then did the double over Chelsea too, with Dennis on target again. To round off a fantastic season, we beat Sheffield Wednesday 2–0 at Hillsborough, with Sayer lashing one in and Hodges getting his 11th goal of the season, a stunning solo effort, which he said was the best he had ever scored. Their manager Howard Wilkinson called us the team of the season, and yes, this bunch of no-hopers, these relegation certainties, had finished 6th in the First Division.

The league table never lies, they say, and 6th place was nothing other than a fantastic achievement, the cherry on the cake following Wimbledon being top of the table earlier in the season. Now that will live with everyone at the club until they die. It was a historic occasion, Roy of the Rovers stuff, and the whole country was captivated by it, especially after the disappointment of the World Cup in the summer of 1986. It was good for English football. Everyone had got used to seeing Liverpool, Everton and Manchester United at the top. We were a novelty. People may have knocked us but I know they were genuinely pleased to see a club like ours doing well. The English love an underdog and, even if we only had an average attendance of 7,810 at Plough Lane that season, there were a lot of fans looking out for Wimbledon as their second team.

Had it not been for the ban on English clubs playing in Europe, we would have been in the UEFA Cup, but we nevertheless harboured realistic hopes that that might lie in the future too. In fact, during the 1985–86 promotion season, we did have a European game, against Swedish side IFK Gothenburg, in a friendly match played in freezing conditions at Plough Lane.

Gothenburg were no mugs – they were on their way to the European Cup semi-finals that season, beating Alex Ferguson's Aberdeen on away goals in the quarters, and had the likes of Johnny Ekström up front and future Liverpool player Glenn Hysén at the back – but we absolutely walloped them 7–3 in front of the watching Sir Alex. Sanch opened the scoring with a screamer of a volley, and two from Leo plus one apiece from Corky, Evans, Wisey and Carlton completed the rout. I'll never forget the faces of the Swedish players as they trooped off the Plough Lane pitch, in their black tights and gloves. It was arctic out there, but do us a favour . . .

So, anyway, it was first England, tomorrow the world. But Wimbledon were going to have to write the next chapter in their history without Harry Bassett and, as it turned out, Wally Downes too. But the likes of Sanch, Beasant, Thorn, Cork, Gayle, Vinnie, Wisey and Fash would go on to be household names across the land. And here's Vinnie with his Crazy Gang memories.

Vinnie Jones

I've known Frenchie since I was seven years old – he lived in the same village. When I was playing for the Bedmond under-12s, John Cornell was our manager, and got Harry in for a training session one night. That was 38 years ago; the connection goes all the way back there. Afterwards Harry said, 'Keep an eye on that kid. I want to see how he gets on.'

Anyway, next thing I'm 16 and have been released by Watford, and Frenchie took me to Wimbledon. He fucking honestly thought I was good enough and wanted to give me a start. 'Come down and see me and we'll have a look at you,' Harry said. I was there for about a week, training with the first team. I remember Wally from then, and I became attached to the team. But then Harry decided, 'No, can't send you out there, son, you're a fucking loose cannon.'

After the trial at Wimbledon, I just went fucking AWOL. I thought it was all over then. My head went up my arse with that rejection. I had a lot of anger issues, not just with the break-up of my family, but with rejection after rejection. I thought I was a bit of a superstar as a footballer – captain of Watford schoolboys, captain of Hertfordshire. I weren't no mug. I didn't just go to Wimbledon to kick shit out of people. I've always needed a home, mates around me. With rejection and a bit of alcohol, you get very fucking punchy.

There were a lot of ex-Wimbledon players at Wealdstone. Chris Dibble was one, and he said at the end of the season, 'Sign for a Norwegian or Swedish club, they'll treat you like a pro.' My ears fucking went up like a boomer-fucking-rang. Get off the fucking building site! I was a gardener up in Bushey then, and used to go up and down with this fucking lawnmower, praying to my grandfather – he was a big Watford fan

– 'Please just give me one chance, I won't let you down.' All of a sudden, boomerang, I got the chance. To cut a long story short, I basically got on my fucking knees and begged Harry. I'd been playing for Wealdstone – I'd had a good run of 18 games at the end of the season and we won the non-league double – and he gave in in the end. I think Frenchie put a bit of pressure on him.

Harry sent me out to Sweden to get some experience, and as soon as I got off the plane, I realized they were treating me like Vincent Jones, from Wimbledon. 'Ooh, fuck me,' I thought. I pulled the old collar up straightaway. They spoiled us rotten. I found that stature again. I was running the show, being a leader. I'm a good follower and I respect the leader, but I'd look to overthrow him if he was a tosser!

I won player of the year in Sweden, in the Third Division, and we beat Djurgården in the Swedish FA Cup – Brian McDermott was there – 4–2, and it was the biggest fucking upset of all time. Roy Hodgson was at Malmö and wanted to take me there. Next minute Harry was on the phone saying, 'Don't fucking sign for them, come back here. I hear you done fantastic.' That phone call changed my life. I went back to Wealdstone and then it all happened very quickly.

My first game in a Wimbledon shirt was at Feltham. Wally played; I was at centre-half. I was dog-shit awful. It was a really windy night – as you ran up to take a free-kick the ball was fucking moving – and it was on fucking Astroturf. It was a stinker – you try your bollocks off and nothing's going right. When I came back, Frenchie was going mad because I was playing centre-half: 'What the fuck are you playing him there for – he's a fucking centre-midfielder!'

Luckily Wimbledon had another midweek game at the training ground, against Brentford. My old mate Bob Booker was playing for them; he was like a hero to me – I played with him on a Sunday morning and next thing I knew he was a professional footballer. We won 3–1 against Brentford, I scored two from midfield, just fucking lit it up. One of them games.

On the Thursday, Wally was there and we were given the blue bibs at training. Harry called me upstairs to his little office and said, 'Right, son, I'm signing you. Year and a half, £150 a week, £50 goal bonus. Try and get in the side. All right, you can fuck off downstairs now.'

And then, fuck me, that Saturday we're playing Nottingham Forest away and Midget is out and Sanchez is suspended and he's looking for someone to play in central midfield with Wally. Frenchie was pushing it again, 'Fucking give him a chance. If you're going to give someone a chance, do it away from home.' I don't remember much about it. Johnny Metgod scored a worldie. I was a little bit rabbit-in-the-headlights, looking at the size of his fucking boots. When I punched the ball away, all the lads looked at me, going, 'Fuck me.' But because I'd met them all when I was younger, I wasn't a stranger.

On the way back from Forest, me and Frenchie

stopped off for a pint at the Bell in Bedmond. Joe McElligott had said to Harry, 'What are you doing putting a fucking builder in midfield?' And I thought that was it, fucking rejection again. I don't know how I played against Man Utd at home. I can't remember much of that – making the run, the ball going in off Remi Moses – but I do remember before the game, I bought a pair of Nikes for £23.50 from Spideys in Hemel Hempstead. They weren't even leather – fucking plastic!

People may have been surprised that I was quiet when I arrived at Wimbledon, but you don't go in as Charlie Big Bananas because you'd get fucking slaughtered. It's first impressions with everything. I knew the rules – I'd spent four years at Wealdstone. You keep your head down. If you do too much talking, people can't talk about you. I was there to be a professional footballer. This was my lifeline, and Harry had thrown the fucking ring out to me.

Frenchie had told me there'd be lots of running, and my first one was A3 to the windmill, a bastard long run. But I was going out there to win the race. I was always a good runner but hated it; I came fourth in the all-England cross-country, and thought, 'Never doing that again.' But this time it was like I was in *Chariots of Fire*. I burst out of the trees, ran round the war memorial by the Common – Alan Gillett, Frenchie and Geoff Taylor were all watching – and I felt about 20-foot tall. Wisey can't have been there, but from then on we used to run shoulder to shoulder.

The tactics on the field were professional with Harry, but the rest of it was like a pub team. Frank at the transport café, with his long black nails, ash from his cigarette falling in your tea, didn't give a fuck who any of us were, but none of us were anybody anyway. When we beat Chelsea away, 4–0 in my third game, we came in on the Monday morning and Frank just didn't give a fuck.

But it was a family atmosphere. When Wally wanted to do the patio at the back of his house, he said, 'Right, Jonah, you're fucking Bob the Builder.' Six of us all turned up one Sunday and then buried the fucking family tortoise under the slabs. Imagine that now! Though as Wally reminds me now, I thought I'd buried the tortoise, but Lightning was too fast for me . . .

The best long-ball team in the country, and the most successful, were Liverpool. Alan Hansen played more long balls than Andy Thorn. They had the swagger of being a glamour club, and big support, but I had no doubt I could have played in that team. Hansen might nudge a couple of little passes to the full-back, but then it was set back and launched and Ian Rush would go through and score – what sort of total football was that? Everton were the same – a great team with Kevin Sheedy and that lot, but they used to hit it long. That was the scene of my famous shout. We were playing them and suddenly I came out with, 'Right, let's take no shit, Wombles!' Everyone looked round and I got hammered.

In central midfield, the rule was – no square balls. Me

and Sanch used to practise, after the centre-halves had knocked it down: swivel, boot it, get it in the final third, then play football. I knew that when it went out wide, I wasn't wasting my fucking bollocks off steaming in there. We could always score goals. The belief was, if you do your job, doubling up with the full-back, we're going to draw 0–0. The only way they could score was if you didn't do your job. We had to protect our livelihoods on a Saturday afternoon.

Even Hodges would work his fucking bollocks off, and he was our fancy dan, the tricky dick, but he could fucking do you. You never pulled out of a tackle. Sanch came to me once and said, 'Someone's going to fucking do you, straight-leg you.' McMahon tried, but it never happened fortunately. But if you didn't go in 100 per cent, you'd get slaughtered from the bench.

We all got obsessed when we went over the line, and we could shut anyone down. Plough Lane was a smaller pitch, and we always did well at Arsenal. Real Madrid were the best at it – all the Spanish teams were good at it. Now I watch Chelsea, or Liverpool, and they get into great positions but I'm going, 'CROSS THE FUCKING BALL!' If you watch *Match of the Day* on a Saturday night, 80 per cent of the goals come from crosses.

Going back to when we beat Chelsea 4–0, that was when people started accusing us of bullying tactics. Doug Rougvie got sent off but he hardly touched Fash; he went down like a sack of shit. That day showed who was really part of the team, though, and we were all in it.

We watched the video on the Monday and there was someone with Pat Nevin in a headlock – I think it was 'Tut Tut' [John Kay] – marching along and punching him at the same time. It was a brilliant feeling because if you hadn't been in there swinging and punching you would have been shown up for not being part of it. Even Lurch ran up the pitch and got involved – Eddie Niedzwiecki shit himself and stayed in his goal. Afterwards Rougvie waited outside the dressing room and we were all giving it, 'All for one and one for all.' The press were there and it all kicked off down the tunnel.

As you go through the lower leagues those things happen more and more often, but they get one tiny paragraph somewhere, or are ignored all together – but then we suddenly found out that we couldn't get away with it. Once we had some success and people realized we weren't just going to roll over and go away, they started to turn on us. Other managers were going to the press and moaning about us. They turned on us very quickly.

Those videos on a Monday morning were so important – if I had gone on to a career in management I would have used them – because if you didn't do your job or you lost whoever you were marking, they exposed you to the other lads for any mistakes or a lack of responsibility. That was what was in your head on a Saturday: 'If I don't do my job, the lads are going to see this on Monday morning.' No one wanted to be seen losing their man and letting them run through and score. Harry never had to say anything because the boys all saw it, and they were on to you because you cost them a win bonus.

I thought I was leaving for Watford too, after Harry left. So I could afford to be a bit lairy with Gouldy because I thought I was off anyway. I thought it was just a matter of time. Wally was banished from the first team; I remember one day Gouldy made Wally train in the gym on his own on a weights circuit – a fucking disgusting way to treat Wally, now I look back on it. So Wally took his little boy in, only a little fucker, and when Gouldy walked in to check on Wally he said that his little boy was doing the dumbbells instead. Gouldy went ape shit and Wally's time was up. What became very clear then was that every 'son of Harry' that was still at the club was going to get bombed. Gouldy wanted to replace them, he wanted me and Wally out, but Sam blocked me leaving.

Sam realized how important I was to the dressing room, and the squad got together, got our heads down and just got on with it. I remember being at Mansfield away at the start of the Cup run – it was muddy as fuck, on a slope and then Terry Phelan scored probably the only goal he ever scored, and somehow we were in the next round. Silly little things like that fell into place. We should never have won against Newcastle away. We spanked them 3–1; Fash scored a brilliant goal, Gayley did too, and then we started building this amazing belief that carried us through, and thoughts of transfers and leaving melted away.

It was hard after Harry. I remember Don Howe coming in and telling us to keep things going; I think Gouldy on his own would have fucked it up, that's the truth. He did not like anything at the club that still had anything to do with Bassett. He wanted it to be his team, and he wanted his players to play. Scalesy was a lovely lad, but when he arrived he was fucking useless. I actually felt sorry for him. Gouldy even wanted his son Jonathan to be a goalie, and he was fucking useless. Wally, me and Wisey used to ping shots past him all day.

In the end I went to Sam and said that I had to get out, and he came back with all the stuff about, 'You can't leave us, we're a family.' But it wasn't my family any more. He said to me, 'If you walk out of here it will happen quicker than you could ever imagine.' With that I told him I wanted to go, and walked out of his house. Before I had even got to Swiss Cottage my in-car phone went and it was Graham Taylor talking about signing me for Watford. In the back of my head my first thought was, 'That cunt Taylor let me go at Watford,' even though he always denied releasing me as a kid. Next thing, the Leeds director Bill Fotherby phoned.

At Wimbledon, after Harry left, we played for Don Howe. With my hand on my heart, we played for Don, and when he came to Chelsea he changed everything for me and Wisey. Chelsea at that time was a shambles, a fucking joke, until Don came and said, 'This place is like a holiday camp. You two are going to be my boys,' and in the first training session he set up some fartlek training.

Before that all we ever did was five-a-side, every single day – it was the most unfit I ever was as a footballer, but then Don came in and we had a great Cup run.

One thing I knew in my heart – I was more sure of it than anything else in my life – was that the minute Wimbledon was not full of 11 players fighting for each other every Saturday, they would be relegated. And I knew that once they were relegated, they would drop down through the leagues. I knew it as sure as anything. I could not see how they could keep replacing players; it was impossible. You don't let three or four players go at a time, it needs to be a transition, and too many were changed in quick succession.

When I re-signed for Wimbledon, under Joe Kinnear, the first season in the Premier League, I finished my first day of training and I realized it was the worst thing I had ever done. After Leeds, Chelsea and Sheffield I just thought, 'What the fuck have I done?' I held my head that night. I went back there full of enthusiasm, and it was knocked out of me. I looked around the dressing room and saw a few good footballers, but I didn't see people I wanted in the trenches with me. Robbie Earle, Warren Barton, Dean Holdsworth – there were good lads, but we didn't have enough. Scott Fitzgerald was a great lad and footballer, but I had to tell Joe that he couldn't play Scotty against players like Mick Harford. Scotty would guarantee you 100 per cent, but he was getting eaten alive by players like Mick. Good footballers with good brains were not enough. We had to rethink and shuffle things about. We needed a few who fancied a fight in a tunnel – if needs be. I ended up becoming the assistant manager, more or less. Joe told me that we had to recreate Bassett's Wimbledon as soon as possible if we were ever going to get out of the shit.

Joe was asking me to organize team-bonding nights for midweek when we had time off – usually a trip to Wimbledon dogs – and every player would be told to come. All would say yes, but when we got down there, there would only be five or six. Suddenly a lot of players were saying, 'This isn't really my thing.' What they failed to realize was it wasn't about the event on a Tuesday night, it was all about Saturday. Those players should have been willing to go anywhere and do anything – ballet, dogs, wrestling – as long as it counted toward doing better on Saturdays. If you can't get your full team down to a night at the dogs on your doorstep, how many of them are you going to have on your side if you end up in a fight? In the old days, the Bassett days, you never worried. But when I went back there it was all a little bit false, and it was forced. I mean, Warren Barton in the Crazy Gang?

I knew what that old gang was about because I knew them. I met them when I was a kid and had played against them. I had my history with the club after being there as a kid, and I knew their history. I didn't get accepted because I scored the winning goal against Manchester United – I was accepted because my foundations were laid years earlier. My first roommate was Wally, and I knew him from my Wealdstone days. They knew I would row for them. Wally put an arm round me straight away.

I've seen people talk about how Wally would slaughter people – rightly so. But it was because they were not cutting it. Harry paid £90,000 for Colin Gordon and he talked about how good he was, he was this and that, but if he could have backed up even a bit of what he went about saying then Wally would have laid off him. He was slaughtered. They tried to make a man of him, but he was shown the Wimbledon way and told, 'You do it this way or you're fucked.' There was no other way.

After the Cup final the Crazy Gang image was played up to, without a doubt. They put it on the shirts and it became a commodity – you could own the 'Crazy Gang'. Second time around, for me, it became embarrassing. The stuff wasn't thought out in advance in the old days. I remember me and Wally going to Lilleshall and causing murders. We followed Gayley and Clemmo up on the motorway once – the M6 – and, once we hit a bit of traffic, me and Wally jumped out and filled their car up with talcum powder through the windows, they couldn't see a thing. They got us back and suddenly there were great big white clouds of smoke dotted down the M6 as a First Division football team conducted a talcum powder war in the fast lane.

We never understood at the time, but whenever we socialized with other players from different teams, we would look at them in awe. We would see them at the bar and be a bit open-mouthed. We didn't realize that they were looking at us thinking the same thing. We'd talk and find out while they were playing five-a-side every Monday morning, we were doing six-mile runs through the woods. We were the paupers but they were looking up to us because we were beating people; you can be as poor as you like, but when you beat people, you earn respect.

When Gouldy came in there was a power struggle between the players. Sanch always got a bit more stick because he was different to us; he was from a different place, same as Scalesy. There were times we went too far and Sanch would stand up for himself – he never took any bollocks. Wally and me would always charge stuff to other people's rooms, and when Sanch and Bez would room together we would always do them. But it was never planned or premeditated. When I went back it was staged. Terry Burton took over and tried to talk about the Crazy Gang – fuck off!

What ended up happening was when Wimbledon won, it was 'the Crazy Gang', but when they lost, it was, 'Forget that old ill-disciplined shit.' There were two sides to the coin, whereas with Harry there was only ever one side. I went through the lot. I went through the changes and saw more than most; me, Corky, Sanch.

I have always felt a sense of guilt and a burden, throughout all these years, that it might have been seen as disrespectful to them other boys. The Micky Smiths, Paul Fishendens, Steve Galliers. I knew all them boys. I have always worried about what they were thinking. They probably saw some of the late Crazy Gang stuff, and players associating themselves with it, and thought they were no crazier than their solicitor. Hanging Carlton Fairweather on the back of a minibus and driving down the motorway was crazy. You didn't think about it at the time, but if it had gone wrong we would have been in serious trouble. Those things were so funny, but once we were in the limelight you could fanny it a bit more.

Most of us were internationals – I could pick a Wimbledon side that could play in the Premier League now. I always felt Corky was underestimated – the shrewdest bloke. If I ever ran a club he would be the first person I would get in to work with the strikers. The little nudges to knock defenders off balance; he didn't beat top-class defenders to balls and headers every week out of luck. He had learned so much coming through those divisions – they all had.

The saddest bit for me was the end, but we could not have stayed together for any longer. I thought it was the end when Harry left. I imagine I spent a few nights crying my eyes out when he first left, worrying I'd be found out!

After we had won at Wembley you can see on the footage where I have the Cup and I'm looking up at Harry pretending to throw it at him, screaming, 'This is yours, this is yours!' That was the most emotional bit, seeing him up there. He should have been sitting next to Sam Hammam in the royal box.

He was a long-ball manager and I was a long-ball player – we will never shake those tags. But you go and ask Gordon Strachan or Mick Harford about me, and see what they say, and then get a list of the managers who have been on to Harry for advice over the last 30 years. The biggest managers have picked Harry's brains.

It was a special time and it should be left at that; the more people try to force it, the more I shy away from it. The Cup final should be the final chapter because the things I dreaded happened after that. I cried my eyes out after I left for Leeds, phoned Fash, telling him I wanted to go back – but when I did go back it wasn't the same. Joe did the best he could, he tried to bring back the good days, but I always felt the burden whenever they tried to use the old Crazy Gang name. I came at the end of the real Crazy Gang, but I knew its history. It meant something very different.

21

Time to Move On

Harry

As the final whistle had gone at Hillsborough on the final day of that 1986–87 season, I knew that was my last game as Wimbledon manager. It sunk in that this was the curtain falling on 14 years of hard, funny, weird, sometimes controversial but always joyful work. I couldn't look in the eyes of the players, many of whom had started out on the journey with me. I welled up, my throat dry, and I needed time for myself. I walked out alone on to the pitch. The crowd had gone. It was just me.

Wednesday manager Howard Wilkinson had invited me into his office for a drink. I had five minutes to myself to get my thoughts together. I had a tear in my eye because I knew it was over, and it had been a wonderful ride. As I walked round the pitch my head was a whirl; memories of what we had achieved came flooding back, the journey through all four divisions. It felt bizarre. 'Did we really do this?' I thought. We achieved so much, and with a wonderful bunch of players who had started out as boys and now were true men in every sense of the word. We had done it all together, and how tremendous they had been to buy into it all. I couldn't hold back the tears. In fact, why should I? I was actually leaving all these boys and all our lives were going to change. I just wanted that moment for myself so I could savour it.

It was a lovely warm day, which was unusual up there, and for five or ten minutes I just strolled around while the boys were showering and getting ready. I knew then it was the last time we would be leaving a changing room together and travelling back on a coach, the things we had done so many times together.

Our dressing room after the game was a mixture of joy and sadness, knowing a new journey was about to begin. I was so proud of them, particularly those who had travelled with me from the start: Dave Beasant, Kevin Gage, Glyn Hodges, Mark Morris, Mick Smith and, of course, Wally Downes, Paul Fishenden and Alan Cork, who didn't play that day but were still close by. There was also Nigel Winterburn, four times player of the year, the underrated Lawrie Sanchez, and then the unique pairing of Vinnie Jones and John Fashanu.

What a time we'd had. So many characters had helped forge the club I loved, both players and fans. It hadn't been like going to work, more a fun palace, but also with a serious side. Who knows what we might have achieved if we had stayed together? This team could have gone places.

We were at our hotel the night before our final game and had told the players to go out and enjoy Sheffield's hospitality if they so wished, but that if there were hangovers the next morning they would be fined two weeks' wages. I went out with Frenchie, Sid, Alan Gillett and Stanley Reed, the chairman, and got back to the hotel around 1 a.m. and asked the duty manager if there had been any trouble. He said no, because the team were still out. So off I went to bed. I pressed for the lift and waited. Eventually the doors opened and inside the lift was almost every item from my room, from the bed to my clothes, the sheets and TV set. You name it. After years of proudly boasting I had never been caught out, I was finally kippered.

I was determined to have a bloody good time on the coach back to London. It just felt like a family breaking up. We had beer and wine, which Sid Neale had bought that morning, some champagne, and the music on.

At the time I didn't fucking realize that eight months later I would be back up in Sheffield. I left on a lovely sunny day – by the time I went back there was six inches of snow on the ground, and that lasted six weeks! Sheffield United turned out to be great – the first six months weren't, but the following years were fantastic. I wouldn't swap that experience for anything – a great club and unbelievable fans (I should do another book!).

Sam would realize in due course what a good job I had done; we bought players for £470,000 and sold them for £7.2 million – fuck me, we made over £6 million profit for him. How many managers can do that now? It would be like turning £4 million into £70 million. But when I had wanted to buy players for the second season in Division One, Sam had wanted to sell four of the ones we had instead. So I thought, 'That's it.' We left. Sam could have kept me if he had really wanted to, but he wanted to go in a different direction.

Even at the start of that First Division campaign, when we were top of the table, Sam was talking about a new five-year contract to keep me at the club, as I was starting the final year of my current three-year deal. I remember I even said at the time, 'I'm happy at Wimbledon, but sometimes I think it would be nice to be at a club with bigger support. It sometimes gets to me that we'll never attract big crowds.' Sam's line was that, 'We are respectful of the manager's ambitions. If he signs a new contract, it must be with full conviction.'

Throughout the season, though, I felt things were going wrong between Sam and me. Our relationship was crumbling. Every time we got close to signing a new deal it was delayed. When it finally came to seeing what he wanted written down I was, to be frank, appalled. The money wasn't right, or the terms, and I felt power was being taken away from me. There was a paragraph saying he would have a say in team selection if he didn't agree with my choices. Over the festive period, I had seriously wondered whether to give him six months' notice. This would have meant I could leave and he wouldn't get any compensation. In the end I didn't and he did.

I felt he wanted me to go. It was becoming difficult for the both of us. I didn't want to leave, but I felt Sam wanted me out. I think he thought I was getting too big for the club, and he wasn't getting enough credit. He had also never forgiven me for leaving to join Palace, albeit for just three days – although he forgot he was also on the verge of doing the same at one stage. My wife, in fact, was at one game when she heard Sam turn to Stanley Reed and ask, 'Why does Bassett get all the cheers and applause?' He saw himself as the club's godfather, someone who should get more reward, more attention.

By the time we played at Hillsborough on 9 May 1987, the players and fans had all become aware that my time at Wimbledon was coming to end. We had committed 698 fouls, won 355 corners, caught our opposition off-side 330 times, had 294 attempts at goal, been top of the table – but as low as 14th six matches later. Dull, it wasn't.

Wimbledon were etched into my soul, yet my final year had been painful, with the off-field battles. Our final home game against Chelsea had been highly emotional. Fans invaded the pitch at the end and sang, 'Don't go, Harry.' I was lifted shoulder-high and carried around the pitch.

Manchester City were looking for a manager in the wake of first Billy McNeill and then Jimmy Frizzell leaving, and I was approached by their chairman, Peter

Swales. We had several meetings at his house, and I still chuckle to this day about the time I first saw it. It was painted sky-blue. What else? Peter was a nice bloke but insisted on one thing, that the existing staff stay on. I wanted my team of Alan Gillett, Geoff Taylor and Derek French with me. We agreed to think about it. In the end it didn't matter, because Elton John and Watford came a-knocking on my door. Frenchie says that Wally was halfway up the motorway to Manchester before the City deal got canned.

There was still the little matter of the few remaining months of my Wimbledon contract to be resolved, though, and I didn't think they would be a problem, after what I had achieved for the club. Wimbledon had plenty of time to replace me, and I believed Sam would release me with instant effect. Sadly, there was another sting in the tail. Sam was demanding £125,000 compensation from Watford, basically the total sum I had been paid in all my years at the club. In effect, I had worked for nothing. It didn't matter that I had built a team costing less than half a million that was now worth almost £8 million and taken them from the bottom to the top. He wanted the final say.

I couldn't believe what I was hearing. We were in London's Inn on the Park hotel, and Sam was asking Elton for money. He eventually agreed to it. I remember Elton saying afterwards, 'When you've got a clinker up your arse you need to remove it.'

Of course I had other reasons to move on. You can't

knock the fans. They were brilliant – year after year, giving us that extra something to pull a result out of the bag when the odds were stacked against us – but you can't massage the figures. The average attendance when we were promoted from the Second Division was 4,578. That first season in the First Division we had 800 season-ticket holders; AFC Wimbledon have more than three times that number in League Two now! Even after we beat Charlton to go top, not one person called the club's offices to get a season ticket – and there were plenty of calls of congratulations, believe me.

Plough Lane was ours – it always will be – but it was still a bit of a shithole with a pub and a nightclub built into it. The rest of the area was all Chinese takeaways, industrial estates, cemeteries, a stream chocka with shopping trolleys, and a dog track. I wasn't exactly used to glamour, but you couldn't stop me thinking, 'Well, I've done something incredible here. Where else might this take me?' I was already in demand from top companies to give motivational speeches based on the Wimbledon story, even going out to Monte Carlo one time with a chauffeur-driven limousine and the rest of the trimmings. Now Watford, with Elton John, were ready to satisfy my hunger. They were a well-organized club with a first-class attitude on the field. They were, I thought, a model for everyone. My Wimbledon days were gone, but never forgotten.

Here's Alan Gillett's recollections of the end.

Alan Gillett

We were joyous reaching the First Division, but that soon wore off when Sam Hammam talked about selling players. I wasn't particularly close to him but Harry had him in his ear all the time. It must have been heart-breaking to see and hear his hard work being written off.

I saw Harry as he came off the pitch after our final game against Sheffield Wednesday. He looked glum. I said, 'Had enough?' and he nodded his head. We had been together a long time but knew things were coming to an end. Even our three days, horrible days, at Palace, could not match our feelings on that afternoon in Yorkshire.

Dave and I went to the FA Cup final a few days later. He had been approached by Peter Swales to manage Manchester City and had gone to see him. He said he would take me with him if he accepted the job. We shook hands. I travelled south to my home, he went north to his – only to see Elton John's Roller in his drive and the singer himself in the kitchen. He asked him to take over at Watford, who had lost Graham Taylor to Aston Villa. Dave phoned and told me the news. My wife wasn't happy. She saw our kids wearing pale-blue shirts, rather than Watford's black and gold.

It was totally the wrong move. Graham had run Watford from top to bottom, from the shop to the kitchens. We were not that kind of management. I recall Kenny Jackett getting into the coach one day and giving me his passport before a pre-season trip. I looked at it and said something like 'nice' and tried to hand it back. 'No,' he said, 'we always had to hand our passports over to Graham.' Then Luther Blissett arrived and did the same and said, 'I would like the *Daily Mirror* and the *Sun* delivered to my room, please.' Graham ran their lives. It was not for us. Wimbledon was so far removed from that. We had a close-knit group, people who thought for themselves. They had been brought up in the school of hard knocks. Great memories.

We made mistakes, too many to mention, but as Lennie Lawrence told us, 'Make one mistake and it's fine. Two and worry. Third, expect the sack.' It was advice we never ignored.

Harry

More than a decade after I left the club, I was back at Wimbledon – well, Selhurst Park in any case – as manager of Barnsley, for a Third Round FA Cup tie. It was the first time I'd ever faced Wimbledon in a Cup competition, so it was a strange experience. They did me the honour of paying tribute to our promotion to the elite of English football in the match programme, which I have kept as a treasured possession. WELCOME BACK, HARRY it says on the front cover, with a picture of us celebrating at Huddersfield. Sam Hammam wrote a message beneath it:

Today we salute Dave Bassett, hero of Wimbledon,

> manager of the Millennium. What you did by taking us from the Fourth to the First Division will never be equalled. Other wonderful managers continued the miracle, but it was you who made it possible. You may well be in the rival dugout today, but there will always be part of us in you and you in us. This will always be your spiritual home. It is an honour to welcome you back.

In an interview in the programme, I reflected both on my Wimbledon years and on the years that had passed at different clubs since then – Watford, Sheffield United, Crystal Palace, Nottingham Forest and Barnsley – as well as on the fact that Wimbledon at the time were enjoying thirteen unbroken years in the top flight, quite a contrast to the yo-yo years.

It was only, I said, after winning promotion to the old First Division for the first time in Wimbledon's history that, 'I felt the time was right to go – the team had achieved perhaps more than I or anyone had really dreamed was possible. In hindsight,' I then reflected, 'perhaps it wasn't the best move I could have made. Graham Taylor had done ten very good years there and I made a bit of an error joining Watford on the day that he left to go to Aston Villa. Graham had been a big favourite with the Watford fans and they didn't really get a chance to mourn his leaving the club. The next thing they know, I'm being revealed as the new boss and I don't think they were really ready. It was just one of those unfortunate things, really. While the chairman,

Elton John, was a different class, I ended up feeling like a square peg in a round hole. The club and me just weren't right for each other.'

It was at Sheffield United where I ended up making a home from home, helped by having a core of Wimbledon players who came up with me, Wally among them, of course. Even if injury would again curtail what he could do on the pitch, he was beside me in the dugout.

Kevin Gage was another who ended up in Yorkshire. Here's more of his memories.

Kevin Gage

I left Wimbledon when Harry left. I felt we had achieved everything we could have done – certainly not go on and win the FA Cup. I played in Harry's last game at Sheffield Wednesday. We won it at a canter; we went one up and they just crumbled. I remember going out on the Friday night because it was the last game of the season and it was a beautiful day, so we went to the wine bar in Sheffield – Hanrahans – in our Spall tracksuits, and I remember people looking at us and they couldn't believe we were doing that before a match. We weren't pissed, it was a few pints, but it was camaraderie. We knew Bassett was going, my contract was up. I never thought, 'This is my last game for Wimbledon,' but I can imagine how Harry felt.

I arrived at Sheffield United in 1991 after playing for

Aston Villa. After being away from Bassett for however many years it was like walking back into Wimbledon. The first person I saw was Geoff Taylor. Then I went to see Harry in his office, which brought back horrible memories. Then I saw Simon Tracey, Gannon was there, Gayley had just signed, Frenchie the physio; it was like a spin-off.

I think Harry proved himself by doing it again there – it wasn't a fluke at Wimbledon. I felt there was some hostility to start with, a north versus south divide, with Bradshaw, Wardy and Whitehouse there. There was an undercurrent, but Harry harnessed that. Harry used it as a conduit. We would play North v South in Friday 5-a-side. I think we all had massive rows with Harry over football at one time or another – I certainly did. But we always knew that he was the manager and we had to get on with it.

Harry

I did have a tendency to try to work with certain players as a manager. When I joined Sheffield United I signed Simon Tracey and John Gannon from Wimbledon. I had seen them develop through the youth and reserve teams and knew what they were all about. When you work with players you get to know their strengths and weaknesses, attitude and commitment. Sometimes it's less of a risk to go out and get the players that you know all about rather than gamble on someone you don't. 'Better the devil you know,' as the saying goes. John and Simon had good careers at Sheffield before he was forced to pack up through injury. Hodges, Gage and Gayle also linked up with me again at Bramall Lane.

Hodges, of course, was another of the players who left Wimbledon when I did, in the summer of 1986, so let's hear him share more of his memories.

Glyn Hodges

The only time I ever encountered a team spirit like Wimbledon was when I went to Sheffield United to play for Harry again, and he had created Wimbledon Mark II. He had taken Frenchie, Geoff Taylor, Gannon, Gagey and Wally up there and got them to mix straight in with all the local Sheffield nutters he'd inherited. It was exactly the same, you knew it was happening – it was a carbon copy, and it worked again because of Harry's recruitment and the people he got in, Frenchie in particular. He was the funniest fella.

When I was the manager at Barnsley we were in administration and the boys weren't getting paid – they weren't getting appearance money, bonus money, loyalty money, and it was hard to motivate them at all. There were so many things going wrong at the time, and I tried to recreate that siege mentality we'd had at Wimbledon. I wanted them to see they had their backs against the wall but to understand they had a load of mates alongside them in the same boat, pulling together. The only way we could affect things was to do well on the pitch. Wimbledon were like that. People couldn't come between us or penetrate us. We had something that was special.

My contract at Wimbledon had been year-to-year for about three years, and I never expected us to go up or be near the top. Every year we turned up we somehow improved. But I wanted to at least see what other offers there were, and that year there was QPR, Watford and Newcastle. When I knew Winterburn and Gage were going it was sort of a good time to draw a line under it. I was quite happy to have those clubs in for me. I went to Newcastle, but it didn't work out – especially when Wimbledon swiftly came up there and beat us, which was a real kick in the bollocks.

I'd scored in the last game for us all at Hillsborough. It was a fantastic goal at their Kop end. On the Friday night we were all in a pub called Hanrahans opposite Hallam hospital and we got absolutely smashed. One of the Wednesday players was in there injured and he must have gone back to them and said, 'Don't worry, fellas, I've just seen the oppo in town bollocks drunk, tomorrow will be a doddle.' But we went and beat them 2–0. I remember it because it was my last game. On the way home it was a drunken blur.

It's hard to really believe what we did – you do pinch yourself. If you didn't know the Wimbledon story and you tried to explain it to someone who watched football these days, there is no way they would believe you, the gap is too big. It will never be done again. To do what we did, in the way we did it and in that space of time – and with the craic we had on the way – was unbelievable, and I hope this book does it justice because I don't think that TV show did.

Wimbledon never hindered me or held me back. It made me the person I am and the player I was. You don't get by on just ability and skill alone, Wimbledon gave me something else. I was probably inconsistent but I knew the heights I could hit, and if I could have hit them more regularly then I am sure someone would have come in and bought me a lot earlier than Newcastle finally did. I would have gone sooner. I was inconsistent – some people had me down as lazy, but I wasn't lazy. I did try, but sometimes Bassett would put me in the team when I wasn't quite fit or ready and, although that's probably a compliment to me, it probably didn't help long-term. It's nice for the boys I played with to talk about the talent and say they feel I had the ability to do more, but they helped me do that; Wimbledon did. I ain't bitter, you won't find me at the end of the bar moaning that I never fulfilled my potential. If I had played at my maximum on a regular basis perhaps I could have played for one of the top teams in the country, but I wouldn't swap what I did or how we did it for anything.

Harry

As I have said, Hodges had a wonderful talent, and it's great to see him doing well in his coaching career, but he also needed managing. A football team is not a democracy. Somebody has to make the decisions, come what may, and that's the job of the manager. If you don't like it, fuck off. Hodges gave the impression of being lazy, and we argued constantly, but I got the best out of him. Leaving him to his own devices was not an option; he needed someone to drive him, and I drove him fucking mad.

After he left Wimbledon and went to Newcastle, he was an unmitigated disaster. He thought he'd arrived, but he wasn't prepared, especially after a summer of eating and drinking. So I took him back under my thumb, and reinvented him at Watford. When he went to Palace, he flopped again, but when I took him to Sheffield United, and later Forest, and as a coach at Barnsley, he was on the money again. He needed me and I needed him, it's as simple as that. Both of us had respect for each other, without admitting it.

I always knew he had excellent technique and talent, but that he had to have a strong taskmaster – otherwise people thought his attitude stank. Yes, he was a very good footballer, but he had a crap disciplinary record and was a difficult character at times. I remember one occasion, in an FA Youth Cup tie at Arsenal, it took him about eight minutes to come off the pitch! It was actually

Glyn's dad who told me that he needed a firm hand. He had to know what the guidelines were or he'd step outside those lines – it was the same with Wally. And when that happened, I'd come down on them with a ton of fucking bricks. When they went over that line, there'd be serious trouble. Both Hodges and Wally had a reputation, and you get a reputation for a reason.

Along with Hodges, other players departing was obviously going to hurt Wimbledon too – although, as it turned out, the players themselves did all right! Nigel Winterburn had been player of the year in every single one of his four seasons at the club, a remarkable run of form, self-belief and consistency. He went to Arsenal for £300,000. On top of the £300,000 Newcastle paid for Hodges, and the £250,000 Aston Villa paid for Kevin Gage, that represented huge money for a club like Wimbledon. Mark Morris joined me at Vicarage Road – for a tribunal fee of £50,000 – along with my coaching staff of Alan Gillett, Derek French and Geoff Taylor, and then Hodges when he decided the north-east wasn't for him.

Sam Hammam's appointment of Bobby Gould turned out to be a masterstroke, and bringing Don Howe on to the coaching staff was a stroke of genius. The players that subsequently joined Wimbledon weren't half bad too. Terry Phelan filled what were thought to be the unfillable boots of Nige at left-back and, along with Bobby's other new signings – Eric Young, Clive Goodyear and Terry Gibson (for a club record of £200,000), plus John Scales coming through – he ended up with an FA Cup winner's medal around his neck.

Fate, of course, decreed that Watford would play Wimbledon in the opening fixture of the 1987–88 season, and I have to confess to having had mixed feelings after the game, the only goal of which was scored by Luther Blissett. By the time Watford were due at Plough Lane in January, I was gone, my contract 'terminated by mutual agreement' as the phrase goes. 'Both parties feel that this agreement is in the best interests of Watford Football Club at the present time,' the official statement released to the press read. I left just days before that Wimbledon–Watford game and, to be honest, that was a blessing.

Here's one of the many players who left Wimbledon for bigger things, and a career in management too. Over to you, Thorny.

Andy Thorn

I left Wembley clutching my FA Cup winner's medal and with my chest puffed out. I was proud. Not just for the club I supported as a kid, not just for me being the only player in the side that had actually started in the youth team, but for all those that made this possible.

The list is endless, from my dad deciding to start a junior football team on our council estate to keep youngsters off the streets, to the likes of Geoff Taylor and Wally Downes, who showed faith in me when others doubted. There was the friendship with Alan Cork that endures to this day, and the countless other youngsters who fell by the wayside but made my footballing life a happy one. And, of course, there was Dave 'Harry' Bassett, the man who gave me my chance, although, to be honest, I don't think he really fancied me at the time.

I was with Harry through all four divisions, but it wasn't until we were in Division Two I made my debut, away to Notts County in April 1985. We won 3–2 and I was up against a name that was to become familiar in years to come, a certain Fashanu, although in this case it was Justin, John's elder brother. He scored that day, but goals from Fish, Sanch and a rare header from Nigel Winterburn gave me my first win bonus. That's a joke, by the way. We didn't get one then.

It had been some journey. It began when my dad, a lorry driver, organized an under-14 youth team called Palma Colts, although where he got the exotic name from is a mystery. We lived on a council estate in Colliers Wood, not far from the old Plough Lane ground. Wimbledon were my side, and I would watch them in the old Southern League days. One of the players in Palma Colts was John Gannon, with whom I later shared my learning years at Wimbledon. Our team were quite good. Dad had by then become friendly with Wimbledon players and, through Les Briley, arranged a friendly between Palma Colts and Wimbledon's youngsters. A few of us impressed the likes of Geoff Taylor and we were invited for trials.

Sadly, it didn't work out well for me. Wimbledon signed seven apprentices that season – I wasn't one of them! I thought that was it. I joined Dad's transport firm and worked in the yard, loading goods for two weeks. Then the phone rang. It was Geoff saying the government had started a Youth Opportunities Scheme, where they pay your wages while you learn a skill. Geoff asked if I fancied joining the club on those conditions.

I later discovered that Geoff and Wally had battled Harry hard to get me to sign. Harry had so many decent central defenders on his books that he wasn't too bothered about taking on another. But Geoff and Wally fought my corner and I got £108 a month on just a year's contract. It was make or break time.

I was so pleased to be there. My first day, I walked from home to Plough Lane and was picked up by Geoff in a mini-van and driven to our Richardson Evans training ground. I couldn't believe it. Here I was looking close up at my heroes, whose pictures I had kept in my Panini stickers book. Boy, was I happy. That day is etched into my soul.

Then the work began. We collected dirty kit, cleaned dressing rooms, put up nets, pumped up footballs, cleaned boots and sometimes, when the ladies who ran it were delayed in getting in, we had to do the washing up in the working-man's café attached to our dressing rooms. It was only then we started training. When that was over it was back to Plough Lane to sweep the terraces (if there had been a game on the Saturday). We'd all start in a line and work our way down. It was synchronized terrace sweeping!

When Harry had his 'head' on he would walk over, inspect our work, and if he wasn't happy would order us to do it all over again! I even helped build our first physio room, knocking down a shower-room wall to make it big enough to get a table in. It was the toughest of learning curves, but undertaken for all the right reasons.

It was on those same terraces I discovered that I was to make my debut at the age of 18. Harry had been hit by injuries and he had doubts over the fitness of Mick Smith and Mark Morris, while Wally had broken his ankle in the previous game against Boro. I was brushing away when Harry came over and said, 'Put the broom down. Go home, you are playing against Notts.' I legged it.

I stayed in the side for the next ten games, then Harry dropped me until he finally decided it was really my time. He was ruthless like that, but in the right kind of way. The same went for Wally, one of the most intelligent footballers I have ever met. He had taken me under his wing. Like Harry, he could be verbally ruthless but, again, it was all done in the right manner. Wally had no room for failure, and if anyone played bad he would tell them. It was a hard school, but the right one. His was the carrot and stick approach: praise one day, slap down another. He was delighted for me when I got my debut, even though it was at his expense. Big man is Wally.

Corky was a man of few words. His longest speeches

were rowing with Harry over money. But when he did speak you listened. He was one of the finest strikers I have met – very, very underrated. Lots of people have got credit for Wimbledon's success, but most of us knew a lot was down to him.

My year came to an end with no word of what the future held. I was certain I was going to be kicked out. Harry left it to the last minute before offering me a four-year contract worth £110 a week, a wage I was still earning when we reached the FA Cup final!

I don't remember too much about why Harry left as he did, but it was a blow to many hearts. Even when he went he still had a hold on me. I was back in my second spell at the club at the time, and he said, 'Don't sign a new deal. I will be in touch. I'm going to manage Manchester City and want to take you with me.' So I didn't sign, I waited. And waited. And do you know what? A funny thing happened to me on the way to Manchester City. I ended up playing for Hearts! I had offers from other Premier League clubs, but I decided to hang on and wait for Dave. Still no call. Then, out of the blue, I got a phone call from Jim Jefferies saying he had three central defenders out, injured or suspended, and they had a Scottish Cup game against Celtic on the Tuesday. I fancied it because Celtic were in their prime and had players like Paolo Di Canio in their side. We won 1–0 and I was man of the match! I hadn't played for four weeks and I was on my knees at the end, but I loved it. Hearts eventually got to the final.

I loved it there and still get letters from Hearts fans.

On my return I got a call from John Aldridge at Tranmere. He said he had a decent side but was short of experience. Did I fancy it? I stayed for two years and met my wife Samantha. My rock. I now live in Chester – a far cry from my south London council flat.

Dave didn't fancy City and joined Forest instead. I never got the call.

Apart from my debut, one game I particularly remember was the occasion we played Newcastle and I witnessed Vinnie Jones grabbing Paul Gascoigne's 'crown jewels'. I had been selected to play for England under-21s, and Gazza was in the side too. We met for dinner two nights later and all he kept saying was, 'Keep that Vinnie Jones away from me. I really am a nice bloke.' He seemed genuinely scared.

My England selection was greeted with delight by Wally, Geoff and Corky. I knew Wally was happy because he simply said, 'I suppose you won't be talking to us now.' From him that was praise. Geoff had been like a father to me and he was also bursting inside with pride. He had fought to get me into the club and had encouraged me all the way. Now it was reward time. He didn't say anything, but we both knew he didn't need to. Corky was so happy for me he personally drove me to the England team hotel, although when we saw the likes of Waddle, Hoddle, Sansom and Gazza getting out of Mercs, he drove round the back to let me out. It wasn't done to be seen in an Opel Manta.

The under-21 fixture was an away game against Yugoslavia. It was at Red Star Belgrade's ground, which was so foggy you could hardly see your hands. We went 1–0 down and I said to Gazza, 'I thought you were a player. Do something.' He said, 'Next time you get the ball give it to me.' I did and he raced into the fog and scored. So every time I got the ball I passed it to him, and off he scampered to score or make a goal. We eventually won 5–1 – I think, not that I saw much because of the pea-souper.

Bobby Robson had encouraged Dave Sexton to pick me for the under-21s. It was a brave decision because I was at unfashionable Wimbledon, the so-called long-booters. They both sat me down and spoke wise words. I left the room feeling 8 feet tall. They were totally truthful, and that was something I carried into management myself.

I witnessed the arrival of both Vinnie and Fash. Vinnie was raw when he arrived, and I mean raw. I looked at him and thought, 'What have we got here?' What he had, however, was a big heart and a determination to make something of himself. Like me, he thought his chance had gone, but he never gave up hope. I got to admire and like the bloke very much.

Fash and Vinnie became icons, which didn't worry me, but they didn't win us games. Fash on his day was unplayable, while Vinnie might knock the odd one in and go into crunching tackles, but the ethics of the side had been established much, much earlier. Harry had forged this spirit within the side, developed a system that worked, and we all knew what we had to do. Harry turned a group of youngsters into winners. We had the nous. There was Glyn Hodges, who could open a tin of beans with his left foot, Corky, who scored from all angles – what price him today? (And what a player he could have been but for twice breaking legs.) Then there was Stevie Galliers, Fish, Sayer, Brian Gayle, Nigel Winterburn and, of course, Wally, who could operate in so many positions. When I went on to the pitch, looked around and saw these men – these mates – I felt pride and confidence.

I was in the side that beat West Ham to win the South East Counties League, at a time when it was usually won by the likes of Chelsea, Arsenal or Spurs. The Hammers could rightly claim their academy had produced a lot of players. So could we. In fact, more of our youngsters got into the first team than at any other club – that will never be repeated. We knew the system we played, and we practised and practised till darkness fell. Our success was no fluke.

Wimbledon made me an FA Cup winner, and helped me return two years later with Crystal Palace. In fact, I have played three Cup finals if you include the Palace replay. Wimbledon also made me England's first £1 million defender when I left and joined Newcastle, where I became their captain. All this from a kid from an estate, who had initially been rejected by the club he supported. There's a moral there somewhere.

After seven knee operations, I eventually retired at the age of 31, but I had no intention of leaving the game. I managed Coventry, who were at the time even more skint than the Wimbledon I joined as a teenager. I had to rely on home-grown youngsters, so it was like Wimbledon all over again. I would have dearly loved to have stayed and seen what we could have achieved. Sadly, it wasn't to be.

I recently watched a re-run of Wimbledon's FA Cup win, and I believe the performance of our back four that day was the greatest I have ever seen. It wasn't won by Vinnie's early tackle on McMahon, or by Fash. You couldn't see Fash on the radar, and when you did it was to kick the ball into touch two minutes into the second half. That game was won by a disciplined defence, one that carried on the traditions instilled in us by Harry, Geoff, Wally, Corky and all the others that turned Wimbledon into a noun.

22

We're the Famous Wimbledon

Wally

WHERE WERE YOU when Wimbledon won the FA Cup? It's a question I'm often asked. And the answer is: I was sitting in a hotel room in Bristol that unforgettable day of 14 May 1988.

By then I was on Harry's playing staff at Sheffield United and we were due to meet Bristol City in the first leg of a play-off the following afternoon. In those days the play-offs involved both teams at the bottom of a division and the ones at the top of the next league down – and having finished 21st in the Second Division, our life-line was against a team that had finished 5th in the Third Division. So, believe it or not, I was fuelled merely by a cup of tea and some biscuits as I watched the Dons beat Liverpool 1–0 in one of the greatest FA Cup final shocks. I saw my old teammates raise the trophy, turned off the TV, left the hotel and went for a walk.

Strange as the whole experience was – not just for me,

I would imagine – I then felt that I could finally stop the clock. I saw Vinnie Jones playing a role I once had, I saw Dennis Wise hit the kind of free-kick we had practised from the 1970s, I saw Lawrie Sanchez head the kind of goal that was once our calling card. Our legacy wasn't wasted.

Sheffield United lost 1–0 at Ashton Gate and fared little better three days later, with a 1–1 draw at Bramall Lane, consigning Harry and me to the third tier of English football. 'We've been here before,' I thought. But the consolation was that for that return leg, seven players from Wimbledon's FA Cup-winning side turned up to support the two of us – and the ex-Dons in the Blades side. Not only were they there in person, but they brought the Cup with them. I kissed it, handed it back and smiled. I knew then I could leave Wimbledon behind. It was closure.

Even though I was still on their books, I hadn't played for Wimbledon that season. I'd just spent a brief spell on loan at Newport as I tried to convince myself I could still play football despite all the injuries. I had broken my leg against Coventry the previous season, but the club had given me a testimonial and an extended year on my contract. I think it was Harry's last deal at the club – he extended it in case they didn't renew it. So when the new manager came in I wasn't high up on his agenda. In fact, as soon as I was out of plaster I was sent to Lilleshall, along with Stevie Galliers, Vinnie, Gayley and Andy Clement. It was a quiet time, really, with only a kidnapping, a failed orgy and a mass punch-up in a disco to keep us occupied!

I think Gouldy wanted Vinnie out as well as me, but when results were going bad Vinnie got called back into the squad and cracked on from there. As a pal of Gouldy's was the manager and I needed to get some games, I was packed off to Newport, with Andy Clement. I scored a couple of goals over Christmas and came back looking for a chance. I played one game against Man City, in a funny Cup competition that I can't even remember the name of. We got done 1–0 and I hit the bar with a screamer, but I clearly wasn't in his plans. I didn't get anywhere near selection – the only thing that kept me interested in training every day was Don Howe, brought in by Gouldy as his assistant.

Don's sessions were terrific and inspired me to want to coach. His enthusiasm was terrific and his sessions ran like clockwork. It was Don's idea to have Dennis screen John Barnes in the final, and Dennis done it great, stopping their best player and sacrificing his own game for the team. He was my man of the match for the way he did that job that day, but it rarely gets a mention. So that was it for me. I suppose I wasn't the player I was, if I'm honest, but I thought I could have been given a bit more of a chance to prove otherwise. But I was a big boy and he was the manager, so off I went to Harry at Sheffield United. I just wish I could have gone back as a player one day, but the ground got sold and I retired.

At least I was still around to see more of the constant

stream of players coming through the youth set-up and into the first team. Another who deserves his place in the history of Wimbledon's rise is Andy Clement. He was the chirpiest of youngsters, who came through the ranks in the wake of John Gannon and Andy Thorn. He was in Gannon's 'mucky youngsters' group but, where John was studious and conscientious, Clemmo aspired to be with the big hitters at the time. He was very versatile as a player, also bird-orientated and loved his looks, so he was devastated when he started going thin on top – hence his nickname of 'Wiggy'. Here he is for you.

Andy Clement

I came through the schoolboys and then as an AP. I would get the train up from Woking and Pat Deller, the driver, would pick us up from Wimbledon station and take us to the training ground and all the South East Counties games – we would burn the clutch out, get through about five clutches each season.

'Intimidating' would be the wrong word to use – it was daunting, but not intimidating. It was exciting. If you were in the dressing room you were in it for a reason, and you had to grow up. The great thing about Wimbledon was what Dario had set up – namely, young players always getting a chance. They must have had more players coming through over a long period of time than anyone else, anywhere. You got a chance no matter what age you were.

If we repeated the things we said to each other to people from the outside I am sure they would think, 'Cor, that's a bit strong,' but that's the way we were. You had to have a thick skin. I never for once ever felt that I didn't want to go training; it was your home, you wanted to get back there. There must have been players who didn't feel like that, because certain people have voiced that, but you always felt part of the group even if you weren't with the first team or even the reserves. There was great camaraderie. I was Wally's boot boy for a season, and it often worked in your favour because if he knew there was going to be a bit of a wrestle going on, then he would give you the heads-up so you could steer clear of it. So if the APs were going to get rushed then Wally would warn you.

We got beat 5–1 in the Southern Junior Floodlit Cup once, and Harry came in the dressing room afterwards. Ballbag was trying to be nice after a right old whooping, but Harry came in, told him to shut up and sacked five players there and then. He said, 'Don't bother coming in.'

There was another heave-ho with Spurs later in that first season in the top flight, when Vaughan Ryan made his debut. He was one of the best youngsters to emerge, but sadly got a bit forgotten when Harry left. Over to you, Vaughan.

Vaughan Ryan

I played for England schoolboys alongside Vinny Samways and Gareth Hall, who went on to join Spurs and Chelsea respectively. I had scouts from all the top clubs knocking at my door . . . so I joined Wimbledon in the Fourth Division.

Why? A gut feeling, and my dad saying I would be given a chance, plus there was the reputation of Dave Bassett.

I had trained with Wimbledon since I was 12 years old, despite being born the other side of the river in Pimlico, a decent kick from Stamford Bridge. I had been taken to the club by Pat Deller, a Wimbledon scout and taxi driver (ironically, because that is now my profession). Then I made the breakthrough into the England schoolboy side and the phone rang. And rang. So when it came to my future I sat down with Dad, Geoff Taylor and Harry. My head was all over the place. Chelsea, Spurs and Arsenal at my fingertips. Harry said nothing until suddenly he stood up, turned to my dad and said, 'Look, if Vaughan's going to be good enough he'll be in my first team.' My dad agreed and the deal was done.

I used to get the Tube to Wimbledon Park and then walk to Plough Lane for night training, then in the school holidays I would jump on the 85 bus to their training ground. I used to travel with Scott Fitzgerald. We went to the same school and lived in the same flats. Scott also made it into the first team. It wasn't so much training on public pitches and eating in a working-man's café, but looking at your peers and seeing similar youngsters who had beaten the odds. It inspired me. I thought, 'I will get a chance here.'

I found everyone warm. Senior pros weren't going to give you an easy time, but they would always come and watch us play on Saturday mornings. Then on Monday they would say, 'You could have done this better, see a bigger picture there.' But they were always constructive, never negative. It was a really wonderful experience, like one big family, and we were the younger members of it. We knew we had to be on our toes, though, particularly in the café, because if you turned your head you would suddenly find your meal doused in salt and vinegar, or Wally would throw talcum powder and it would go all over you and the food.

If you got too big for your boots they would put you in your place. I remember coming in one day with my England schoolboy bag and Glyn Hodges asked, 'What's that?' So it disappeared. Not to be seen again. We were always being educated in the right way. Geoff Taylor was always protective of us, but not overprotective because he also knew we had to stand up for ourselves. He wouldn't let anyone take liberties. We were a group who just wanted to be in the first team. We could see that happening in front of us and we wanted to go out and do it.

We all looked out for Wally. I loved him. Still do. There should be a shrine to him. He was Wimbledon. He was bright, could be a test – actually, a big test – but overall he wanted you to do well, emulate what he had done. Climb through the ranks. Beat the odds. He was extremely helpful to all the kids, particularly me.

I remember when I first got into the first team at the age of 17 I suffered a lot of injuries. Wally came to me and said, 'You can't control the ball, that is why you are getting hurt. You are trying too hard to get it back.' So in the afternoon he would have me whacking balls, controlling balls, learning. Even when he left he would watch me and tell me what I was doing right or wrong. You could talk to him about anything. He does have another side of him, maybe a bit wild, but I found him protective of us apprentices. He was trying to show us what the future held. He sometimes couldn't look after himself, but he never failed us. He wanted us to do well.

Mind you, he let us know when we were shit. I remember one time when we played in the reserves at Orient. I had not been expecting to play, and I was useless, I was an embarrassment. I had the biggest 'mare ever and, at half-time when Alan Gillett went to have a go at me, Wally said, 'Leave him, he's dizzy.' Then he came and sat next to me and told me to liven myself up. He said whatever I do next, smash the bloke I'm up against to give me a boost. So the next time the ball came near me and there was a challenge to be had, I went for it and completely missed him and Wally shouted, 'You're fucking having one!' Luckily Guppy got hold of me and told me to calm down, to ignore Wally and focus on my own game – it would be all right. A minute later I did something dreadful and Guppy screamed, 'He's right, you're fucking having one!' That's how bad I was – but that's how it was. It was blinding.

Dave Bassett was separate to us. We knew he was always about, who he was, and we knew he also could be approached. But we were only kids and that wasn't the done thing. I joined the club at 12 years of age but there was always the air of him being approachable. He would always watch youth-team games and come in and have his say; he would always give you information, but you also knew you could not step out of line.

We also knew money was short. When Harry offered me my first pro contract, he said, 'You're on £120 a week and £150 in appearance money.' I said, 'But—' and he replied, 'No buts, that is what you are getting. If you don't like it then go.' He didn't change when he took me to Sheffield United, and to start off with I stayed in a hotel. I had everything deducted out of my wages – phone calls, meals, the lot. I just wanted to play football, and I don't know to this day whether it was a good or bad thing.

The biggest compliment I can give Wimbledon is that when I left after a day's work I couldn't wait to get back. I never bought into the bollocks of bullying, the type John Fashanu talked about during that infamous show. Nothing like that happened during my time at the club. *The Crazy Gang* film was a poor portrayal of a unique journey. What has never come across in real terms is that we had very good players, very well coached and very well organized. It wasn't that we just turned up and worked our magic; we were ahead of the game. We had stats long before other clubs did it. Harry took us to Lilleshall to get our coaching badges. Something not heard of at other clubs. He wanted us to know football from every angle. Our army-camp trips were hard work. Funny, but knackering at the end of it. I didn't realize what they were about until I had gone. It was bonding, putting people in different holes and seeing how they could adapt.

One of our training programmes was virtual hide and seek. The youngsters were ordered to duck into the woods and warned the first team was going to find them. When we got found they stripped us naked. We didn't want to get caught.

We even achieved the impossible once. We got Wally after a South Eastern Counties game. We used to use the first-team dressing room and he came in one morning and insisted he would use it too. Geoff told him to get out, but Wally refused to budge. So we cut up his clothes. He wasn't happy. He went mad. We went back to the ground and eventually an apprentice arrived dishevelled. We asked what had happened and he said Wally had bashed him up! He said Wally had declared out and out war on us. So on the Monday we were ready. No Wally. But then Geoff came out and said, 'Get back to your dressing room. Wally is in there and has locked himself in.' We got a key off the groundsman only to find Wally totally naked, covered in eggs and flour and dancing on our clothes.

Nothing was half-cock with Wally. After we had hammered Gothenburg in that friendly, Wally said we had to lump all the money from the players' pool on Aberdeen beating them. He did our players' pool money in one hit.

I played the year after the Cup final and started getting it from the crowd, partly because Vinnie had gone and I wore his shirt. Harry was at Sheffield United then and wanted me to play for him, but Bobby Gould wanted too much money for me. Harry being Harry didn't want to pay any money. In the end I played under Harry, Gould, Ray Harford, Peter Withe and Joe Kinnear.

Great days.

One in particular sticks out. Us kids got back to Plough Lane and were bored and decided to fire water pistols at the first person who came through the door. It was Harry. We drenched him. He wasn't happy and ordered Geoff Taylor to round us up in the dressing room. Harry went berserk, calling us everything under the sun. He got so fired up he kicked in the dressing-room door. Sadly, his foot got stuck. He couldn't get it out and there he was dancing around on one leg, cursing us and the door until Geoff quietly told us to leave before helping Harry remove his foot.

You can't buy those moments.

Wally

While I was watching the Cup final on telly, Harry was in the ITV commentary box with Brian Moore and Ian St John, and full of pride at what he saw unfolding before an unbelieving public's eyes. 'I was so pleased and Ian St John was so fucking gutted,' as he reminded me recently. Wimbledon had already finished 7th in the league, proving our first season in the First Division was by no means a fluke or beginners' luck, and now a game plan was executed in true Harry fashion to bring Liverpool down to size, and spawn that infamous 'the Crazy Gang have beaten the Culture Club' line.

And what joy it was too to see Lurch save John Aldridge's penalty and go on to lift the Cup. Along with Corky, he'd been there almost from the start, or so it seemed. Vinnie was, of course, by then a best mate of mine, while Andy Thorn had, like me, started out as a kid at Wimbledon, Wisey was practically family and, as for Sanch, well, who else should score the goal but my old midfield mucker. It's fitting then to give him the stage here for the penultimate batch of Crazy Gang memories, before we turn to the skipper, Dave Beasant. After me, he was at Wimbledon the longest too, so he gets the final word! But before I go, let me say just one more thing. I would go ANYWHERE, ANY TIME and do ANYTHING for ANY ONE of these people in this book!

Lawrie Sanchez

I made my debut for Reading on 1 October 1977 as a 17-year-old schoolboy against Wimbledon, and Gary Peters was playing for us then. It was Wimbledon's first year in the league and playing against us in centre-midfield were Bassett and Galliers. We drew 2–2 and I hit the post. I made my senior debut for Reading before I played in the youth team. I used to go to training after school.

The season I left I finished runner-up in the player of the year vote and second in the highest scorer list, with ten from midfield. I went in to see the manager Ian Branfoot to get my rise, as you did at the end of the season – usually a fiver or tenner – and was asked how I thought I had done. I said I thought I had done quite well, and he said, 'I don't,' and by around October I was dropped from the team and they tried to sell me to Swindon.

I agreed a deal to go to Swindon, who were managed by Lou Macari, but then I got a call from Vince Craven (the video analyst) who said, 'Don't sign for Swindon, we'll have you.' I said, 'Who's we?' and he said, 'Wimbledon.' At the time Reading were in the Third Division, Swindon were in the Fourth and Wimbledon were starting their first year in the Second. I was told to go to a hotel near Heathrow, where I met Alan Gillett. I had been at Reading for seven or eight years, since school, and I was being forced out, but I didn't really want to leave. Gillett just kept insisting that I wait for Harry, speak to Harry, listen to Harry. In the end I got angry and said, 'Fuck Harry, when is Dave Bassett turning up?'

We sat in the bar talking, and in the end I finally got offered the same money I was offered at Swindon, but I got a signing-on fee. Harry was shouting my wages all over the bar – because he can't talk normally – despite me telling him to quieten down. In the end I asked what I should do, should I go back and discuss things with Reading? Harry said, 'No, just come with me, I'll meet you at Richmond in the morning.' The first day was OK, the second day he never turned up, so I had to find my own way across Richmond Park and to the training ground, but I never went back to Reading. I never even went back to get my boots in the end. Harry said, 'Fuck 'em.'

On my very first day I remember wondering how much of a step-up it would be from Division Three and Division Four. I kept thinking about how much harder it would be, what the standards would be like. Then I sat next to Corky in the dressing room and he said, 'What are you doing here? It's a shit club, the manager's shit and we're getting relegated.' I thought, 'Fuck me, that's their star striker talking, and I've just signed a two-year deal.'

Richardson Evans was a park, there were no windows in the dressing room – this was supposed to be glamorous Second Division football? I signed around Christmas and watched the team on Boxing Day and thought they were brilliant – and that I would never get in the side. I did make it for the next match, though, and I thought I had done quite well with a few neat touches, but at half-time Harry said to me, 'Are you fucking fit or what? Run about! Liven yourself up!'

I think I played pretty much from the time I came in. Wally was a centre-midfielder but had a lot of injuries, Fish played a bit in midfield, and so did Gagey to start. I think I played 20 odd games and by the time the next full season came around I knew everyone, and vice versa, and it was a different story. Wally christened me 'the Mexican'. I slotted in, the style of play suited me, I played midfield with Galliers. I played more than every game that season, because the Bradford fixture happened twice. There was a bit of cash floating about back then, so the deal was I got a £50 goal bonus, five goals was £250, and 10 was £500. I had scored nine and we were playing Bradford and it had rained non-stop before the match. Once it started I scored, but then the game got abandoned despite me telling the ref there was nothing wrong with the pitch, it was just more puddles than grass. We went up again and it rained again and was called off, then the third match happened after we were promoted, on 8 May. A lot of the other players didn't bother going up for the game, but I had that £500 riding on it. I didn't score this time, but told Harry that, in effect, because of the abandoned game, I had scored 10 goals that season so was due the big bonus. Harry, of course, said I only scored nine and then he only gave me £50!

The only person who possibly underachieved or had a bad time at Wimbledon was Ian Holloway – people forget he played for us. He went to Brentford then back to Bristol Rovers and then did ten years at QPR and was an outstanding Premier League player. He would run all day – he would beat anyone over Richmond Park – but when it came to Saturday he would blow up. People thought it was psychological, but by the time he had gone he was diagnosed as having had glandular fever, as John Gannon said.

People were always interested in Wimbledon, wherever you went, or when you went on international duty – like my three times with Northern Ireland! People would ask you about it because we were always in the papers and people had read about us. If the channel had been around back then we would never have been off Sky Sports News; the world was a lot smaller in those days.

We got more physical as it went on. John O'Neill at Norwich would not disagree, because Fash finished his career in December 1987. Gary Stevens wouldn't tell you it wasn't physical, because between Fash and Vinnie they nearly ended his career. John O'Neill tried to sue Fash; it was settled out of court. It got more physical and it revolved around two players, mostly.

Wisey was the worst tackler at the club but he only weighed five stone. I used to cringe at his tackles, but they could rarely hurt anybody – he jumped in two-footed on people all the time but luckily he bounced off them. When you're 12 stone, doing some of that stuff, it went beyond the pale.

I bridged the gap, I think. When I came in it was a group of young players – it became more cynical, later on, because the rewards were getting bigger. There was a moment when Wimbledon moved from being that friendly, perhaps aggressive, little club to a level above.

Sam once told me the Wimbledon story through managers. Allen Batsford got them in the Football League; Dario took over and introduced the youth system that created Fish, Gannon, Hodges, Gage, Sayer; then Harry came in and started the 'up and at 'em, take no shit' mentality at the club; Gouldy bought half the team that won the Cup final, and sold on people like Eric Young, Terry Phelan and Keith Curle; then Joe Kinnear came in and had all the money to spend and ended up spending £8 million on a player on a million pounds a year. The John Hartson signing was both the peak and the trough for Wimbledon; it was the beginning of the end.

There is the story of the non-league team that almost beat Leeds in the FA Cup, with Dickie Guy in goal; there's the story of the side that went from the Fourth to the First Division. Then there's the Cup final and beyond team. There isn't one continuous story. I bridged the last bit, the end of the promotion team and the team that stayed there for 12 years.

The difference between players' wages during the years of Gary Peters in the early eighties and when I came in wouldn't have been much, but once we got in the First Division it all changed. Fash changed his name overnight from 'Fash the Bash' to 'Fash the Cash' and I remember he put a story out that he was in the top five of the highest-paid players in the league. I remember saying to Sam, 'Why do you let him get away with saying he earns two or three times more than the rest of us? It really pisses people off.' Sam just said, 'You know and I know it's a lie – everyone else knows it's a lie – but it might just help us bring another top player to the club who thinks we pay big wages!' That was Sam's attitude.

At Reading my performances were so erratic I would be either sky high or rock bottom, I had no consistency at all. At Wimbledon we knew exactly what our jobs were, and that if – even if I felt crap about myself or was lacking confidence – I kept doing as I was told, what we had planned and practised, then I would be helping the team.

We knew Harry was leaving after that Sheffield Wednesday match, because he came down the night before and told us all that we could have a drink before the match. It had been going on for a while. But I remember, even though it was the last game of the season and the outcome was irrelevant, Gary Megson said to me, 'Don't any of you lot ever stop running?' We just ran teams into the ground.

By the time Vinnie and Wisey and those players came Wally's influence had waned; he wasn't in the team because he had broken his ankle again. And when you are not in the team you cannot have that influence or sway any more. He was still a big part of things, but not like he had been in the early eighties.

The only thing I remember after my goal beat Huddersfield to send us up to the First Division was June Whitfield being in the dressing room afterwards, ending up shaking Lurch's cock. She still came back for the semi-final of the FA Cup at White Hart Lane, though!

My most memorable game for Wimbledon happened in the middle of winter at Plough Lane, in front of about 500 people on a Tuesday night – the game against Gothenburg that others have mentioned. They came out in gloves and tights and we thought, 'We'll smash these,' and we did. They had their first team out against us and we bombed them.

I played two parts in the rise of Vinnie: he got his break in the side because I got suspended. The next game at home against Manchester United he scored and climbed up on the cage in front of all the fans, and both him and the fans were going wild and I remember thinking, 'He's going to be a legend here.' Then I came back and we started playing together. The next season Gouldy called me up into his office – I might have been 27, 28 at the time – and he told me we were playing Newcastle and they had this tasty little midfielder who he wanted me to man-mark, his name was Paul Gascoigne. I said, 'Who the fuck is Paul Gascoigne?' I told Bobby I wouldn't be very good at that job, I was getting on, and told him that Vinnie would be the ideal candidate for the job. THAT photo followed and the rest was history.

We were on a boat once somewhere between Finland and Sweden in July 1986 and Lurch and I were having to sort out the bonus system we wanted in place for the coming season. We were sure we were going to get relegated so we just wanted the most we could get for every point, goal and clean sheet. Suddenly Sam says, 'Lollie, I give you one million pounds if you win the FA Cup.' At the time we thought we didn't have a chance of winning the Cup, so we ignored it. The next morning Sam said that offer was a bit strong so we scrubbed it out and just got FA Cup appearance money, with all the bonuses focused on the league. And just over 18 months later we fucking won it.

It's a tag people know – when I get asked who I played for, and I tell them 'the Crazy Gang', their interest multiplies. If I were to say 'Wimbledon' they probably wouldn't know that much. It was encapsulated by John Motson at the Cup final, 'the Crazy Gang beating the Culture Club'.

Originally it was the crazy gang with a small C – that was just our day-to-day lives – then when Tony Stenson coined the phrase, and Motson said it in his commentary, it was real and it became 'the Crazy Gang'. And then some players felt they had to live up to this title and pastiche it and recreate what the real original crazy gang had done ten years earlier.

Dave Beasant

My first wage at Wimbledon was £25 a week, my last wage was £500. If I had been at another club in the First Division, I could have been earning five grand. And in the run-up to the Cup final, money was an issue, as there were no bonuses in the offing – all we got was appearance money. That affected our performances too; in the weeks leading up to Wembley, from the semi against Luton onwards, we could hardly win a game – just the one win at Norwich in the final ten matches of the league campaign. In the last of those, at Old Trafford, on the Monday night before the Cup final, Man Utd beat us up, and it was the first time that had ever happened. People like Gordon Strachan were saying, 'What, you want to play in the Cup final?'

We won the Cup not just with the players on the pitch. There were other players not at Wembley that day who were a major part of what we achieved, and a major part of that 1–0 result. And the good thing was, when we were going round with the trophy after the game, I remember Vinnie was holding it and he pointed up at the gantry and said, 'There's Harry.' We were all waving; it was Harry's team, even Gouldy will own up to that.

At the end, people realized what a good team Wimbledon were, even if Harry would never tell us we were any good. And it was because we won the Cup that people slaughtered us for that match; if we had lost to Liverpool, no one would have said that we were bad. But that was the beginning of the end. It showed what good players Wimbledon had produced, and suddenly they were being plucked by other clubs. Not just that, but other managers were saying, 'I want a bit of Wimbledon spirit in my team!' And I was one of that number.

Harry had made me his captain, saying I was a sensible lad – 'one of the boys but also level-headed'. He was such a good motivator. In our first season in the First Division, I conceded five goals in the first two games and went to see him, saying I didn't know if I was cut out for this. He told me not to worry about it – we won the next game 1–0, and the rest is history. When Harry left, Bobby Gould kept me as skipper. Like Harry, we had known Gouldy as a player – 'the mole' we used to call him – but when I told him I felt I needed to go somewhere else to get to the next stage in my career, he guaranteed that he would let me know if anyone came in with an offer, and was true to his word. We had played against Newcastle in the Littlewoods Cup earlier that season – Gazza at his magical best – and that was where I was headed.

We grew together at Wimbledon, and we were together for a long time – you don't get many teams that spend seven or eight years with each other. People say to me, 'You missed out on a lot of money,' but I wouldn't swap my time at Wimbledon for anything. If you ask me whether I'd prefer to have started my career, day one, with a club in the First Division, or with Wimbledon in the Fourth Division, I'd say, 'Wimbledon in the Fourth

Division' every time. I've got medals at home, and the one with a '4' on it from a promotion means as much as the one with 'FA Cup winner'. Medals are all the same – it's what you achieve with a group of people that matters. They were, and are, my mates.

Wimbledon made me the person and the character that I am, with what I went through in those years. I had tougher times later, especially at Chelsea, and I don't think I'd have got there and got through those times if I hadn't been through the process of what happened at Wimbledon, the mentality it gave me. It also made me a better footballer. When Harry first suggested my dribbling the ball out of the area, I told him to fuck off – even if I fancied myself as a player and used to play centre-forward until I was 16 or 17. But I loved that role, and the year we won the Cup, Wisey got about 75 per cent of our assists and I got the rest. The trick was to hit the ball high, so as it didn't go too long.

The memories are so good. Even when we were running on Wimbledon Common, from the A3 to the windmill, we'd get Harry or Dario and roll them in the mud. Magaluf every summer. Stevie Parsons throwing plant pots in the air and headbutting them from the top of a ladder at a place in Willesden on my 21st birthday. And that time in France that Gary Peters mentions – it was actually Crystal Palace who were meant to be there, but we went in their place, and were instructed to tell everyone we actually were Palace. That was asking for trouble. I remember Fish – who fancied himself as Tony

Hadley from Spandau Ballet – hanging upside down from a beam, singing 'True' with a big fat cigar in his mouth. When he fell head-first, it was like watching something from *Tom and Jerry*, the cigar squashed flat on the floor beneath his face – one of the funniest things I've ever seen.

Having a nightclub 40 yards from the pitch was also asking for trouble. One year, Harry made us come in on Sunday mornings for the rest of the season, not deigning to show up himself. We trained for a couple of hours, Nelson's would open, and by the third week we had the strippers in there. The boardroom was used for more than meetings, I can tell you. And alcohol made very little difference to the way we played. By the way, it was me and Sanch that stitched Harry up in Sheffield – he blamed everyone bar the two of us!

What the Crazy Gang was all about, though, was those early days, going to reserve-team games on a minibus and stopping off for a pint and to pick up fish and chips on the way back. That, and nicknames – it's the secret to a team. Yes, Wally used to pick on me – he didn't have too many names but 'Big Gob' was one – but he could make you feel that big too. There's a Wally in most clubs, but no one quite like him. Now when I do strange things as a football coach, people think I'm fucking mad. 'No I'm not,' I say. 'Meet Wally.'

Epilogue

Harry

As I SAID, a lot of people said some nasty things about the Crazy Gang, even if I couldn't help thinking that secretly they admired all our achievements. I'm not much of a one for keeping old books and photos about those days, but I do have some old match reports and newspaper cuttings that obviously had a special meaning for me at the time. And I want to reproduce here what Eamon Dunphy once wrote about Wimbledon in the *Sunday Times*, when we were top of the league in September 1986. You have to respect Dunphy's opinion – he wore his heart on his sleeve as a player and still does as a pundit – and don't forget that he wrote one of the all-time great football books, *Only a Game?*, about his time at Millwall, who agonizingly missed out on promotion to the First Division by a single point in 1972. Here it is. Thanks, Eamon.

There are those who claim that what Wimbledon play isn't really football. Ted Croker, the secretary of the Football Association no less, is one of them. He has even stated that Wimbledon should not be in the First Division at all. But what Croker and others in English football should be doing is extending to Dave Bassett and his Wimbledon players the respect and admiration they deserve. Not because they are top of the First Division, not because they are 'marvellous', but for the very good reason that Bassett, his players and Wimbledon Football Club epitomize all that is good in English football.

That people, inside and outside the game, fail to appreciate Wimbledon's achievements – not just these past few weeks but for several seasons – is proof of the degree to which English football has lost its way and its sense of values. Proof that those who would presume to tell us what football is or should be about have been consumed by pretentious guff (their own) about style and entertainment.

What football is about is winning teams, their creation, development and achievement. What football is not about is style. Football is conflict not entertainment.

English league football is about a number of other things – or ought to be: living within your means; spending time, as Dave Bassett has done, working with your players on the training ground; improving them rather than wasting money on the transfer market. It is also, in the age of freedom of contract, when players are liable to be free to the point of irresponsibility, about fostering loyalty within your club. This Bassett has achieved. His players identify with their club, are proud of it, see their own fate as being inseparable from the club's.

Wimbledon are not a corporation, they are a football club. The major shareholder may be a wealthy Lebanese businessman, but Sam Hammam is recognizably human sitting on the team bench with his kids. Hammam is not your flash boardroom tycoon, your *nouveau* businessman feeding his ego on publicity and half-time brandy.

The point about Wimbledon's success is not their style of play but their style of thinking. The philosophy is what counts. And not just off the field. The difference between Wimbledon and Manchester United at the moment is a difference of attitude rather than style. I have seen United twice in recent weeks. They are losing games because they have a couple of elegant conmen in the side. Entertainers, no doubt, when in the mood, when the grass is green, the sun shining and the long elegant balls are finding their targets.

To win football matches at any level, to go on winning them home and away, autumn, winter and spring, you need more than long balls and aggression. You need team organization, players who concentrate and accept responsibility, a willingness throughout the side to step up the pace when you go a goal down away from home.

You need lads who will get on the ball when they are having a bad time, mark the man they should be marking, stick their head in where the boots are flying. If, like Wimbledon, you rise and rise you need players who aren't complacent but are willing to work harder the more successful they become. Lads like Alan Cork, Steve Galliers, Kevin Gage. Lads like Roger Hunt, Nobby Stiles, Jack Charlton, Geoff Hurst and George Cohen. Remember them? Yes, England 1966 and all that.

England didn't win the World Cup in style. They just won it. They won it the English way, grafting, being competitive, finding inspiration and moments of real grandeur. But at the core of that achievement, which was much maligned at the time, was a willingness to compete, to concentrate, to take responsibility and above all a sense of commitment to Alf Ramsey and England.

The same values distinguish Wimbledon. They are in the best English tradition, a team of honest men. Led by an outstanding manager who, like his team, has been patronized rather than appreciated.

Having spent a few days with Wimbledon last spring I wondered, not about whether they were ready for the First Division, but whether the First Division was ready for them. I am still wondering.

If that doesn't make you proud, nothing will. The Crazy Gang were a team to be proud of. Yes, we were silly buggers but we worked bloody hard. Wimbledon could not have gone up through all the divisions, won the FA Cup, without that. We have never been given proper credit for what we achieved. But I hope now that this book proves what a special team we were, and that it wasn't all about one game, the 1988 FA Cup final.

Finally I will say what Wimbledon achieved is one of the greatest success stories in the history of the game, going from the Southern League to the First Division in nine years and winning the FA Cup in ten years will never ever be equalled or beaten!!!

Appendices

Wimbledon FC league record, 1977–88

1977	Elected to the Football League
1977–78	Division 4
1978–79	Division 4 – promoted
1979–80	Division 3 – relegated
1980–81	Division 4 – promoted
1981–82	Division 3 – relegated
1982–83	Division 4 – promoted
1983–84	Division 3 – promoted
1984–85	Division 2
1985–86	Division 2 – promoted
1986–87	Division 1
1987–88	Division 1 – won FA Cup

Wimbledon FC first-team players, 1977–88

Glenn Aitken
Gary Armstrong
Gary Barnett
Dave Bassett
Dave Beasant
Kevin Bedford
Mick Belfield
Brian Bithell
Joe Blochel
Paul Bowgett
Terry Boyle
Dave Bradley
Les Briley
Peter Brown
Jeff Bryant
Andy Clement
Dave Clement
Roger Connell
Alan Cork
Fran Cowley
Laurie Cunningham
Tommy Cunningham
Geoff Davies
Roy Davies
Paul Denny
Chris Dibble
Dave Donaldson
Wally Downes
Phil Driver
Mark Dziadulewicz
Terry Eames
Billy Edwards
Mark Elliott
Wayne Entwistle
Stewart Evans
Carlton Fairweather
John Fashanu
Phil Ferns
Paul Fishenden
Kevin Gage
Steve Galliers
Dave Galvin
John Gannon
Brian Gayle
Paul Geddes
Terry Gibson
Ray Goddard
Clive Goodyear
Colin Gordon
Dickie Guy
Phil Handford
Lee Harwood
Steve Hatter
Paul Haverson

Ian Hazel
Glyn Hodges
Ian Holloway
Billy Holmes
Dave Hubbick
Billy Hughes
Steve Jones
Vinnie Jones
Francis Joseph
John Kay
David Kemp
Steve Ketteridge
Bryan Klug
Ray Knowles
Paul Lazarus
John Leslie
Ray Lewington
Dave Martin
Doug McClure
Paul Miller
Mark Morris
Paul O'Berg
Steve Parsons
Steve Perkins
Gary Peters
Terry Phelan
Paul Priddy
Craig Richards
Vaughan Ryan
Lawrie Sanchez
Andy Sayer
John Scales
Don Shanks
Mick Smith
Willie Smith
Brian Sparrow
Peter Suddaby
Phil Summerill
Dave Swindlehurst
Tony Tagg
Richard Teale
Dean Thomas
Keith Thompson
Andy Thorn
Kevin Tilley
Robbie Turner
Micky Welch
Nigel Winterburn
Dennis Wise
Eric Young

Index